W9-CBD-663

MAXIMUM SEX!

DDM Press
1040 Avenue of the Americas • New York, NY 10018 • 212.302.2626 • http://www.maximonline.com

For more information on Maxim Books, call 888-328-4380

Maximum Sex!

Portions of this text have been adapted from *Maxim* and *Stuff* Magazines.

ISBN 0-9675723-9-8
Printed in Canada

Cover photograph: Charlie Langella • Cover model: Katja Hilgendorff

MAXIMUM SEX!

BY THE EDITORS OF MAXIM

MAXIM
BOOKS
DDM Press

MAXIMUM SEX!

Senior Editor
Rosie Amodio
Senior Writer
Shane Mooney
Art Director
Jane Mella
Photo Editor
A.S. Brodsky
Interior Photographers
Charlie Langella
Jennifer Robbins
Illustrator
Lyman Dally
Writers
Kimberly Flynn
Laurina Gibbs
Elaine Heinzman
Rich Hoxsey
Copy Editor
Kenneth Gee
Proofreader
Carmen Armillas
Fact Checker
Elaine Heinzman
Additional Production
Murphy Fogelnest

DDM PRESS

Chairman
Felix Dennis
President
Stephen Colvin
Chief Financial Officer
Paul Fish
Publisher
Steven Kotok
Group Creative Director
Andy Turnbull
Executive Editor
Robert Simpson
Direct Marketing Manager
Joanna Molfetta
Directors
Robert G. Bartner
Peter Godfrey

CHAPTER 1

CHAPTER 2

CHAPTER 3

CHAPTER 4

CHAPTER 5

CHAPTER 6

CHAPTER 7

CHAPTER 8

FOREPLAY

Letters? You betcha we get 'em! And not just PETA and NOW hate mail. Since its inception, Maxim has become the one true authority on sex—the opposite sex, sex ed, and even the occasional sextuplets (boo-yea!). Every time Freddy from the mail room brings our bundles of letters, they're bursting with pleas from men (and their women), begging for help on the finer points of the Love Tango. A sampling: "How can I get my girlfriend to do a three-way?" "What does it take to really please a woman orally?" and our favorite, "If I occasionally find myself admiring a guy who's really cut at the gym, does that mean I'm gay?"

Naturally, we feel it's our civic duty to share our vast wealth of sexpertise with the masses. So after one particularly intense session of, um, editorial brainstorming, we decided we should gather all our carnal knowledge about sex into convenient book form. And the result, my friend, is you are now weighty tome you're cradling so lovingly in your hands.

What can you expect from this piece of useful art? We cover the whole sexual spectrum, from guy parts to girl parts to putting those parts together (Insert Tab A into Slot B. Repeat). Not only do we cover the finer functioning of the male and female bod (like just where the hell that G-spot is), but we detail everything your typical sex manual is afraid to touch: what fisting is, how to make your own porn film, and whether it's true there are women who get off on being dressed up in full pony gear and ridden around the backyard like a frisky filly (apparently there are—hey, we can't make this stuff up, folks).

Best of all, the book's contents page breaks down the lay of the land in bite-size chunks. Go ahead, flip right to the dirty parts if you want (just like with *Playboy*), or if you're worried you might miss some key nugget of info that'll forever turn you from Bill Gates Geek into Don Juan Stud, you can read it all the way through.

Naturally, a book of such sexual weight doesn't happen overnight. In fact, this carnal chronicle of copulation was millennia in the making. Don't believe us? Here's a time line of the events that led up to this historic moment:

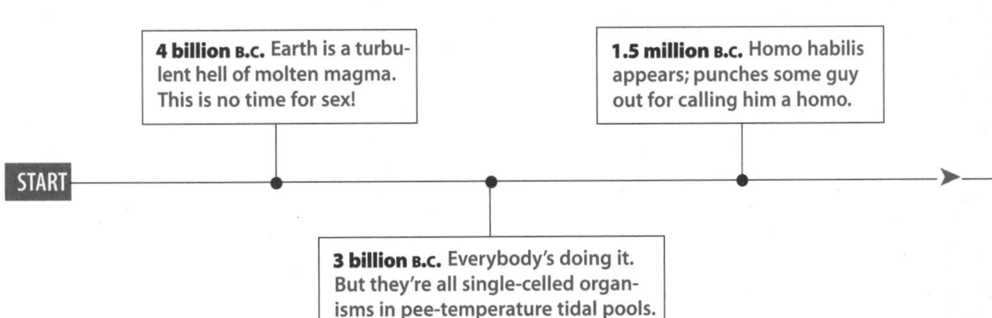
START
4 billion B.C. Earth is a turbulent hell of molten magma. This is no time for sex!
3 billion B.C. Everybody's doing it. But they're all single-celled organisms in pee-temperature tidal pools.
1.5 million B.C. Homo habilis appears; punches some guy out for calling him a homo.

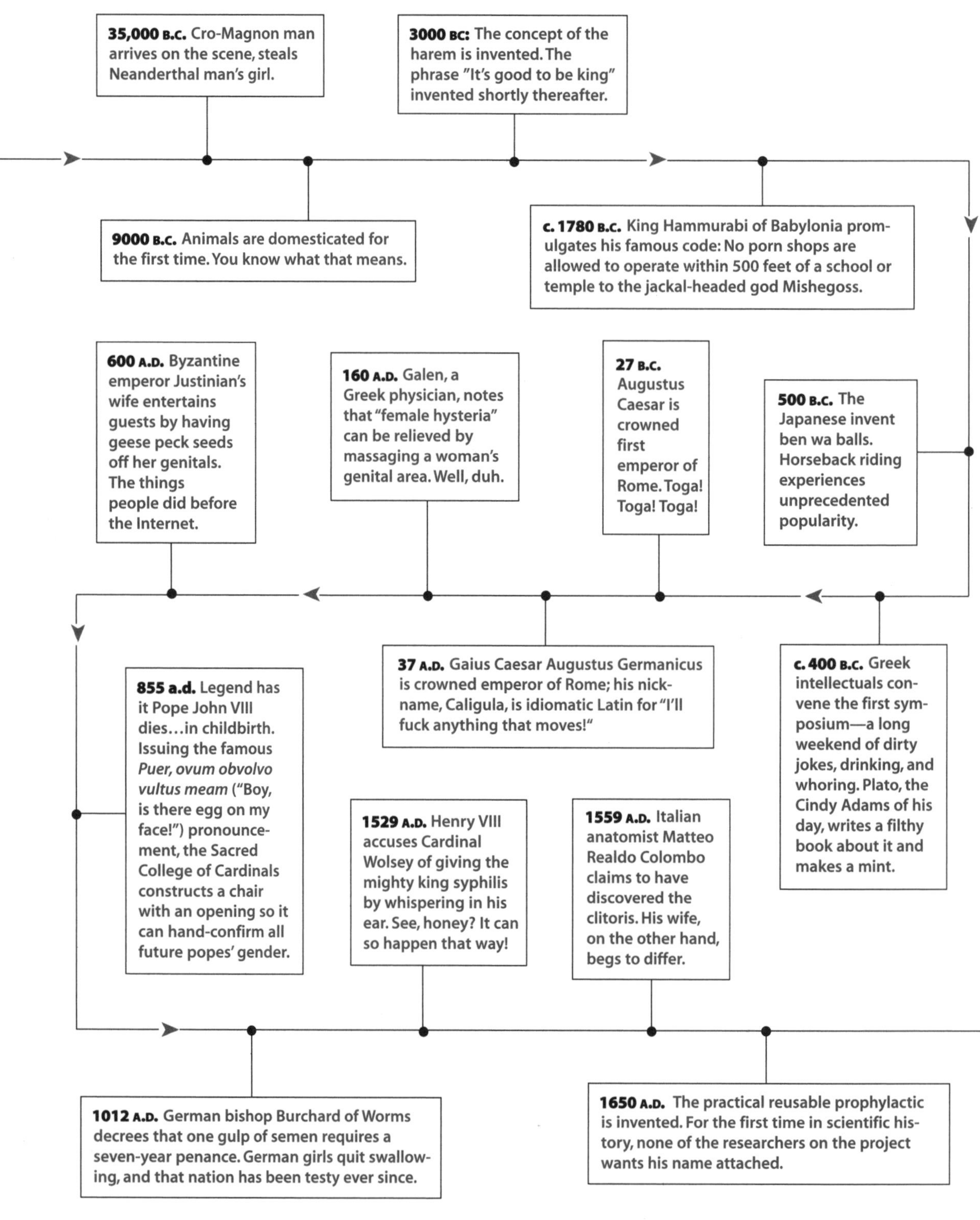

35,000 B.C. Cro-Magnon man arrives on the scene, steals Neanderthal man's girl.
9000 B.C. Animals are domesticated for the first time. You know what that means.
3000 BC: The concept of the harem is invented. The phrase "It's good to be king" invented shortly thereafter.
c. 1780 B.C. King Hammurabi of Babylonia promulgates his famous code: No porn shops are allowed to operate within 500 feet of a school or temple to the jackal-headed god Mishegoss.
500 B.C. The Japanese invent ben wa balls. Horseback riding experiences unprecedented popularity.
c. 400 B.C. Greek intellectuals convene the first symposium—a long weekend of dirty jokes, drinking, and whoring. Plato, the Cindy Adams of his day, writes a filthy book about it and makes a mint.
27 B.C. Augustus Caesar is crowned first emperor of Rome. Toga! Toga! Toga!
37 A.D. Gaius Caesar Augustus Germanicus is crowned emperor of Rome; his nickname, Caligula, is idiomatic Latin for "I'll fuck anything that moves!"
160 A.D. Galen, a Greek physician, notes that "female hysteria" can be relieved by massaging a woman's genital area. Well, duh.
600 A.D. Byzantine emperor Justinian's wife entertains guests by having geese peck seeds off her genitals. The things people did before the Internet.
855 a.d. Legend has it Pope John VIII dies…in childbirth. Issuing the famous *Puer, ovum obvolvo vultus meam* ("Boy, is there egg on my face!") pronouncement, the Sacred College of Cardinals constructs a chair with an opening so it can hand-confirm all future popes' gender.
1012 A.D. German bishop Burchard of Worms decrees that one gulp of semen requires a seven-year penance. German girls quit swallowing, and that nation has been testy ever since.
1529 A.D. Henry VIII accuses Cardinal Wolsey of giving the mighty king syphilis by whispering in his ear. See, honey? It can so happen that way!
1559 A.D. Italian anatomist Matteo Realdo Colombo claims to have discovered the clitoris. His wife, on the other hand, begs to differ.
1650 A.D. The practical reusable prophylactic is invented. For the first time in scientific history, none of the researchers on the project wants his name attached.

1677 A.D. Using his homemade microscope, Dutch scientist Antonie van Leeuwenhoek discovers sperm. Till then they had thought it contained microscopic men, but nobody had really wanted to look that closely at a puddle of spooge.

c. 1774 A.D. Giovanni Giacomo Casanova is expelled from a seminary when tales of his sexual exploits get around. The Catholic Church then misses the boat on royalties from Casanova's sizzling 12-volume memoirs.

1799 A.D. To avoid being caught rogering the wife of an employee at his Mount Vernon estate, the original George W. is said to have jumped out a window with no pants on, subsequently dying from a chill a few days later.

1814 A.D. The Marquis de Sade, host of innumerable celebrity orgies, croaks in an insane asylum.

1829 A.D. Arguing that a spicy diet could tempt young men to masturbate, Dr. Sylvester Graham invents the wholesome, inoffensive cracker that still bears his name. Unrepentant gherkin-jerkers are forced to look at naked pictures of Mark Twain.

1883 A.D. The term lesbian is first used to describe a homosexual woman. Prior to this the word had been associated with fellatio, as it was said that the women of Lesbos were without peer in this regard. The Greeks, it's worth noting, also gave us irony.

1894 A.D. Thomas Edison introduces the first peep-show machine. The animated flip-book short "Marie Curie's Radioactive Sweater Meat" is a hit.

1919 A.D. More WWI troops are hospitalized for VD than for all other injuries combined. Talk about trench warfare.

1921 A.D. Sixteen-year-old Margaret Gorman wins the first Miss America contest, despite having measurements of only 30-25-32.

1930 A.D. Thin latex condoms are introduced, replacing bulky, tire-grade rubber sheaths. Suddenly sex feels almost lifelike.

1940 A.D. Japanese prostitutes pioneer the breast implant. To lure higher-paying American GIs, they inject their bosoms with saline, goat's milk, and even paraffin wax. And you thought the Japanese were only good at miniaturizing things.

1943 A.D. Dow Corning begins selling silicone. Proves infinitely more sexually inspiring than its other products: napalm and Agent Orange.

1946 A.D. The residents of tiny Bikini Atoll watch as the U.S. military turns their beaches into sheets of glass with a nuke test. We compensate the natives by naming the two-piece swimsuit after their island!

1948 A.D. Biologist Alfred Kinsey follows up his book *Edible Wild Plants of Eastern North America* with *Sexual Behavior in the Human Male*. Suddenly his car payments are not a problem.

c.1949 A.D. Dr. Robert L. Dickinson confirms the dimensions of the largest medically verified penis. The record still, uh, stands at 13.5 inches long and 6.25 inches in circumference, though anyone who's seen a John Holmes film knows this is total crap.

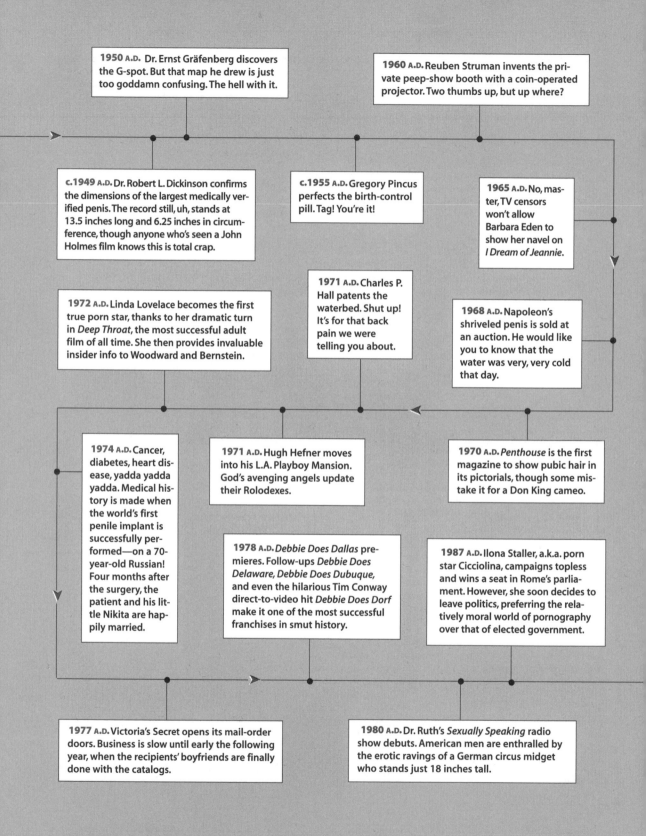

1950 A.D. Dr. Ernst Gräfenberg discovers the G-spot. But that map he drew is just too goddamn confusing. The hell with it.

c.1955 A.D. Gregory Pincus perfects the birth-control pill. Tag! You're it!

1960 A.D. Reuben Struman invents the private peep-show booth with a coin-operated projector. Two thumbs up, but up where?

1965 A.D. No, master, TV censors won't allow Barbara Eden to show her navel on *I Dream of Jeannie*.

1968 A.D. Napoleon's shriveled penis is sold at an auction. He would like you to know that the water was very, very cold that day.

1970 A.D. *Penthouse* is the first magazine to show pubic hair in its pictorials, though some mistake it for a Don King cameo.

1971 A.D. Charles P. Hall patents the waterbed. Shut up! It's for that back pain we were telling you about.

1971 A.D. Hugh Hefner moves into his L.A. Playboy Mansion. God's avenging angels update their Rolodexes.

1972 A.D. Linda Lovelace becomes the first true porn star, thanks to her dramatic turn in *Deep Throat*, the most successful adult film of all time. She then provides invaluable insider info to Woodward and Bernstein.

1974 A.D. Cancer, diabetes, heart disease, yadda yadda yadda. Medical history is made when the world's first penile implant is successfully performed—on a 70-year-old Russian! Four months after the surgery, the patient and his little Nikita are happily married.

1977 A.D. Victoria's Secret opens its mail-order doors. Business is slow until early the following year, when the recipients' boyfriends are finally done with the catalogs.

1978 A.D. *Debbie Does Dallas* premieres. Follow-ups *Debbie Does Delaware, Debbie Does Dubuque,* and even the hilarious Tim Conway direct-to-video hit *Debbie Does Dorf* make it one of the most successful franchises in smut history.

1980 A.D. Dr. Ruth's *Sexually Speaking* radio show debuts. American men are enthralled by the erotic ravings of a German circus midget who stands just 18 inches tall.

1987 A.D. Ilona Staller, a.k.a. porn star Cicciolina, campaigns topless and wins a seat in Rome's parliament. However, she soon decides to leave politics, preferring the relatively moral world of pornography over that of elected government.

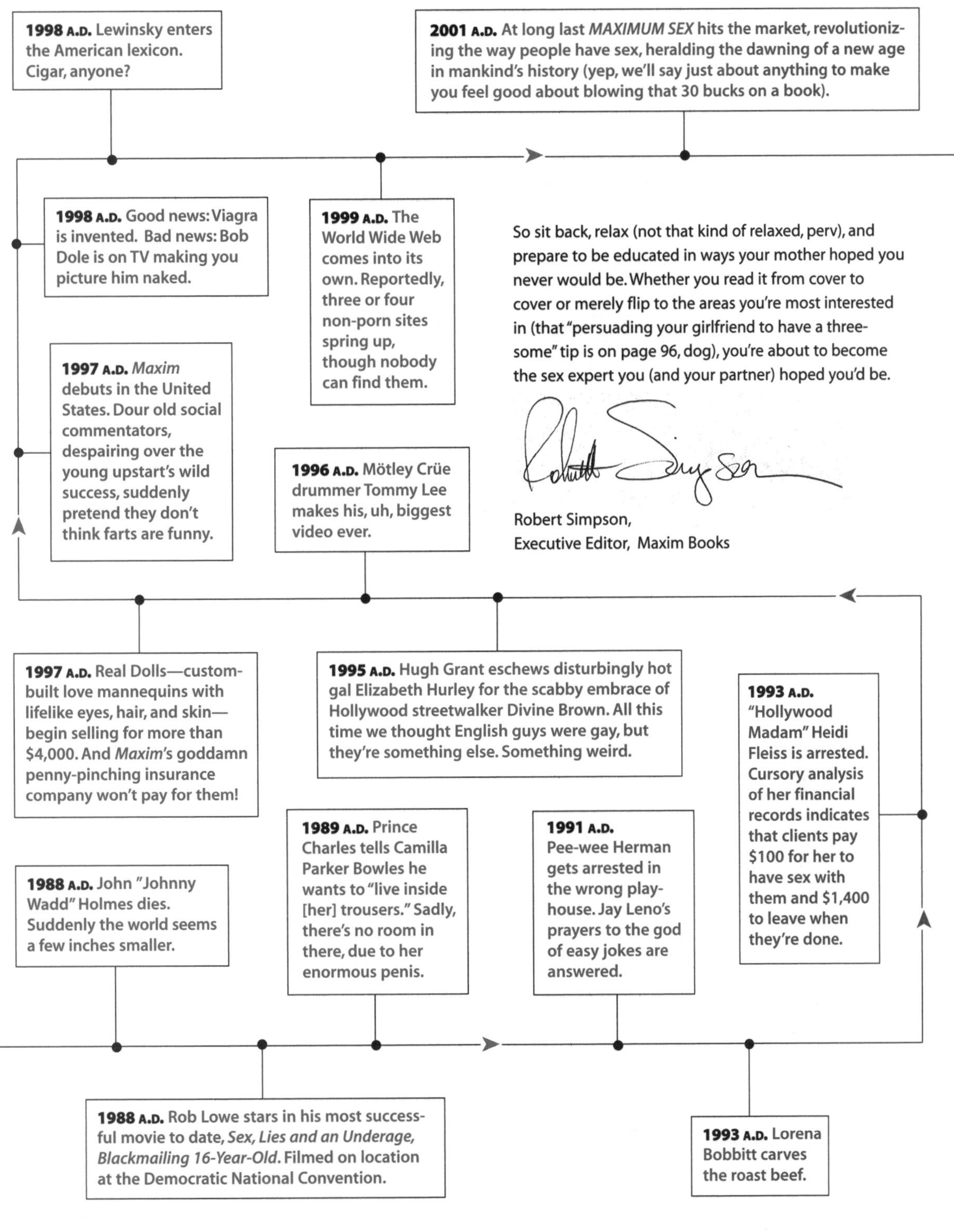

1988 A.D. John "Johnny Wadd" Holmes dies. Suddenly the world seems a few inches smaller.
1988 A.D. Rob Lowe stars in his most successful movie to date, *Sex, Lies and an Underage, Blackmailing 16-Year-Old*. Filmed on location at the Democratic National Convention.
1989 A.D. Prince Charles tells Camilla Parker Bowles he wants to "live inside [her] trousers." Sadly, there's no room in there, due to her enormous penis.
1991 A.D. Pee-wee Herman gets arrested in the wrong playhouse. Jay Leno's prayers to the god of easy jokes are answered.
1993 A.D. Lorena Bobbitt carves the roast beef.
1993 A.D. "Hollywood Madam" Heidi Fleiss is arrested. Cursory analysis of her financial records indicates that clients pay $100 for her to have sex with them and $1,400 to leave when they're done.
1995 A.D. Hugh Grant eschews disturbingly hot gal Elizabeth Hurley for the scabby embrace of Hollywood streetwalker Divine Brown. All this time we thought English guys were gay, but they're something else. Something weird.
1996 A.D. Mötley Crüe drummer Tommy Lee makes his, uh, biggest video ever.
1997 A.D. Real Dolls—custom-built love mannequins with lifelike eyes, hair, and skin—begin selling for more than $4,000. And *Maxim*'s goddamn penny-pinching insurance company won't pay for them!
1997 A.D. *Maxim* debuts in the United States. Dour old social commentators, despairing over the young upstart's wild success, suddenly pretend they don't think farts are funny.
1998 A.D. Good news: Viagra is invented. Bad news: Bob Dole is on TV making you picture him naked.
1998 A.D. Lewinsky enters the American lexicon. Cigar, anyone?
1999 A.D. The World Wide Web comes into its own. Reportedly, three or four non-porn sites spring up, though nobody can find them.
2001 A.D. At long last *MAXIMUM SEX* hits the market, revolutionizing the way people have sex, heralding the dawning of a new age in mankind's history (yep, we'll say just about anything to make you feel good about blowing that 30 bucks on a book).

So sit back, relax (not that kind of relaxed, perv), and prepare to be educated in ways your mother hoped you never would be. Whether you read it from cover to cover or merely flip to the areas you're most interested in (that "persuading your girlfriend to have a threesome" tip is on page 96, dog), you're about to become the sex expert you (and your partner) hoped you'd be.

Robert Simpson,
Executive Editor, Maxim Books

The Penis: Tool of the Trade

One-Eyed Trouser Snake, Foaming Beef Probe, Rumpleforeskin. Your love dart goes by many names, but its function remains the same—and you're not going to have much sex without it. After all, a man without a penis is like a carpenter without a hammer or a refrigerator repairman without his exposed butt crack. But even though most men are on a first-name basis with their love handle, many have a better knowledge of the inner workings of their car's fuel-injection system, and this lack of knowledge can be detrimental to a man's overall performance and effectiveness in the sack. The bottom line is that if you expect to be a master of the sex domain, you must first learn all there is to know about the workings of your flesh toy.

KNOW YOURSELF: HOW IT ALL WORKS

When it comes to what we know about penises, we're pretty much limited to what we can see, and considering that the view isn't the best (especially with that gut, humongo), there may be a few things you overlooked. Just to be sure, we'll take it from the top:

■ **Glans** (Head, Helmet)
The tip of your mighty love spear is better known by scientific types as the glans. For the uncircumcised, it usually spends its off hours covered by what's called the prepuce (foreskin to us regular Joes).

■ **Prepuce** (Foreskin, Turtleneck, Cock Warmer, Monk's Hood, Meat Casing)
While the jury is still out on whether this unique sheath that covers the glans is necessary or just God's way of showing that people will take a knife to most anything to stay in His good graces, this skin is what covers the glans on most non-American penises.

FACT OR FACTOID?

The longest erect penis, confirmed by reliable medical data: 13.5 inches long and 6.25 inches around, documented in the early 20th century by the esteemed Robert L. Dickinson, M.D. Soon after the term "penis envy" became widespread.

Since you're probably not privy to a pouch, we'll give you the scoop. While the outside is composed pretty much of regular flesh, the inside layer that comes in contact with the mushroom cap is a moist, mucosal layer that protects the glans from abrasions and maintains its sensitivity.

Foreskin champions claim that this natural reserve of skin gives their hog the slack it needs to slide in and out friction free during the humpty-hump. And anything which helps that ol' piston action go smoothly can't be bad.

■ **Corona**
This is the "crown," or ridge of flesh where the glans (see above) joins with the shaft (see below). Also, for those who like to spend their free time shaking their fist at their ex-girlfriend, it's called a hand stopper.

■ **Shaft**
Who's the black private dick that's a sex machine to all the chicks? That's right (well, yours may be more pinkish): shaft! This is the actual penis part, minus the glans.

■ **Frenulum** (Frenum)
If you're a member of the uncut, this is the thin strip of highly sensitive flesh on the underside of the penis that keeps the foreskin in place. If you went under the neonatal knife, the beardlike strip of wrinkled skin is all that remains. Some (mostly the uncircumcised) say it's the male equivalent of the G-spot, which gives us yet one more reason to resent our parents.

FACT OR FACTOID?

In 1995 a Hong Kong Chi Kung master Mo Ka Wang lifted over 250 pounds of weight two feet off the floor with only his penis.

■ **Urethra**
This is the major multi-use highway of the penis that runs from the bladder to the outside world. Urine, semen, sperm, pre-ejaculate, and if the gods be especially unkind to you, kidney stones, all travel this route at some point or another. While dozens of on-ramps converge with it, there's only one exit ramp at the very end of the road. Coincidentally, Urethra Franklin is the name of the popular diva that sang "Freeway of Love."

■ **Meatus** (Pee Hole)
The opening at the tip of the penis that allows the passage of both urine and semen. It is also part of Meat Loaf's Latin name, Meatus Loafus.

■ **Smegma**
Yes, it's as gross as it sounds. Among the uncircumcised, smegma is the cheesy by-product of natural lubrication. You only need to worry about this if you're uncut.

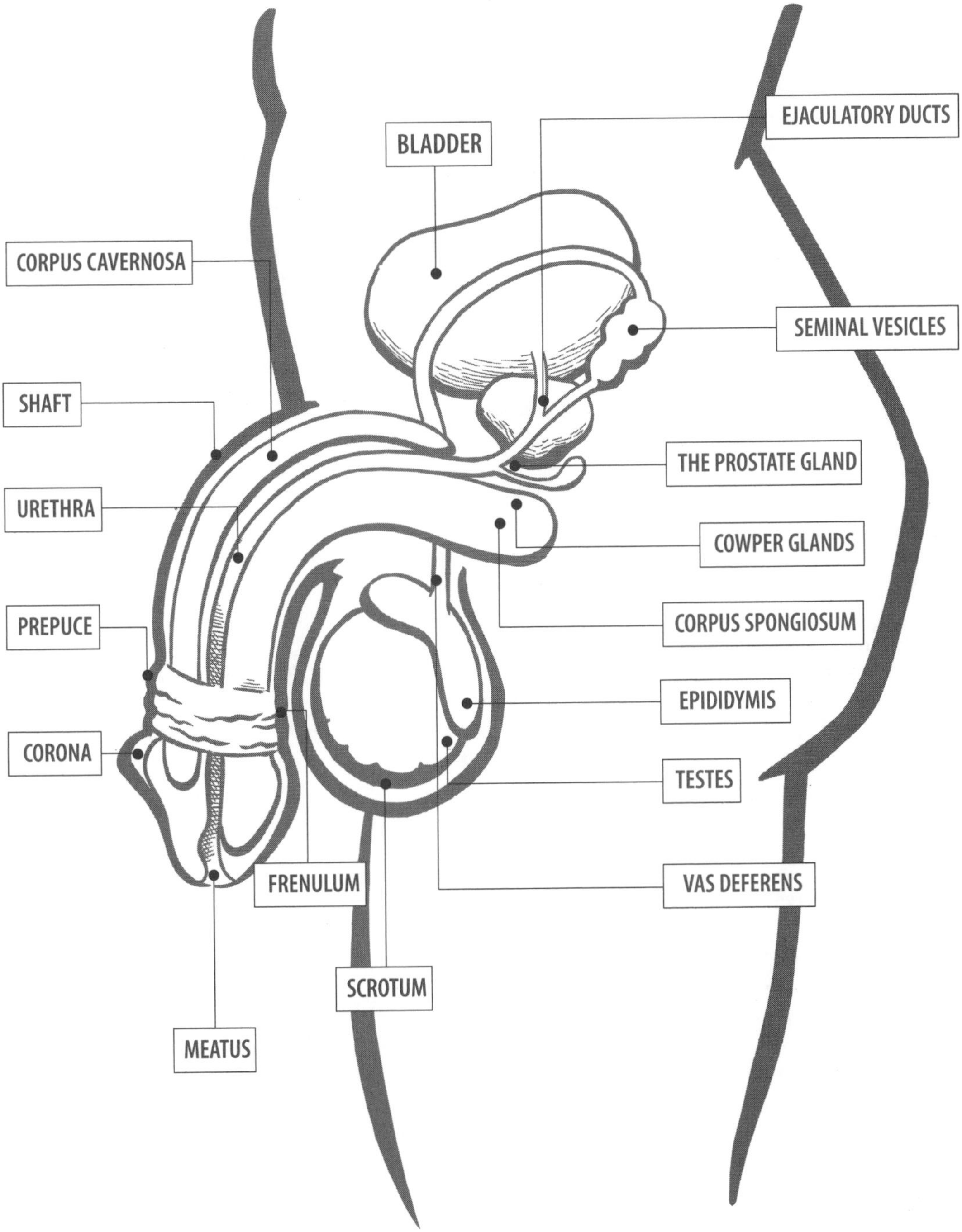

EJACULATORY DUCTS
BLADDER
CORPUS CAVERNOSA
SEMINAL VESICLES
SHAFT
THE PROSTATE GLAND
URETHRA
COWPER GLANDS
CORPUS SPONGIOSUM
PREPUCE
EPIDIDYMIS
CORONA
TESTES
FRENULUM
VAS DEFERENS
SCROTUM
MEATUS

■ **Scrotum** (Ball Sack, Jewel Purse)
The wrinkled skin sac that hangs down, behind, and below the penis and keeps the family jewels relatively safe. Its main purpose is not to serve as Target No.1 when being attacked, but to maintain the testes at approximately 94 to 96 degrees Fahrenheit, the temperature at which they most effectively produce sperm. A thin layer of muscle fibers on the inner wall of your scrote draws your bridge up when it's too cold and relaxes when it's too warm, allowing your testes' sweet chariot to swing low.

FACT OR FACTOID?

In the 1920s, to keep some unmarried men chaste, doctors would pierce the foreskin and inserted a thin wire, then solder the ends together. A vasectomy doesn't look nearly as brutal anymore, now does it?

■ **Testes** (Testicles, Balls, Nuts, Family Jewels)
Each nut holds about 800 tiny convoluted pipes called the seminiferous tubules, which generate sperm. If you laid these tubules end to end, they'd stretch to nearly six and a half football fields in length. Each testicle produces about 15 million sperm every 24 hours.

■ **Epididymis**
Kinda like a little wine cellar, the epididymis is a holding pen where sperm produced by the seminiferous tubules mature. The sperm kick back here waiting for the fire alarm to ring, hoping that when the time comes, they'll be racing to fertilize Ms. Egg, and not end up running down the center spread of the latest issue of *Hustler*.

■ **Vas Deferens**
The ducts leading from the epididymis loading dock to the prostate (see below). These bad boys are the ducts that are cut and tied when your wife and 13 children finally convince you to have a vasectomy.

■ **Seminal Vesicles**
The seminal vesicles produce about 70 percent of your (surprise, surprise) semen, the stuff that carries and protects your sperm. Your ejaculate consists of about 97 percent semen and only 3 percent sperm. Semen is high in fructose, a simple sugar that acts as sperm food.

■ **Corpora Cavernosa**
The corpora cavernosa are the two spongy bodies of erectile tissue on the top side of the penis that become engorged with blood from arteries that lead to the penis, thus causing an erection.

■ **The Prostate Gland**
No, its sole purpose is not to afflict men with prostate cancer (the most prevalent type of cancer). The chestnut-sized gland secretes fluids that balance the pH in the urethra and vagina to make the environment less hostile (meaning, less acidic) to sperm. An internal sphincter, it also squeezes the urethral duct shut during ejaculation to keep urine out of the mix. If you're a male over 30, it's a good idea to make annual visits to Dr. Jellyfinger to keep an eye (a finger, actually) on the health of the prostate. Also considered the male G-spot.

FACT OR FACTOID?

Blame it on the wank: During the Victorian Era, many noteworthy maladies were associated with masturbation, such as impotence, epilepsy, tuberculosis, alcoholism, blindness, paralysis, heart disease, gout, hernia, curvature of the spine, imbecility, sexual deviancy, insanity, rheumatism, gonorrhea, priapism, tumors, constipation, hemorrhoids, headaches, female homosexuality, death, and a really bad case of carpal tunnel syndrome.

■ **Corpus Spongiosum**
Like the corpora cavernosa, the corpus spongiosum fills with blood during an erection, the only difference being that it is found on the underside of the penis. The third spongy body-contains the urethra.

■ **Ejaculatory Ducts**
The paths through the prostate that sperm travel during ejaculation.

■ **Cowper's Glands**
The Cowper's glands secrete small amounts of pre-ejaculate fluid prior to orgasm. This fluid neutralizes the acidity within the urethra to make the road to glory more sperm-friendly.

SEX MYTH: Wearing briefs instead of boxers will lower your sperm count.

SEX TRUTH: Not unless they're permanently shrink-wrapped around your balls. Anyone who's ever been hit in the crotch with a baseball doesn't need to be told that the family jewels are sensitive creatures. These fellas must be kept at an average temperature of 94 degrees, almost five degrees lower than body temp, a process that would become every guy's primary hobby if not for the magical, mystical scrotum. But does wearing tighty-whities, which draw the nuts unnaturally close to the abdomen, lower your sperm count? Researchers at UCLA exaggerated the effect of briefs by trapping guys in polyester and even molded aluminum cups. Result: a rise of less than two degrees in the scrotum swimmers.

HOW IT ALL CUMS TOGETHER

Now that all the puzzle pieces are in place, what's the big picture? Well, depending on who you're talking to, the main functions of the penis are procreation and urination. In terms of procreation, all you probably know is that the whole act feels really good. The reality is that to blow your wad, your little buddy and his parts go through a process akin to a battle plan. Here's what happens, from hard-on to shoot.

FACT OR FACTOID?

The origin of the word *dick* has nothing to do with Richard Nixon. Since a man killed by hanging often develops a major woody after death (or beforehand, if you're Michael Hutchence), witnesses to an execution used to laugh and point at what they cruelly called the "derrick" (after the long cargo arm that protrudes from a ship's mast), which gradually shortened to "dick."

Sound the Alarms!

With the exception of "morning wood," everything starts with arousal. Whether by being led by the hand to a dimly lit bedroom or you just got a peek down Judy Wonderstuff's amply packed shirt, the part of your brain dedicated to sexual response gets flicked on like a light switch by your stimulus of choice. Your pulse quickens, and your testicles become large (or larger, depending on the size of your ego) and elevated. The brain begins the production of endorphins, the neurotransmitters responsible for that Dr. Feelgood sensation you're about to be bombarded with, and voilá! You are aroused.

Commander Sulu, Arm the Torpedoes!

At this point, a series of electrical impulses travel from your brain down the spinal cord, which tells a set of arteries valves to dilate, allowing the spongy tissues in the penis to fill with blood like a sinking submarine. Simultaneously, the set of valves in your veins, which will later drain the blood from your penis, clamp shut. As the arteries continue to pump blood into your Li'l Elvis, the opening and closing of these valves ensures that it'll soon be your Big Elvis, ready and raring to go like it was time for your big comeback special. At the same time, your testicles increase in size by as much as 50 percent ("Whoa, I'm gonna need a bigger pair of pants!"), as they too fill with blood and are slowly drawn up toward your body. Your blood pressure is also on the rise, and your heart rate is getting quite the workout.

As more and more blood is pumped into the penis, the various glands receive the call to get to work. The prostate enlarges, and a light goes on in the Cowper's gland, which begins to release its slippery pre-ejaculate, designed to keep you—and her—pH balanced.

Closer, Closer . . .

As the big moment draws nearer, your pulse has gone from stopwatch to jackhammer and you're getting ready to blow, thanks to whatever external penile stimulus you're currently enjoying. You are now approaching the inevitable point of no return. Your pee hole has dilated, and the testes become harder and harder and drawn closer to the body.

WHEN "DICK" JUST WON'T DO

In a world filled with all too many Michaels and Jonathans, it's nice to know that when it comes to alternative names for our love hammers, we prefer to take the road less taken.Top Ten Penis Names: Drumroll, please…

10. Mr. Happy
9. Jack (in the Box)
8. Willy
7. Harry and the Hendersons
6. Saint Peter
5. Old Blind Bob
4. Gladius Maximus
3. Big Jim and the Twins
2. Vlad the Impaler
1. Russell the One-Eyed Wonder Muscle

FACT OR FACTOID?

The size of your testicles has a direct bearing on the amount of sperm you produce, which is why a horse can produce 22 billion serm per rendezvous, while even the most ball-heavy human is lucky to squirt out 500 million.

Fire the Torpedoes!

The part of the brain that controls sexual response, the limbic system, is now swimming in endorphins. You feel really, really gooooood. Sphincter muscles contract and close off the part of the urethra that goes through the prostate. Then, along with causing a series of major involuntary muscle contractions akin to a full-body sneeze, the brain sends the signal to fire. Sperm has already left the epididymis and is heading down the vas deferens. The prostate adds its contribution as the penis pumps the mix of semen and sperm to its final destination (whether that's a condom, a tissue, or even an actual vagina). The Big O is followed by a series of smaller convulsions, and the whole deal takes about 45 seconds. (Hopefully, though, you usually last longer than it took you to read this section.)

Postmortem

The valves that maintained the erection now open to allow the blood to drain out of the penis. Conversely, the arterial valves that opened to allow the influx of blood close, and Big Elvis has left the building. Unless you need to reciprocate the favor to a partner, you can have that cigarette now.

HOW BIG IS BIG?

OK, now that we've gotten the mechanics out of the way, it's time to get to the real reason you're reading this chapter: to find out how big your dick is compared to everyone else's, right? While the answer is usually at least two inches longer than whatever *you* happen to be sporting, there are several studies that, while giving a very general idea as to what is average, can't all agree and pinpoint the precise, universal average. Here's what the penis pros say:

■ Click "Dick"

According to the Internet's popular and surprisingly thorough sixth edition of *The Definitive Penis Size Survey*, which has surveyed over 3,100 certainly honest Web surfers, the average size is 6.4 inches long (when erect) and five inches in circumference. Though the survey and results are considered as professional as many other studies, we are talking about lonely, anonymous males detailing the correct measurements of their endowments. And while it's probably true that the members of society most intimately familiar with the size of their erect member are probably those who spend an inordinate amount of time on the Internet—c'mon, we know they aren't spending time researching the armor thickness of WWII battleships—who isn't going to fudge a little when asked to anonymously reveal the size of his member?

■ Old-School Sizers

The Kinsey Institute (the usual yardstick, er, ruler by which most surveys are measured) and a study where they saw the surveyed men taking matters into their own hands and re-emerging from their private measuring area to report the results. The average erect penis proved to be five to seven inches long and between four to six inches around. That college frat boys were doing the self-measuring may also explain why there were a few claims of nine-inch-long schlongs with fire-hose-size girths.

FACT OR FACTOID?

Though most everyone believes women and men couldn't be more different, at the time of orgasm, they both experience contractions at exact 0.8-second intervals, or at least that's what women tell us.

A Pile of Rubber-ish?

The Durex condom company was also interested in men's penis size, though their motives were purely capital. In a survey of 2,935 mostly British and American men under the age of 25, the Durex folks determined an average erect size, unsheathed, of 6.4 inches among its respondents, and a 5.2-inch circumference erect. Durex also was able to determine that it wished more people bought Durex products.

Academic Achievements

Another study involving 60 men conducted by the University of California at San Francisco determined that the average size of their erect penises was 5.1 inches long and 4.9 inches in girth, the results of which most men will like a lot more than the study spearheaded by a Brazilian urologist who measured 150 men and reported that the average size of their erections was 5.7 inches long and 4.7 inches around. We say that you take whatever study fits your particular situation (or better yet, underestimates it) the best and use that one as gospel.

BIG DILL OR BABY GHERKIN?

So if you're wondering how your own tube steak measures up in the grand scheme of things, here's a look at the infamous survey (sorry—of white college males only) from *Kinsey Data*:

Length (inches)	% of Men
3.75	0.2
4	0.3
4.25	0.2
4.5	1.7
4.75	0.8
5	4.2
5.25	4.4
5.5	10.7
5.75	8
6	23.9
6.25	8.8
6.5	14.3
6.75	5.7
7	9.5
7.25	1.8
7.5	2.9
7.75	1
8	1
8.25	0.3
8.5	0.3
8.75	0.1
9	0.1

SIZE: DOES IT REALLY MATTER?

Now that you know where you stand, it's time to find out if any of this really matters. We polled a bunch of real women to see how they feel about size. Is the saying "It's not the size of the boat, but it's how you disembark the passengers" just that—a line to make the baby carrots of the world feel better—or is it indeed how women really feel? Overall, we did find a couple of size queens, but most of the women agreed that when it comes to penises, more is not necessarily merrier.

■ "I had to break up with Keith because his 11 inches kept giving me urinary tract infections and a good dose of pain when he tried to deep-thrust. Not to mention, I couldn't go down on him without the gag reflex kicking in."—Alisa, 28, architect

■ "I was with a guy once who was too big, like in the width, and it was really painful. But I don't think there's really such a thing as too small."—Nina, 31, graphic designer

■ "I don't really think the size of a guy's penis is important. I would say anything that hurts is too big, but nothing is really too small. There's definitely such a thing as too big, though. After a point it's just painful and doesn't feel good. I would never-dump someone based on penis size. That's just ridiculous. I've found that guys with smaller penises tend to be better in bed. Maybe it's because they're insecure, I don't know. But they definitely seem to try harder and make sure I feel good."—Jessica, 24 marketing coordinator

■ "I would never choose to be with a man based on the size of his penis. It wouldn't even be a factor. For the most part bigger is better, to a point. I was with a guy once who had a huge penis, and sex was really difficult. He was really careful not to

hurt me, but that also meant he was always holding back and never really letting go."—Laurie, 25, exotic dancer

■ "I prefer not too long but with some girth. If it's too small, it's not feeling so much during the actual sex part that's disappointing; if it's really big, it makes foreplay really exciting. Just the thought of 'Oh, my God, he's so big.' But I think during sex it doesn't make a big difference. The worst thing is too long, 'cause it hurts like crazy."—Megan, 30, production editor

■ "I wouldn't say I've never dumped a guy because his penis was too small, because it's never gotten that far. Once I found out what I was in for, I just never called him back. I am a bit of a size queen. I've actually slept with guys I didn't know that well because they told me they had a big penis."—Liz, 33, sales manager

■ "There is absolutely nothing worse than a Crayola. You know, the dick that is so thin, you feel like you should thread it rather than suck it. Giving head should in no way resemble flossing."—Amanda, 29, bartender

PENIS PANIC

Financial woes and a tepid love life, getting you down? Cheer up! At least your penis isn't shriveling away. Not so for victims of shrinking-penis panic attacks, due in some cases to *koro*, the psychological delusion that Mr. Happy's saying bye-bye. Some examples:

INDIA, 1982: Spurred by the rumor of a shrinking-penis epidemic, thousands of concerned mothers bring their sons to hospitals en masse. First, however, they bind the poor boys' penises with string to prevent further shrinkage—"Aw, Mom! You're embarrassing me!"—a preventive measure that produces a multitude of lacerations and ulcers. Quick-thinking docs quell the hysteria by conducting large-scale public penis measuring.

UNITED STATES, 1996: An immigrant from Guinea, enraged by the prosecution of O.J. Simpson (who turned out to be innocent, by the way), comes to believe that his penis is shrinking. To raise public awareness of his predicament, he does the only sensible thing: He kidnaps a nursing-home patient. (Anyone else smell sitcom here? Get UPN on the phone…)

WESTERN AFRICA, 1997: A mob from Senegal and Ivory Coast rounds up 20 or so "magicians" accused of casting penis-shrinking curses on villagers. When a quick demo proves that everyone's penis is in fact perfectly normal, magicians obviously repaired the, ah, shortage when no one was looking. And without further ado, the mob burns the bastards alive.

FACT OR FACTOID?

Women say penis size is only 10th on their What-We're-Looking-For list.

GIRTH IS WHAT IT'S WORTH

As everyone knows, it's not the length of your flagpole that counts, it's the girth; great for guys hung like tuna cans, not for men hung like licorice ropes.

Circumference (inches)	% of Men
1.5	0.3
1.75	0.4
2	0.4
2.25	0.2
2.5	0.3
2.75	0.3
3	0.4
3.25	0.4
3.5	0.9
3.75	1.1
4	6.3
4.25	6.3
4.5	17.1
4.75	11.7
5	24.1
5.25	9.9
5.5	11.5
5.75	3
6	3.9
6.25	0.5
6.5	0.5
6.75	0.1

DICKS OF THE ANIMAL WORLD

There's no debate as to who's the world's smartest animal, if we do say so ourselves. But as we learned in high school, a big IQ doesn't always land women. With information from Jim Knowlton, whose 'Penises of the Animal Kingdom' poster you probably remember from Sunday school (Scientific Novelty, 888-264-6255), we measure up the equipment of our critter pals.

■ **Humans** Be proud—we're the biggest of the primates, with 90 percent of our species measuring between five and seven inches long.

■ **Gorillas** For all their chest thumping, the big apes reach a pathetic 1.5 inches when erect.

■ **Chimpanzees** A chimp's banana is about four inches long, but narrow, like a pencil. Not bad for a little guy.

■ **Horses** A galloping two and a half feet, which undoubtedly helped keep those masculine Wild West pioneers humble.

■ **Pigs** Porky packs a 20- to 30-inch sausage, only half of which is exposed (and shaped like a corkscrew, just like his tail).

■ **Dogs** Big fellas, like Great Danes, can have seven- to nine-inch doggy paddles, while shrimpy little Chihuahuas can be all but microscopic. Fun fact: Dog boners have actual bones in them.

■ **Elephants** Pachyderm puds are the largest of any land creature's, reaching a whopping four and a half feet and tipping the scale at 65 pounds. (Can a porn movie titled *Cumbo* be far behind?)

■ **Blue whales** Their 10-foot underwater drilling equipment is by far the largest in the animal kingdom, no matter what Bruce Willis says.

■ **Fleas** He ain't big, but when a flea's ready to dog, his seventh leg reaches a third of the length of his body.

■ **Barnacles** These seafaring suckers have the largest mast relative to body size—a barnacle's boner is several times longer than its body.

FAMOUS PENISES Don't believe that all big dicks go on to be porn stars; some go into politics, while others enjoy fame in less titillating fare. From the exhaustive research compiled in Gary Griffin's tome *Penis Size and Enlargement*, here are the alleged measurements of some famous folks (believe it if you will):

Ernest Hemingway	"30-30 Rifle Shell"	David Letterman	9 inches
Bill Clinton	5 inches long, with a circumference like a quarter	Groucho Marx	9 inches
		Robby Benson	9 inches
Humphrey Bogart	8 inches	Donald Sutherland	9 inches
Michael Caine	8 inches	Jim Brown (football great)	9 inches
Cary Grant	8 inches	Shawn Cassidy	9–9½ inches
Steve Martin	8 inches	Mikhael Baryshnikov	9½ inches
Tom Brokaw	8 inches	Jim Nabors (Gomer Pyle)	9–10 inches
Rock Hudson	8½ inches	Milton Berle	10 inches
Randy Travis	8½ inches	Liam Neeson	10 inches
Lorenzo Lamas	8-plus inches	Ed Begley Jr.	10 inches
Eddie Murphy	8–9 inches	Charlie Chaplin	12 inches
Willem Dafoe	9 inches	Grigori Rasputin	12¾ inches

HOW TO MAKE YOUR PENIS LOOK BIGGER

If there were a magic potion to make your penis larger, we'd have it in the office water cooler. Surgery can enhance and enlarge your Johnson, but even if successful, "surgery doesn't necessarily lead to a bigger erection," says Maggie Paley, author of *The Book of the Penis.* "You'll simply look better in the shower." And that will only impress the guys at the gym. There are, however, a few ways to cheat. Here's the skinny (sorry).

> **FACT OR FACTOID?**
>
> **Of the penis' overall length, one-third to one-half lies within the body, where it connects to the pubic arch. It can be felt at the perineum, the space between the testicles and the anus also known as the taint ('tain't the balls,'tain't the...butthole.)**

FAKING IT: COSMETIC METHODS

■ Shorten Your Short Hairs

We're not talking a full shave here, only a little off the sides. Trimming around the tallest tree in the forest will let your scraggly larch mimic a mighty oak—just be careful with those electric hedge clippers.

■ Take to the Treadmill

If you're chunky, your belly may have swallowed up to an inch of your fire hose. Get rid of that gut and you'll have a comeback special taking place in your pants.

■ Wear Makeup

Apply your girlfriend's foundation to the tip of your penis and the front of the shaft. Then, if need be, dye your newly cropped pubes black. The contrast will accentuate what little length you have. (We don't have to point out how pathetic actually doing this is, do we?)

■ Buy a Funhouse Mirror

Another way to supersize your Mini-Me is to stand naked in front of a funhouse mirror. Of course, your distorted reflection might also reveal feet the size of Volkswagens, but you know what they say about guys with big feet.

■ Move to France

OK, so it won't actually make you look bigger, but you'll instantly sound bigger thanks to their confounded metric system: Four scrawny inches becomes a more-than-manly 10 centimeters. And in France that's more than enough to make you the next Long Dong d'Argent.

THE REAL DEAL: SURGICAL PENIS ENLARGEMENT

If cosmetic cheats don't give you the yardage you want, and you've got a masochistic streak wider than a side show fakir who hammers nails into his nose—not to mention a bank account that'd impress even P.T. Barnum—then you might consider putting Willy under the knife. Sure, it sounds like a dream—you go in as Tiny Tim and come out the other side as Big John—but most methods of penis-enlargement surgery are so excruciatingly painful, they could have been developed by the Grand Inquisitor of the Spanish Inquisition.

In addition to the pain factor, the risk of a botched surgery is unusually high. In 1994, a cosmetic surgeon in Miami was convicted of manslaughter after his patient bled to death following a penis-enlargement operation. If that's the kind of risk you're willing to take, here are some of your options.

■ The Bihari Procedure

There is a ligament that supports your penis when it's erect, but also manages to keep part of it hidden within your body like a frightened turtle. In the Bihari procedure, the ligament is snipped, which can add between one half and two inches to your overall length. In some cases the ligament halves reunite, so it is suggested that postop patients actually wear weights on their wang to prevent this from happening. Once these ligaments have been severed, your soldier will never again stand at attention, but you'll always be able to find due south. If you've ever seen a football player snap a ligament during a game on one of those NFL highlight reels, you may want to think twice about this one.

■ Hot Fat Injections

Sure, snipping ligaments may add an inch or two to your length, but everyone knows girth is whats got worth. In an attempt to add girth to your newly elongated schlong, doctors will suck fat out of your thighs, stomach, or ass and inject it into the base of your penis. The biggest risk in this procedure is infection, and the only cure for gangrene is amputation. Kinda puts you waaay behind square one we'd say. If you clear the infection hurdle, you may need several expensive injections for the girth to take permanently, as the fat has the annoying habit of being reabsorbed into your body, leaving you with hard nodules all over your penis (ribbed, for her pleasure).

■ Calico Penis Quilting Bee

To avoid that nasty fat-reabsorption problem, some doctors have taken an even more drastic measure. First, the skin along the shaft of the penis is slit open. Then patches of skin are removed from your ass and the layers are *sewn in along the shaft*. This is a highly effective method if you're attempting to achieve that sought-after Frankenpenis look that's all the rage this year on the fashion runways. Furthermore, the skin on the penis is highly specialized with unique stretching qualities found nowhere else on the body. The mixing of non-spandex skin to the natural spandex dermis will make your meat rope look like it was tied in knots. And this is if the procedure goes as planned. For an extra added bonus, the graft might not take properly, so you end up with a horrifyingly scarred wiener instead of the old "just fine as it is" model.

HELP! THEY MANGLED MY PENIS!

Meet a desperate man who went in to get his banana stretched and came out with fruit salad.

To explore the sinister side of a trendy but unproven penis-enlargement operation, we found a guy in his 20s whose innocent effort to increase his swing went horribly, horribly wrong. To spare him any further mortification, we'll refer to him as Bob Dangle…although his real name is John T. Hopkins of Kalamazoo, Michigan. (Just kidding.)

Bob, a manager at a major department store chain, is very willing to talk about his ordeal. "One of my employees and I saw the ad in the paper, and we were joking about it," he says. "Privately I said to myself, Let me give 'em a call and see what it's all about."

Though he'd never had complaints from any of his partners, Dangle himself had always been unhappy with the size of his penis. "So I gave 'em a call and went in for the orientation. I talked with a salesman, not a doctor, which was just a little strange," he continues. "But he told me all about the procedure and reassured me. I found out later that he left out a lot of major, major information about the after-effects of the procedure."

At the time, however, armed with what he thought was all the information he needed, Dangle decided to go ahead with the $6,000 operation. It still bothered him that he hadn't spoken to an actual doctor, and when he arrived on the morning of the operation (after shaving his nether regions per instructions) and he and another patient were told that the doc wouldn't speak to them until after the surgery, they drew the line. Following a small waiting-room fuss, the doctor emerged and answered some of their questions.

As Dangle lay on the operating table waiting for the anesthesiologist to put

FACT OR FACTOID?

The first illustration of a surgical procedure dates back to 2200 B.C., Egypt. The doctors were performing a circumcision, apparently not wanting anyone but the pharaoh to have his own little pyramid.

FACT OR FACTOID?

In 1993 the *Bangkok Post* reported on quacks operating in Thailand who performed at least 100 bogus penis-enlargement operations. The surgery involved injections of a mixture of olive oil and chalk, among various other substances. One hospital official noted that he had even seen victims' penises containing portions of the Bangkok telephone directory.

him out, he had mixed feelings. "I was nervous but also excited, because I was looking forward to the fantastic outcome that the doctor had promised me," Dangle recalls. "I couldn't wait for it to be over with, because I was going to be better than before."

Dangle's surgery involved the first two of the procedures listed in the previous section—procedures that cause intense groin pain even when you merely read about them—but his lingering fears were eased by the doctor's postop enthusiasm. "I remember him saying 'I think I've done the best job on you I've ever done,'" says Dangle. "The first thing I wanted to do was to check my new penis. But the whole thing was bandaged, penis and scrotum. Plus, I was in so much pain, I couldn't even bend down."

He had been warned to expect discomfort, but nothing like the agony that was in store. The doctor's orders were to keep the bandages on for seven to 10 days, but Dangle took it upon himself to

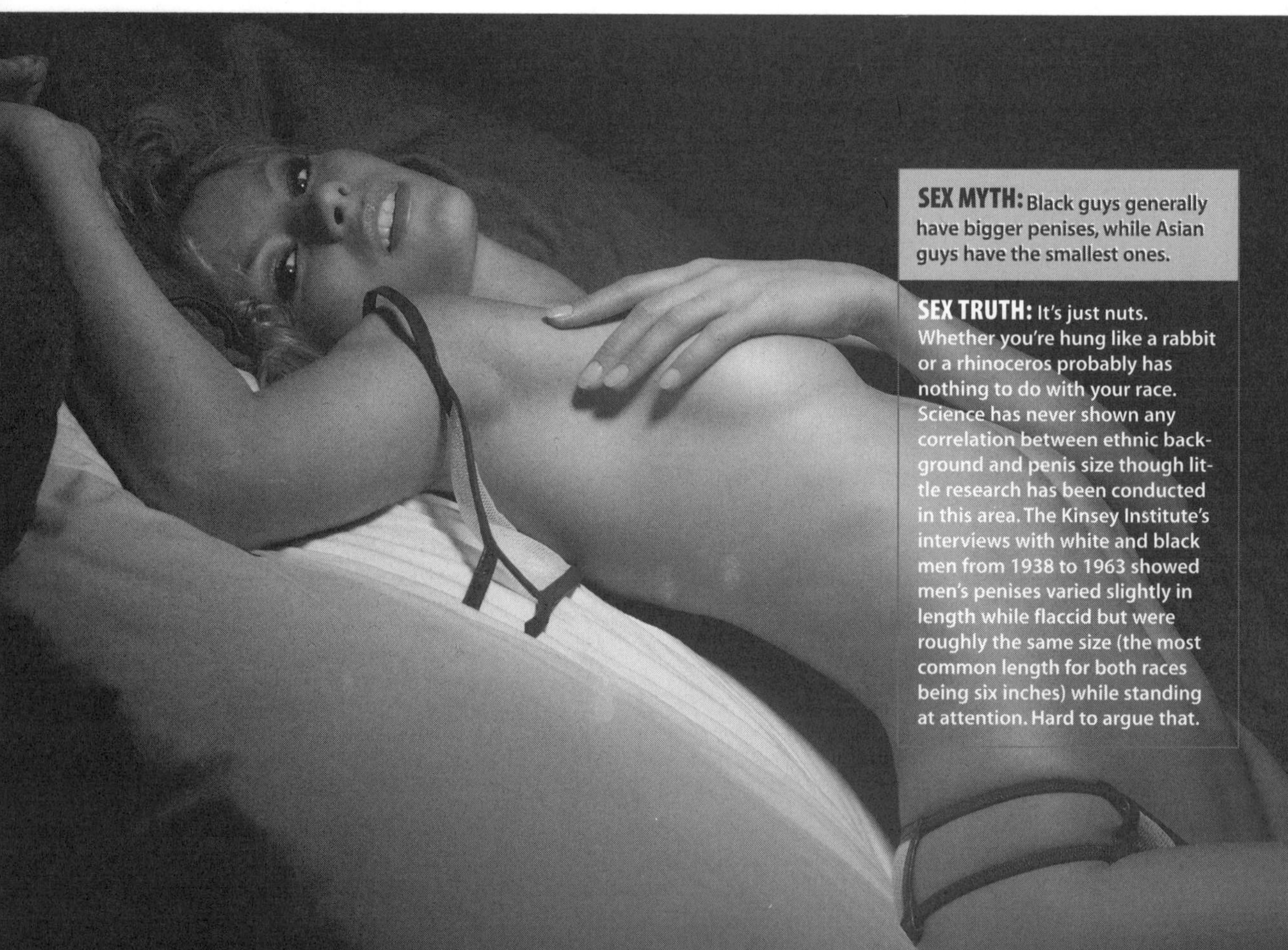

SEX MYTH: Black guys generally have bigger penises, while Asian guys have the smallest ones.

SEX TRUTH: It's just nuts. Whether you're hung like a rabbit or a rhinoceros probably has nothing to do with your race. Science has never shown any correlation between ethnic background and penis size though little research has been conducted in this area. The Kinsey Institute's interviews with white and black men from 1938 to 1963 showed men's penises varied slightly in length while flaccid but were roughly the same size (the most common length for both races being six inches) while standing at attention. Hard to argue that.

remove them the very next day. The way he saw it, he had no choice: They were saturated with blood.

"Clearly, I was bleeding from my incisions," says Dangle, "and my testicles had swollen to an unreal size. They were blue and velvety, like blood was building up in them to the bursting point."

His doctor was out of town, and the covering physician didn't return his what-the-fuck-is-happening-to-my-weenie calls until the following day. He hadn't been prescribed any pain medication after the surgery because his doctor *didn't have the right notepad with him* (we can't make this stuff up, folks). Luckily, his waiting-room efforts to pick up the receptionist paid off: A phone call to her secured Dangle some much-needed relief (well, she got him the painkillers, anyway).

Now that the bandages were off, Dangle was devastated by what he saw. "It was grotesque, because of the swelling and everything else. The doctor said it would go down after a few weeks, and it did. But the swelling gave way to lumps at the top and bottom of my penis."

Then things started to get bad. One of the bits of information Dangle claims he never received from his doctor was that he should wear weights on his new penis to keep it from *retreating back into his body!!!* The weights, on which is clearly printed THIS PRODUCT IS SOLD AS A NOVELTY ITEM ONLY, are about three pounds. "You're supposed to wrap 'em on and leave 'em there to dangle," says Dangle. "It's very painful, to the point where you feel like your testicles are popping out of place."

The lumps at the top and bottom of his penis, the result of injected fat coagulating instead of spreading evenly, are a disturbingly common side effect. "All I can say is that my penis is deformed," says Dangle. "It's the same length as before, only now it's like there's a golf ball inside my penis when I'm erect."

Appearance is only half the story; functionality took a big hit as well. For weeks after the operation, it hurt Dangle to urinate—to this day, a few seconds after he thinks he's done pissing, he'll have to go a little more. But that's just an annoyance; sex is now a nightmare. "It's painful to have an erection, not to mention to ejaculate," Dangle says. "I feel as if someone came along and just massacred me."

Still, ya gotta try, and after a few months, Dangle was cleared to road-test his flawed new unit. He crashed hard. "My first partner was grossed out about how deformed it looked," says Dangle. "We were trying to have oral sex, and she actually said to me, 'I just want to get up and leave.'"

"Naturally, I was humiliated beyond belief." He gamely persevered with a second partner, but although he got further, it was still not what you'd call pleasurable. "When I put it in her, it was very painful, especially at the top and bottom of my penis, where the lumps were." The pain was so intense, he had to keep stopping the action; finally, swimming in agony and mortification, he had to call it off.

After spending an additional $7,500 on surgery to fix his penis' appearance, Dangle sued his doctor, and they reached a settlement for an undisclosed sum. He claims he's unhappy with the amount, and we believe him. How much cash would you accept in exchange for a permanently fucked-up sex life? "It's very hard when a sex partner actually makes you feel worse about yourself," says Dangle. "When they see it and go to touch it, you can watch them getting turned off. And that makes you feel like dirt."

Dangle's is an extreme case, certainly, and there are no doubt many examples of happily elongated customers. But it's worth noting that the American Urological Association "considers subcutaneous fat injection for increasing penile girth, and division of the suspensory ligament of the penis for increasing penile length, to be procedures which have not been shown to be safe or efficacious." In other words, get the surgery and you're taking your dick into your own hands. And not in a particularly enjoyable way either.

DO-IT-YOURSELF KITS

The bulge in your back pocket no bigger than the one in front? Save bucks with these quacky nonsurgical options... if you dare.

THE CIRCLE DEVICE

The Plan: A hinged pewter cock ring gradually stretches your member as you go about your day.
The Pitch: "The longer you wear it, the longer your penis will become. There is no limit!"
The Price: $275
(www.penis-enlarger.com)
Freeware Version: Duct-tape rock to member. (Don't forget: Remove with quick pull, not the slow rip.)

FACT OR FACTOID?

Lost your balls? New silicone testicles can be had for $2,000 a set at the Clinique de Chirurgie Esthetique St. Joseph, in Montreal. They're only for looks, but imagine the fun you'll have when someone kicks you in the package and you just smile.

MAGNUM EXTENSION SYSTEM

The Plan: An elastic band ties the tip of your cock to your thigh, loaded-catapult-style, pulling your member away from your body.
The Pitch: "John Holmes, American porn star, apparently used this method of penis enlargement and kept it a secret."
The Price: $19.95
(www.largerpenis.com)
Freeware Version: Knot old pair of tighty-whities around penis and favorite leg. Act nonchalant in public.

DR. JOEL'S ELECTRICAL VACUUM PUMP

The Plan: Vacuum pressure draws blood into your love muscle, expanding it.
The Pitch: "Like bodybuilding, the capillaries will dilate, breaking down and rebuilding. Eventually the penis becomes bigger permanently."
The Price: $199
(http://www.drjoelkaplan.com/)
Freeware Version: Fit hungry python over penis. Wait.

PENILE ENLARGEMENT HYPNOSIS FOUR TAPE SET

The Plan: You convince your penis to grow by means of autohypnotic suggestion.
The Pitch: "This tape will begin to increase tissue growth and adjust the hormonal release and blood flow for maximum size."
The Price: $79
(www.biggerisbetter.com)
Freeware Version: Slap dick silly until it finally agrees to grow up. Tough love really works!

THE RELEASE FORM

Still think we're being alarmist assholes? Wait till you see the surgical consent form. The following is excerpted from an actual consent form for penis-enhancement surgery that a Robert Stubbs, M.D. (yes, that's his real name, and, yes, he's heard all the jokes) uses before operating.

Special Consent to Penis Lengthening Surgery

1. I hereby request Dr. Robert H. Stubbs to perform "penis lengthening" surgery on:

____

(Name of patient) or (Myself)

2. The procedure listed in Paragraph 1 has been explained to me by the doctor and/or his staff and I completely understand the nature and consequences of the surgery. The following points have been specifically made clear:

a) That medicine is not an exact science and complications such as death, although extremely rare, may occur.

b) That swelling, bruising and mild discomfort usually occur.
c) That no guarantees with respect to the final outcome can be offered.
d) That infection is possible.
e) That sensation may be altered or completely lost.
f) That function may be altered.
g) That delayed wound healing and/or poor scarring may occur.
h) That revisions may be necessary.
i) That the healing process takes time and the final result will not be readily visible for many months.
j) That bleeding may occur and should blood collect (a hematoma), this may require further surgical treatment.
k) That skin loss may occur and that smoking may cause this problem.
l) That chronic or persistent problems may occur which require treatment.

3. I authorize and request that the above-named surgeon, his assistants or his designees perform such procedures as are, in his professional judgment, necessary and desirable, including, but not limited to, procedures involving pathology and radiology.

4. I consent to the administration of anesthesia, and/or deep sedation.

5. I am aware that the practice of medicine and surgery is not an exact science, and I acknowledge that no guarantees have been made to me as to the results of the operation or procedure.

6.. I consent to be photographed before, during, and after treatment; that these photographs shall be the property of Dr. Robert H. Stubbs and may be published in scientific journals and/or shown for scientific or educational reasons.

WHAT'S THE DEAL WITH PENIS PUMPS?

There are a ton of penis pumps available to those damned with a short stick, in a wide variety of price ranges. Some are approved by the FDA, and some aren't, but they all work on a simple vacuum principle. By sucking the air out of the pump cylinder once it's donned on your johnson, the vacuum pressure draws blood into your penis and expands the blood vessels and connective tissue in the spongy tissues of the corpora cavernosa and corpus spongiosum (if you're confused by the vocab, go back to the beginning of the chapter). But most legitimate experts agree that these pumps are only temporarily effective, and continued use is the only way to guarantee "permanent" largeness. As Joel Kaplan, Ph.D. claims with his several-hundred-dollar pump, the penis is like a muscle—the more you pump up, the bigger it gets. Some pumps purport to work only with special creams or vitamins that the manufacturer sells (surprise) at extortion prices, while other pumps are downright dangerous, and you run the risk of popping your own balloon. Something to consider before tackling your tackle.

SPEAKING OF SCALPELS, LET'S TALK ABOUT CIRCUMCISION

Think God doesn't have a sense of humor? One need look no further than the deal he made with Abraham (the original Jew) that all future generations would "take a bit off the top." But circumcision in this country didn't become the most popular medical surgery until around the turn of the century, and it had nothing to do with religious beliefs or with personal hygiene. The reason can best be summed up by one of its main proponents, John Harvey Kellogg, M.D. (yes, the cereal guy):

"A remedy [for masturbation] which is almost always successful in small boys is circumcision…The operation should be performed by a surgeon without administering an anesthetic, as the pain attending the operation will have

CUT OR UNCUT: WHAT DO WOMEN PREFER?

Whether a woman prefers cut or uncut has more to do with what she's used to (which is hopefully two inches shorter than whatever you're sportin'), and so for most all-American women, the choice is clear-cut. However, the remaining 3 billion women in the world approach circumcision like we approach eggplant: wholly unnatural and unfit for human consumption. But as a service to our readers (and in keeping with the highly unscientific methods used elsewhere in this book), we decided to poll scores of beautiful women on what they like better: cut or uncut.

"I've been with both circumcised and uncircumcised men, and there doesn't seem to be a big difference during intercourse. It looks and feels different during foreplay and oral sex, of course, but I like both equally well."—Missy, 29, Lawyer

"I've never been with an uncircumcised man, so I can't say."—Jane, 26, Accountant

"I prefer circumcised. I think it's just cleaner."—Sarah, 24, Waitress

"Circumcised, definitely. Uncircumcised men are like those Chinese Shar-Pei dogs with all the skin hanging off." —Jennifer, 32, Investment Banker

"I have been with uncircumcised men, but I prefer circumcised. Although the uncircumcised men were sort of fun because there was more to play with."—Cindy, 35, Controller

"Well, I've seen a lot of foreskin in my day, and when I was with a guy who was uncircumcised I tried to concentrate on the positives. My German girlfriend summed it up best when she said, 'You know, on those long road trips when you pull over and he wants to screw and you don't want to do it in the car, you can just give him a handjob and it's so much easier when they have foreskin [thanks to all the extra loose skin].' However, oral sex with uncircumcised men is much more preferable. So I'd have to say uncircumcised wins the day."—Suzanne, 26, Journalist

a salutary effect upon the mind, especially if it be connected with the idea of punishment."

If you hadn't guessed, Kellogg was quite the hit at parties. And just so the ladies didn't feel left out, Kellogg also advocated the application of carbolic acid to a girl's clitoris to prevent her from diddling.

These are bold words from a man who never had sex with his wife. It has even been postulated that he was a *klismaphiliac*, or one who derives sexual pleasure from enemas. He was particularly obsessed with his own bowels, and had several enemas administered to him a day, sometimes with hot water, sometimes with yogurt. His favorite device was an enema machine that could irrigate a helpless bowel with 15 gallons of water in a few seconds. Nonetheless, people still listened to his *scheisse*-freak quackery.

As it happens, the U.S. is the only industrialized country that still regularly does the snip-and-tuck to young male newborns for nonreligious purposes. Circumcision became routine in the U.S. in the 1940s because it was thought that uncircumcised penises were much more at risk for urinary tract infections and penile cancer. Doctors now know this is not the case, as circumcision offers virtually no medical benefit (the procedure itself also causes negligible medical harm). The procedure saw its peak in the 1960s and 1970s, with approximately 85 to 90 percent of male newborns getting their turtlenecks altered to crewnecks.

Those who've been circumcised their whole life really can't comment on the before and aftereffects, but those who've waited until adulthood to have the procedure done have typically complained of decreased sensation relative to how it was before. In *The Journal of Sex Research*, Money and Davison (from the Johns Hopkins

University School of Medicine) reported on five such men. One typical response: "The greatest disadvantage of circumcision is the awful loss of sensitivity when the foreskin is removed…On a scale of one to 10, the intact penis experiences pleasure that is at least 11 or 12; the circumcised penis is lucky to get to three."

The reason for this is that the glans is not covered with skin as we know it. Like the inner layer of the foreskin, the glans is covered with a highly sensitive, self-lubricating mucosal layer. When the foreskin is removed, this mucosal surface of the glans develops a thick keratin skinlike surface to protect it from abrasions and other unwanted stress. This process results in a desensitization of your helmet-head.

In some cases the surgical damage done by circumcision goes far beyond desensitization. These extreme (and rare) worst-case scenarios include extensive scarring, curvature of the penis, deformities of the glans, shaft, and urethral meatus, as well as extreme mutilation. Inappropriate cauterization of the wound after circumcision can also result in the loss of the entire member. In John Colapinto's book *As Nature Made Him: The Boy Who Was Raised as a Girl*, the author recounts the sad and horrible saga of David Reimer, who lost his penis after a botched circumcision. As a result, he was "sexually reassigned" and given strict behavioral modifications. He was then named Brenda and raised as a girl.

Of course, whether you were circumcised or not had little to do with your own personal feelings on the matter, though, believe it or not, you can still take matters into your own hands if you're not happy with the way you are, i.e., get yourself circumcised or uncircumcised (more on that later).

UNCIRCUMCISION OR "GETTING IT BACK"

It goes without saying that when you were first faced with the decision to get circumcised you probably weren't able to make up your own mind, so the decision was left to those least likely to have your sexual well-being in mind: your parents. But for those bemoaning their unhooded monk, circumcision need not be forever. There is actually a 10,000-man-strong movement pioneering "foreskin restorations." You too can have what some faceless doctor took from you with simple surgery, or, if you have two to four years to spare, the same results can be had through extensive stretching of the remaining foreskin.

BUT WHY, DEAR GOD, WHY?

Men who wish to restore their foreskins do so for both psychological and physical reasons, says nurse Marilyn F. Milos, executive director of the National Organization of Circumcision Information Resource Centers in San Anselmo, California, a non-profit organization that opposes circumcision. "Men who are trying to stretch their foreskin are trying to take back control, to get back something that was taken away from them," says Milos. "We can't give their foreskins back to them. The best we can do is act as passionate observers, so they can heal their wounds and won't pass this act on to the next generation."

There are actually a number of drop-dead-serious organizations devoted to the "healing of their wounds," sporting such clever names as NOCIRC (National Organization of Circumcision Information Resource Centers), NORM (National Organization of Restoring Men), NOHARMM (National Organization to Halt the Abuse and Routine Mutilation of Males), and DOC (Doctors Opposing Circumcision).

But lest you think this idea is a product of the same misguided generation that gave us hair implants and tofu burgers, the first known methods of uncircumcision actually date back to biblical times and are detailed in the

Old Testament in 1 Maccabees 1:14–15. Back in the day when public nudity was more popular during athletic competition and in public baths, circumcised Jews were widely ridiculed for their abridged penis style. To avoid public scorn, circumcised Jews either kept their genitals covered, or were forced to stretch their shortened foreskin with a special weight called the Pondus Judaeus. These weights, made of either bronze, copper, or leather, were attached to the shortened foreskin, a sort of ancient skin expander not too different from the methods used today by advocates of foreskin restoration.

CUT CELEBRITIES

If you are bemoaning your fate as one of those without foreskin, the folks at www.sleepy.net have compiled this somewhat dubious list of celebrities who may be half the men they used to be (believe at your own risk):

Muhammad Ali	Alice Cooper	Sigmund Freud
Woody Allen	David Copperfield	Mel Gibson
Kevin Bacon	Kevin Costner	Wayne Gretzky
Warren Beatty	Tom Cruise	Woody Harrelson
Milton Berle	Rodney Dangerfield	Ernest Hemingway
Larry Bird	Ted Danson	Pee-wee Herman
John Wayne Bobbitt	Robert DeNiro	Kareem Abdul-Jabbar
Ray Bradbury	Michael Douglas	Bruce Lee
Terry Bradshaw	David Duchovny	Sugar Ray Leonard
Tom Brokaw	Clint Eastwood	David Letterman
Mel Brooks	Albert Einstein	Carl Lewis
President George Bush	John Elway	Mark Messier
Dick Butkus	Harrison Ford	Joe Montana
Chevy Chase	Michael J. Fox	Bruce Willis

HOW IS RESTORATION DONE?

Once circumcised, you can get back the look and feel of an original foreskin through restoration. The methods are similar to the penis-enlarging ones we talked about earlier. Nonsurgical stretching of the shaft skin is the most commonly used method, which is based on the fact that the skin is a pliable organ that can be coaxed into becoming longer over time without considerable thinning of the skin. (Think about fat people. If the skin did not have stretching properties, there'd be a bunch of near-translucent gordos waddling around.) This kind of skin expansion is extremely time-consuming, but with patience and several hundred yards of medical tape, many have achieved marked results, with total glans coverage.

Here's a rundown of some popular stretching techniques:

Taping: Using the type of first aid tape that works best on one's skin, one pulls whatever shaft skin he has over the glans and tapes it closed. Gentle pressure from the glans will start stretching the skin.

Manually: Some men use gentle manual stretching of the shaft skin on a daily basis, which will eventually achieve the same results as taping.

Extension Devices: When sufficient skin length has been obtained, various extension devices (weights, elastic straps, cones, etc.) can be used to augment the stretching. These modern Pondus Judaeus, however, are most effective when utilized in a standing position. One effective "advanced" expansion device is a garter belt with an elastic strap that maintains constant tension on the foreskin.

Surgery: Surgical reconstruction is not recommended. Surgery may seem to be faster, but it is riskier, with results that are usually less than satisfactory. It is costly and has not had good results in most cases. Think Frankenpenis. No safe, effective surgeries have been developed.

Many men get back a healthy amount of foreskin through manual and taping methods, then seek minor touch-up surgery to contour the tip of the foreskin for a more natural, snug fit and/or to reconstruct the frenulum. NORM maintains a list of medical referrals for those who wish to have contouring surgery after the stretching process has been completed.

HOW LONG DOES IT TAKE?

The time frame to recover the glans skin varies. Factors include: how much shaft skin remains after circumcision, how diligent and persistent one is with stretching, and the amount of foreskin coverage desired. Some men achieve restoration after months, while for others, it can take several years.

UNCUT CELEBRITIES If you are uncircumcised and tired of being different than all your chopped pals, take some heart in this list, straight from the "researchers" at www.sleepy.net, that claims you and your intact member have plenty of famous company:

Hank Aaron	Francis Ford Coppola	James Earl Jones
Desi Arnez (Jr. & Sr.)	Bill Cosby	Martin Luther King, Jr.
David Bowie	Larry Czonka	Elvis Presley
Marlon Brando	Erik Estrada	Vincent Price
Yul Brynner	Lou Ferrigno	Ronald Reagan
Richard Burton	Clark Gable	Keith Richards
Michael Caine	Hugh Hefner	Tom Selleck
Johnny Carson	Jimi Hendrix	Sting
Johnny Cash	Charlton Heston	Mr. T
Charlie Chaplin	John Holmes	Eddie Van Halen
Sean Connery	Anthony Hopkins	

PICKLED PETERS

Despite the penis' somewhat diminutive stature, mankind has filled his history with sonnets, holy shrines, and federal indictments aplenty dedicated to his most treasured organ. But, until now, there have been no museums devoted to man's favorite toy. Thanks to the efforts (and personal collection) of Icelander Sigurdur Hjartarson, as well as funds from the Icelandic government, members now have a club they can truly call their own.

A mere 400 kronas (about $4) gains entry into The Icelandic Phallogical Museum, which boasts the world's largest collection of penises and penis parts under one roof (outside of Elton John's home). While most of the 124 specimens that have been hung, pickled, mounted, and stuffed are of the local aquatic variety, such as the right testicle of a mink whale, there's a fair number of land-based love muscles as well, including those of boars, bulls, horses, and rats.

Alas, some of the collection specimens were gathered from butchers, not biologists, resulting in preparations that'd make even Lorena Bobbitt wince. A whale phallus that's had its skin tanned for neckties, bow ties, etc; the bull who had his scrotum's skin worked into a purse, and another bull whose little bullfighter was salted, dried, and made into a walking stick. You may uncross your legs now.

But what's an overseas excursion without tacky souvenirs and, thankfully, the museum brags a gift shop featuring all sorts of "artistic oddments and other practical utensils related to the museum's chosen theme," (i.e., dicks). Skillfully carved by Hjartsarson himself, such necessities as phallic-shaped key rings, salt and pepper shakers, and even toilet roll holders (perfect for the mother-in-law you lovingly left behind) are available. (For museum hours, call 011-354-566-8668.)

Under Her Hood

Ask a man where the nearest sports bar, golf course, or auto parts store is and he'll probably answer without batting an eye, with detailed directions to boot. But hold up a diagram of a woman's nether regions and ask him for the most direct route to her G-spot and you might as well be asking him to locate The Lost Dutchman's Mine. In all likelihood, most guys' knowledge of female anatomy has come from fumbling around in the dark in the heat of the moment after an evening of beers and tequila shots—not unlike a blind man trying to milk a cow.

GETTING TO KNOW HER

Just as you can't become a master mechanic without first learning the name, location, and function of a car's many components (all the important ones anyway), so too will you never be a genuine sexpert unless you are familiar with all of her parts. In this chapter we show you what few have seen before in the bright light of day and peel away the mystery often associated with a woman's sexual functions. The good news is, her reproductive system is far less complicated than your average fuel injection system (though only slightly).

■ Vulva

This is where it all begins, what every man thinks of when he thinks of her privates, though he probably has a crude name for it. The vulva encompasses the entire outer area of her sex organs: the *labia majora* (the outer lips), *labia minora* (the inner lips), clitoris, urethral opening (that's her pee hole), and the vaginal opening (you know, her hole majora). Typically, you won't see much more than the labia majora in her unaroused state, but if you do your job well, the vulva will open, like a glorious flower, revealing the rest of her. But as with penises, women's features, while somewhat the same, come in an assortment of shapes, sizes, perks, and quirks.

■ Mons Veneris

Latin for "hill of Venus" (Roman goddess of love and sex), this is the pad of fatty tissue that covers her pubic bone just above the vulva. The good news is that this area is usually pretty sexually sensitive in most women while at the same time it protects the pubic bone from the pounding of sexual intercourse (you animal). For women who enjoy it, take the heel of your hand and, push down on it and rub it in a circular motion. Don't worry, she'll let you know if she doesn't like it.

■ Labia

Actually, she's got two sets of these. There are the outer vaginal lips, known as *labia majora* (Latin for "big lips"), and then, once you get past those, there are the inner lips, known as the *labia minora* (Latin for, you guessed it, genius: "small lips"). The outer lips are typically covered with pubic hair, and they completely cover the vagina so no dirt or sweat can get in. The inner lips are smooth and (hopefully, please, dear God) hairless. They fill with blood and swell during arousal so that they can get a stronger grip on your penis.

If you come across some lips that look a little different, there's nothing wrong with her. Like breasts, labia vary widely in physical structure (and even color). Some women have labia minora that actually extend past the labia majora, while other women have not the usual pink, but brown or even black.

> **FACT OR FACTOID?**
>
> The labia are made of the same kind of tissue as the lips of your mouth.

■ Clitoris (pronounced *clit*-er-us; it does not rhyme with Delores)

Women have all the luck. The clitoris is the only part of the human body (male or female) with the sole function of sexual pleasure. (Think about that one the next time you debate which sex God gave the short end of the stick, especially considering how short your stick really is, Junior.) While you may like to think the sole purpose of your love dong is sexual, it does have one other very important nonsexual purpose (and if you consider that a sexual function, you are in need of some help!).

It is true that many experts consider the clitoris the female equivalent of the penis. (Interestingly enough, the clitoris can even have a foreskin also called the clitoral ood.) The typical clitoris measures around three-fourths of an inch in length, though some can be as long as two inches. When a woman becomes aroused, the clitoris fills with blood and gets an erection the same way a penis does. Then the hood that usually covers the clitoris recedes, leav-

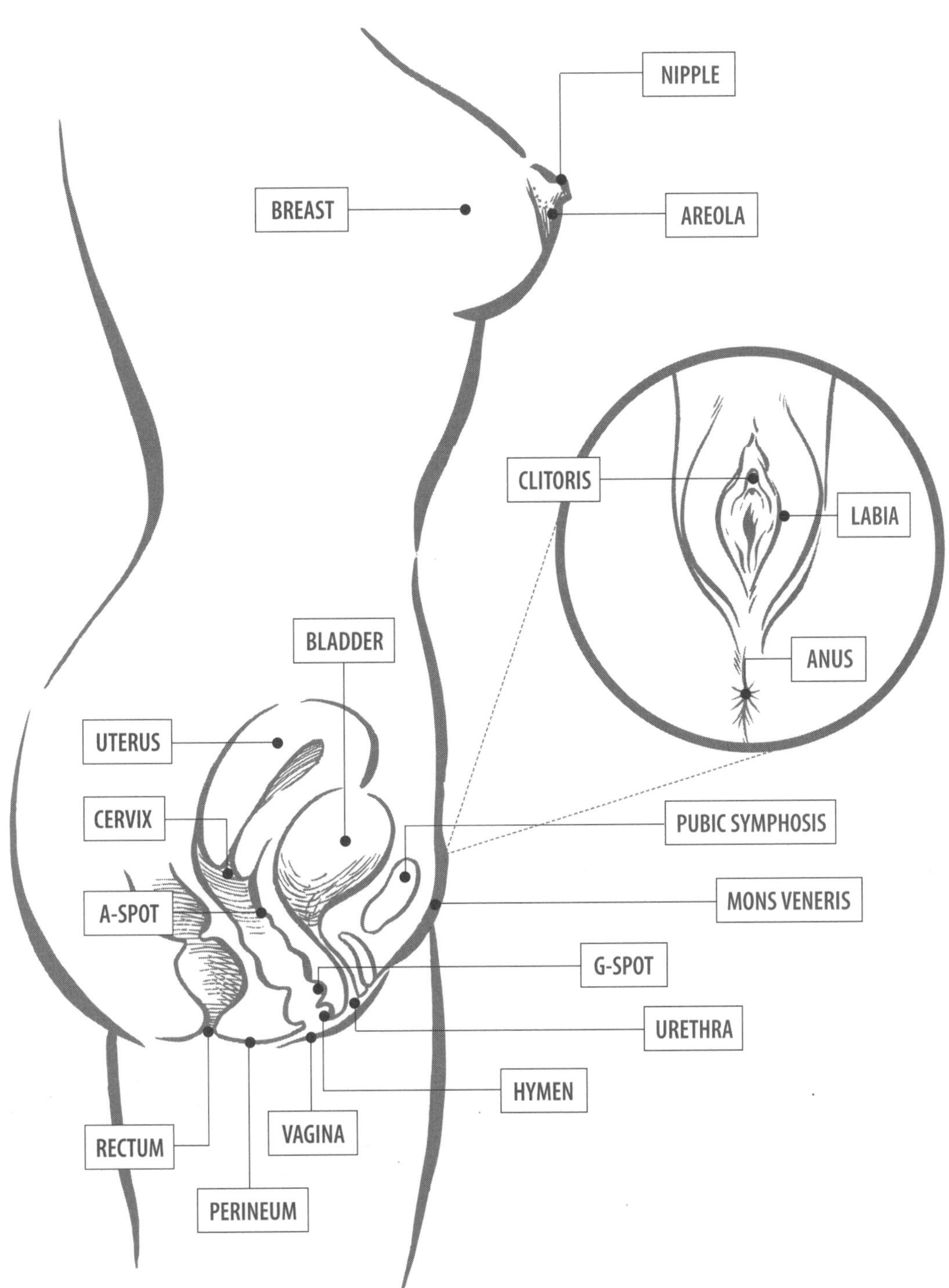
NIPPLE
BREAST
AREOLA
CLITORIS
LABIA
ANUS
BLADDER
UTERUS
CERVIX
PUBIC SYMPHOSIS
A-SPOT
MONS VENERIS
G-SPOT
URETHRA
HYMEN
RECTUM
VAGINA
PERINEUM

ing it exposed to stimulation. It can be an extremely sensitive spot for women, and many find direct stimulation painful, especially early on while getting it on.

■ Vagina

This is the oft-elusive holy land for your penis, and the exit for babies and menstrual blood (it's a virtual Grand Central Station down there). In its unstimulated state, the vagina is a three-inch-long canal that's lined with mucous membrane and reaches from the vulva's vaginal opening to the cervix. When you've worked your mojo on your woman, the walls of her vagina expand as much as eight inches and become covered with lube to accommodate your giant schlong (yeah, right).

FACT OR FACTOID?

The largest medically documented clitoris measured 12 inches long, only an inch and a half shorter than the world's largest penis. No word on whether that was on an East German Olympic swimmer.

Just before she has an orgasm, the outer third of the vagina swells with blood and narrows, then contracts repetitively during orgasm at 0.8-second intervals, coincidentally, the exact same interval as in a male orgasm. Afterward, the blood drains and the vagina returns to its normal size and shape in about 15 minutes.

■ G-spot

No, it's not a myth like the Easter Bunny, Santa Claus, or a brainy blonde; it actually does exist, at least in most women. And contrary to popular opinion it's not named after the loud sounds a woman makes when her man marks the spot. (If that were the case, it'd be called the Oh-my-sweet-Jesus spot.) It's named after the researcher who published a paper on it, Dr. Ernst Gräfenberg in 1950.

For those fortunate enough to be blessed with one, it's located directly behind the pubic bone in the upper front wall of the vagina, approximately two inches inside the vaginal opening. It's tough to locate while she's lying on her back, so try having sex from behind or with her on top . If you're going exploring with your finger, apply firm upward pressure to the front wall of the vagina. You may feel a small lump or swelling, and don't be alarmed if the first thing she feels is the need to urinate. The G-spot's near the opening of the bladder. Keep applying moderate pressure, and that urge will be replaced by a much better G-that-feels-terrific sensation.

Debate is fast and furious over whether the G-spot even exists, but the women who've found it tell men everywhere it's worth looking for. For more detailed information, see "How to Find Her Friggin' G-Spot" in chapter 6.

■ Perineum

Long ignored by men everywhere, this is the area between her genitals and her anus. While most wouldn't even think about paying much attention to this no man's land of sexual delights, it has a high concentration of nerve endings, making it highly sensitive to touch. Men have this, too, and it can be stimulated through direct pressure with a finger through the rectum, or—for her—through deep penetration of the vagina.

■ Anus/Rectum

Sure, the poop chute is the center for the body's waste disposal, but Mother Nature also made it an area of highly concentrated nerve endings, so it's ripe for sexual play on both men and women. Granted, some women are turned off by the idea of you exploring "back there," but many love it. It's a matter of making it pleasurable, not a pain in the ass. Generally, we encourage a bit of advanced discussion beforehand with your partner about exploring this area of sexual stimulation, rather than waiting until the heat of the moment and pretending you "slipped" during sex. Take it from us, that's a sure way to bring the session to a rapid close.

The rectum doesn't have natural lubrication like the vagina does, so always use a water-based lubricant before penetrating her with your finger or penis. And *always* wash immediately after, as bacteria from the rectum can cause infection if it comes into contact with the vagina (or even the unsheathed penis). For more info on anal sex and anal play, see chapter 7.

■ Urethra

The pipe that carries urine from the bladder and out of the body (no, Virginia, she doesn't pee out of her vagina). Its opening is located within the vaginal lips and just in front of the vagina. Many women say that this and the area between it and the vagina are perfect spots for oral sex maneuvers.

■ Hymen

This is a thin mucous membrane that or partially covers the opening of the vagina, though this isn't necessarily the case with every woman. It's usually pretty flimsy and can easily tear, sometimes without any sexual activity whatsoever. Often a girl simply horseback riding, masturbating, or inserting a tampon can break the seal. Many are under the impression that the presence of an intact hymen is a surefire indicator of whether she's a virgin or not. (The breaking, and the subsequent bleeding, of the hymen is how we got the term "pop her cherry.") But the lack of a hymen in no way proves that a girl has had sex before. In fact, some women are even born without a hymen, while others have a hymen that is so elastic it doesn't even break during sex. The only way these stubborn shields are broken is through childbirth.

Still, the belief persisted for years, even to the point where prostitutes at one time surgically had their hymens fixed so that they could appear as virgins to higher paying customers.

■ A-spot

Way more elusive than the G-spot is the A-spot (short for anterior fornix erogenous zone), though 95 percent of women who had their A-spot tickled in test groups were able to experience multiple orgasms. According to researchers, it can be found between the G-spot and the cervix. In layman's terms, that's on the front vaginal wall between the midpoint and the *tippy-top*. (You won't find *tippy-top* anywhere else in this book, we promise.)

■ Breasts

If the Eskimos have at least 200 names for snow (reportedly due to its strong importance to them), then the American male must have at least 2,000 names for breasts. This seems puzzling, considering the sole function of female breasts is to provide nourishment for her young. C'mon, do men get as excited dreaming about giant jars of Gerber strained peas?

But despite the intense scrutiny, men tend to be pretty ignorant regarding her ta-tas. To us boobs are kind of like art. We may not know much about it, but we know what we like when we see it. But handled with care—and sometimes not—working her boobs

WHAT IS "TIGHT"?

We've been hearing about it practically since we first heard about sex; i.e., how "tight" a woman is. While adolescent locker room banter may have you believing that the tightness of a woman's vagina is dependent on her loose morals or her ethnicity, how snug she is down there has very little to do with how much she sleeps around, says Lauri Romanzi, M.D., clinical assistant professor of obstetrics and gynecology at Cornell Medical College. "The vaginal capacity correlates with her overall pelvic shape and the strength of her pelvic muscles," Romanzi says.

Nearly all women have thick pelvic muscles before childbirth, making them feel tighter than women who've had kids. Of course, this all changes after she's had a kid or two (especially if she's done so later in life) and as she gets older, though the degree to which her muscle bulk deteriorates differs from woman to woman. And Romanzi says rumors like "Asian women are naturally tight" have no clinical basis.

Women can help keep their vaginas as tight as possible by doing Kegel exercises, says Romanzi, or by having orgasms. Orgasm contractions are like mini-exercises that will keep her muscles strong. You can tighten the screw, too: "It behooves a man to make sure his partner has plenty of orgasms if he's interested in keeping her tight," says Romanzi.

can up the sexual satisfaction all around. So let's try and lift the mystery off the mammaries.

■ **Areola**

(pronounced uh-REE-uh-luh)
This circle of pink or brown that surrounds the nipple, like the breasts themselves, runs the whole gamut of size, shape, and color, all of which have nothing to do with her sexuality. However, when a woman is aroused, her areolae swell so much they seem to bury the erect nipples. Speaking of which…

■ **Nipples**

No one knows why men have an obsession with sucking on a woman's nipple. Sure, some speculate it's because a woman's breast is often man's original source of nourishment, but if that were the case, women would be just as obsessed with breasts as men (lesbian fantasies aside, this ain't the case).

Some women love to have their nipples sucked (many to the point of orgasm), while some can barely stand it because of extreme sensitivity. For some women it's not the actual sucking that arouses them—it's watching a man get excited as he sucks them that really floats their boat.

Sometimes you'll find that if you suck, a sweet-tasting fluid will come out, even if she's not breast-feeding. No one knows exactly why that happens, though it's been found that the leakage sometimes occurs with women who use Norplant (a hormone-releasing birth-control device that's implanted under her skin) or women who have high levels of prolactin, a hormone secreted by the pituitary gland that affects milk production. Don't fret: The stuff is harmless, and if you do encounter this, it doesn't necessarily mean she's pregnant.

Surprisingly, the nipples aren't the most sensitive parts of her breasts. According to researchers at the University of Vienna, the upper breast is the most sensitive spot (studies say especially—and we're not making this up—between the hours of 9 A.M. and 3 P.M.). The outer rim of the nipple is the second most sensitive area, with the nipple itself the least sensitive.

WHAT IS CUP SIZE?

Basically, it's the difference between her breast size and her band size. While we promised no math in this book, a woman's cup size is actually quite easy to figure out, if you can add and subtract.

A woman measures twice: first around the flat part of her chest just under her breasts, to which she adds 5 inches to get her band size, then around the fullest part of her breast. Subtract the first from the second and you've got her cup size.

Less than 1 inch = AA cup
1 inch = A cup
2 inches = B cup
3 inches = C cup
4 inches = D cup
5 inches = DD cup

BOOB FACTS

As you know, breasts do indeed come in all shapes and sizes. While some believe that the bigger the knocker the louder the answer, science has found no direct link between the size of a woman's breasts and the size of her libido. In fact, there are plenty of small-breasted women who are even randier than Austin Powers. Here are some fun facts you should know:

There also isn't a correlation between the size and shape of her breasts and how much she enjoys having them fondled, kissed, or sucked; that is, there's no relation between size ad pleasurablity.

Never automatically assume that a woman with implants has a pair of numb knockers. Of course, the more surgery done on them the less sensitive they'll probably be. But believe it or not, women with breast reduction surgery are more likely to lose feeling, since the nipple may have to be moved or completely reconstructed.

Breasts get bigger not only when a woman becomes pregnant but also when she gets turned on—as much as 25 percent bigger if she hasn't breastfed any children and far less if she has.

HER EROGENOUS ZONES

As far as men are concerned, there is essentially only one spot on her body that she wants stimulated during sex. But a woman is loaded with erogenous zones, many more than the ones listed above. And since this is a sex book that details all it takes to get her going, we'd be doing a grave injustice if we didn't let you know what other hot spots she has. But don't take our word for it—listen to these women's advice:

"The back of my neck and the base of my head—a rub there gets me every time; and my feet, especially the ball of my foot, under the big toe, the right amount of pressure and I'm jelly. And hand massages give *me* a hard-on." —Jo, 27, human resources manager

"Touch the soft area of skin behind the ear and shock my senses!"—Donna, 22, actress

"I love when I'm lying on my stomach and he slowly runs some ice down along my spine."—Karen, 26, writer

"The first time we got together, he ran his fingers through my hair, slightly tugging at the hair at the back of my neck. There's nothing like it, really." —Eloise, 24, bartender

"I love it when my guy turns me over and bites me on the back of the neck. I just squirm beneath him. Then he nibbles along my sides, kisses, bites my hips, and licks and kisses the space where my thigh and ass cheek meet. And I love it when he licks and kisses my inner thighs, where the thigh and labia meet. Heaven."—Lauren, 27, assistant editor

"Nibble and kiss my neck. It's so good. The hairs on the back of my neck just stand up." Laura, 27, editor

"My boyfriend usually has to be reminded that there *are* other erogenous zones besides the obvious. I do love it when he brushes my collar bone with his hand or mouth on his way south. Kissing the small of my back will also send me into overdrive."—Marie, 28, office manager

"I love when he lightly scratches my arms and back. The insides of the elbows and backs of my knees are sensitive and often overlooked." —Karen, 24, teacher

"Earlobes, earlobes, earlobes! Nibble them, please, and don't forget to feel the 'foot clit' (the spot directly below the balls of the feet, dead center)." —Janine, 21, student

"I have to say, ass biting gets me off. Not a chomp, more like a succession of nibbles. The ass cheeks are so often ignored, and wrongly."—Stephanie, 28, lawyer

"I'd say the entire body's a G-spot. You lick and nibble right and she'll be good to go. I know my boyfriend will rub my legs slowly, nibble along my sides, turn me over and kiss my back, bite the back of my neck, run his fingers through my hair...Just don't slobber, make a lot of sucking noises, or bite too hard."—Jennifer, 30, hairdresser

FLYING SOLO: FEMALE MASTURBATION

No matter how well you know a woman, she's always putting on a bit of a show when you're having sex. But when the lovin' involves just her, she can really be herself. You can learn a lot on how to turn a woman on by learning what she does when she masturbates, how she does it, and what she thinks about while doing it. But the important thing to remember is that first you need to forget everything you know about masturbation.

"It's a mistake for a man to assume that women like the same kind of stimulation," says Tracey Cox, a psychologist and sexpert. Men and women touch themselves very differently, and the only way to find out what she likes is to go to the source. Ask her questions about what she does and what she likes, says Cox. If she's comfortable enough to answer those questions, she might even be comfortable enough to do it in front of you. "The way she masturbates will be the way she orgasms most easily and quickly. The man who knows this is one step ahead of the rest," Cox says.

If you're lucky enough to convince her to masturbate in front of you, make sure you use the opportunity to learn as much about her as possible. Observe her technique, speed, sequence, and hand placement, says Cox. Let her fly solo the first time, then next time ask if you can join in. Have her put her hand on top of yours and guide you while you pleasure her manually. You'll learn a valuable lesson about pleasing her.

INTERPRETING HER MOVES

Now for the method behind her masturbation. Here's what Cox says it means if your woman does the following:

Her Move: Rubs Against a Chair or Pillow
What It Means: She doesn't like direct stimulation on her clitoris. It may be especially sensitive, so she avoids it somewhat. She may also use the water in the shower, which provides indirect pressure.
Your Move: Stimulate the whole labia area and avoid focusing directly on her clitoris or else she won't enjoy it.

Her Move: Inserts a Finger or Two
What it Means: She likes to be filled up and wants more than just clitoral stimulation.
Your Move: Pay close attention to how long she waits before moving inside—that's how long you should wait, too. And watch to see whether she stimulates her clitoris at the same time. You may need to learn to extend a helping hand during sex.

Her Move: Reads Erotica
What it Means: Unlike women in porn films, most women don't usually spend hours sitting around masturbating. If they feel aroused, they'll do it, but usually in less than five minutes.
Your Move: If she does woo herself, pay

SPOTS WE WISH SHE HAD

Sure she's got a veritable alphabet of sexual hot spots, but if we were in charge, we'd throw in a few more buttons, switches, and functions.

Fast-Forward Key: So she can just get to the point of the story already!
Not-So-Selective Hearing: So when we tell her something that can be taken one of two ways, she picks the one that doesn't get her upset.

Boyfriend B-Gone: One flip of this switch and all memories of her previous relationships, such as his prowess in bed, his godlike dimensions, and his constantly romantic behavior, will immediately disappear.

Sperm Burner: A button that, when activated, actually causes her body to take sperm and make it an unrivaled fat-burning chemical. More sperm = less fat.

Short-Term Memory Switch: Once she starts remembering shit from five years ago, you can stop her dead in her retreading tracks.

Mute Button: Need we say more?

attention. Whatever she does to herself is what she wants you to do. If she reads erotica, try reading some to her or telling her a story, making her the star.

Her Move: Uses a Vibrator
What it Means: Women who use vibrators are able to orgasm in about two seconds flat; there's nothing you can do to match the firepower. Women should try to use their fingers some of the time so that they don't become dependent on the battery power.
Your Move: Ask her to switch to manual in front of you. It's the only way you'll learn anything.

WHEN, WHERE, WHY...

To help us poor saps understand, a few nice gals share some sordid details about their masturbation sessions.

"I do it at home, in bed, during stressful and frustrating times." —Sarah, 25, art assistant

"I do it at home, on vacation, even at work—sometimes you need a bathroom break. And there's no better stress reliever." —Elizabeth, 31, occupational therapist

"I masturbate when I have nothing to do, because when I'm busy, all sexual thoughts—including masturbation and intercourse—go out the window." —Lisa, 33, police officer

"I used to masturbate alone with a vibrator when I was horny and there weren't any men around. But ever since my boyfriend and I started masturbating together—a little kink's been added to things." —Marie, 28, office manager

"I swear by vibrators and by lubrication, as a girl can't always depend on her own juices. I especially like to rub two fingers up and down, one finger on each side of my clit, slowly. Then I move them in a circle." —Nancy, 23, musician

"When I masturbate, I think of very kinky things, stuff I'd never do in real life. Like having sex with a bunch of guys at once." —Amy, 28, office manager

"I get off when I think of giving it to a woman with a strap-on." —Janine, 21, student

"I think of having sex with two guys—one below me and one above me. I only fantasize this because I know if it were really to happen, my body probably couldn't take it. But it's fun to think about. I also think about being picked up by a woman in a gay bar and having sex with her in the bathroom. Or of him having anal sex with me—hardcore." —Adrian, 29, publicist

97 EUPHEMISMS FOR FEMALE MASTURBATION

We think one of the main reasons women's masturbation is "the sin that dares not speak its name" is because, face it, there are no really cool euphemisms for it. Unlike us guys, who have as many synonyms for "tossing off" as there are Kleenex in a box, women are left high and dry, so to speak. While we can "bop the bishop," "rough up the suspect," or "buff our helmet," women are stuck with simply "rubbing off." But we're here to correct this egregious situation with the list that follows. Be sure to use your newfound knowledge to impress the in-laws at Thanksgiving.

- 5-Digit Disco
- A night in with the girls
- Audition the finger puppets
- Backslappin' Betty
- Bailing out the gravy boat
- Beaver bashin'
- Bouncing the bearded clam
- Buffing the beaver
- Buffing the box
- Buffing the jewel
- Buttering the muffin
- Buttering up the whisker biscuit
- Buzzing the honey hole
- Clam twiddlin' jamboree
- Clean her fingers
- Come into your own
- Couch hockey for one
- Critter crammin'
- Damming the beaver

97 EUPHEMISMS CONT...

- Dialing "O" on the little pink telephone
- Diddling Miss Daisy
- Diggin' for clams
- Digitis erectus
- Do handiwork
- Douse the digits
- Drilling for oil
- Engage in safe sex
- Fan the fur
- Feeding the bearded clam
- Fingering the fountain
- Fingerpainting
- Fist fucking
- Flicking the minnow
- Fluffin' the muffin
- Friday night lip service
- Frosting the love muffin
- Genital stimulation via phalangetic motion
- Get a date with Slick Mittens
- Get a fat lip
- Get a lube job
- Get to know yourself
- Give yourself the finger
- Going for the gooey duct
- Grab the goatee
- Grease your hips
- Grope the grotto
- Have sex with someone you love
- Hitchhike to heaven
- Hitchhike under the big top
- Impeaching Bush
- Juicing the clam
- Leglock the pillow
- Let your fingers do the walking

MAXIM SAT (SEXUAL APTITUDE TEST)

OK, You read the chapter, but were you paying attention? To make sure you don't get a big fat "F" the next time you hit the hay with your honey, take the following test to make sure you know a G-spot from an O-ring.

1. The vulva is...

a) An extremely safe car made in Sweden

b) The external female genitals, including the labia and the clitoris

c) Spanish for "evolve"

d) The real name of Jerry Seinfeld's mystery girlfriend

2. A woman prefers to have her nipples...

a) Twisted as if they were the knobs on an Etch A Sketch

b) Pushed into her breasts so that they're inverted

c) Ignored

d) Gently caressed and sucked

3. The G-spot is so named thanks to...

a) The letter shape one needs to twist into to reach it

b) The exclamation that often accompanies its successful location

c) Dr. Ernst Gräfenberg

d) The response men give when asked to try and locate it

4. The clitoris is the only body part, male or female whose purpose is...

a) To remain a mystery

b) To frustrate oversexed teenage boys

c) Solely for sexual pleasure

d) To keep people guessing as to how it's really pronounced

5. A woman can lose her "tightness" after she's had...

a) The whole team

b) A few too many

c) A sex change

d) A baby

6. Her perineum can be located...

a) In the garden, next to her annuals

b) At the mall, next to the Orange Julius machine

c) Halfway between millennia

d) Between her vagina and her anus

7. You can tell a woman masturbates if...

a) She has a detachable showerhead

b) She's able to orgasm only by giving you precise instructions

c) She gets tendinitis in her elbow

d) All of the above

8. Women are more sexually excitable when...

a) The moon is waxing

b) The moon is waning

c) The moon is full

d) You're out of town

9. The part of a woman's breast that is most sensitive is:

a) Her nipple
b) The upper breast
c) The lower breast
d) The part you're not touching

10. The Mons Veneris is:

a) A mountain on Venus
b) Yet another Latin legal term you've forgotten since college
c) The pad of fatty tissue that covers her pubic bone just above the vulva
d) A rare Pokemon

11. Women are typically against experimenting with anal sex because:

a) You really, really want it
b) The high possibility that it'll hurt like hell
c) You're just too darn big, stud
d) The fear that she'll never be able to control her bowel movements again

97 EUPHEMISMS CONT...	
Lip smacking	Shuck the oyster
Lube the labia	Solo sex
Manual override	Spanking Lucy
Menage à moi	Stinky pinky
Mowing the lawn	Stir the yogurt
Petting the kitty	Stroking the newt
Piddly diddler	Stuff the taco
Playing the clitar	Taking a dip in the lake
Playing the squeezebox	The art of unisex
Pokin' the pie	The virgin's release
Polishing the little pink pearl	Thumb the button
Pumping the kooter	Tickling your fancy
Punchin' the chipmunk	Ticklin' the taco
Reading in Braille	Tissue tickling
Riding the unicycle	To "jill off"
Riding the clitorisaurus	Twirl the pearl
Romancing thy own	Unbuttoning the fur coat
Row the little man in the boat	Warming the wrist rocket
Rub one out	Wash the carrot
Rubbin' the nubbin'	Wash your fingers
Self-guided tuna boat tour	Water the hot spot
Shagging the carpet	Wax the saddle

From First Dating to First Mating:

Foolproof Dating Strategies

If we haven't banged this into your head yet, women and men are not created equally. Make no mistake, they love sex as much as we do; it just takes a little more than a heartbeat to get them fired up for the deed. While men too often think that foreplay starts when they start touching her breast, it's actually a woman's brain that needs to be properly stimulated long before you lay a finger on them. That's why women love foreplay. Sure 'Wine-Dine-69' makes for a clever shorthand guide to easy sex, but in reality you're going to need more than a bottle of Chianti at L'Idiota to achieve your goal. But don't fret, fellow travelers. In this chapter we give you our foolproof step-by-step dating tips, which show you how to prep yourself for the big date, what to say, what not to say, and all the little things that'll have her begging you to take her to bed — all without having to liquor her up!

PRE-DATE PREPPING: TOP 5 THINGS TO DO BEFORE YOUR DATE

OK, hotshot, it's going to take a bit more preparation for your date than merely peeling yourself off the couch, slapping on some cologne, and relying on your natural good looks to woo her into a more intimate encounter. The fact is, getting lucky has little to do with actual luck and a lot to do with how prepared you are. What follows are five things you must do, according to our official experts (i.e., women), to truly impress her (besides picking her up in a Ferrari).

1. Hit the Showers

A dirty date is a lousy date, so before you dress, Caress. "I definitely prefer a guy who knows his hygiene," notes Adrian, 29, echoing a sentiment unanimously shared by the women we talked to. And we're not just talking about your weekly shower, whether you think you need one or not. Even if you've already showered once that day, shower again before your date if at all possible. "I love a fresh, clean guy," says Julia, 25. It should be noted that the cleanliness rule also applies even to the long-married man who merely wants to rev his wife's engines. Even though she may be used to your stink and sweat, give her a break from it if you expect any kind of special treatment from her in return.

2. Pride in Groom

You've showered, but this should only be the beginning of your grooming ritual. Why? Because women notice details, pal, so it helps if you pay 'em some attention as well.

"Make sure to clean those fingernails. Dirty hands and nails are a definite turn-off," says Marie, 28.

While you don't have to set up an appointment at Foo Foo's Nails 'N' More for a pedicure, hopefully you've mastered the finer points of trimming your nails and cleaning out whatever godforsaken gunk lies beneath. And while it goes without saying that you should have a decent haircut, do not ignore other facial areas known to have errant hair growth.

"It sounds silly, but if a guy's eyebrows are growing together, I fixate on it," notes Patty, 27. "I can't look away, so do us both a favor and buy a pair of tweezers," she adds.

We don't advocate going that far—we'll leave the masochism to the women, thank you—but at least run a razor or electric clipper between them. The unibrow look may work for Tom Cruise, but you, my friend, are no Tom Cruise. And don't forget those stragglers growing out of your nose and ears, which the female radar will instantly home in on. Get rid of 'em! Finally, while one would think oral hygiene would be an automatic, apparently some guys need to be reminded of this, as Michelle, 29, attests: "I dated a guy once who liked onion bagels as an afternoon snack, but didn't brush afterward. Like I said, I dated him once."

Yuck. Remember, not only do women notice these things, they also tell their friends. So unless you want to be the subject of a chain of e-mails amongst her circle of friends, you'd better clean and polish yourself with as much vigor as if you were buffing the finish on a vintage Jaguar.

3. Dress the Part

Instead of rummaging through your clothes hamper to find your cleanest dirty shirt, put some thought into what you're going to wear, and make sure that it is clean. If you're going on a first date, you need to put even more thought into your clothing decisions. The old adage that first impressions are the most important is absolutely true.

"Wearing jeans on a date tells me a guy just isn't trying," says Julia, 25. At the same time, you don't want to be something you're not. "Dress appropriately for whatever we're doing and for whatever your real style is," adds Beth, 24, "as long as your style is neat and pleasant in appearance."

Obviously, if you're going white-water rafting, you can leave the blazer and Gucci's at home, but again pay attention to the details. "Put on the right color socks—no tube socks on a date," notes an obviously frustrated Rosa, 34. "It's those subtle details that we're looking for. Make sure there are no weird stains on your clothes. If you have to ask yourself if you can get away with wearing it, then you probably can't."

4. Have Some Common Scents

Believe it or not, your own manly aroma may not be enough to sweep her off her feet. Make sure your aroma is pleasing, either on your own or with help from a good cologne. Of course, this doesn't mean you should take a bath in a tub of Old Spice, as Maria, 28, warns, "Be very careful about application! One side of the neck is enough!" And for the sake of your date and all those forced to sit downwind from you, wear only one fragrance. Scented deodorant and aftershave plus cologne do not a pleasant combo make.

5. Prep the Whole Package

No, not *that* package, you perv. We're talking about being fully prepared for the evening. A woman wants to know that you put some thought into the evening and that you're prepared to show her a good time.

"Have a plan!" insists Beth, 24. "Don't order me around, but have a good idea of what you want to do on the date. And be on time, *please*." A couple other things that are sore points with females: when you have to stop at the ATM on the way to dinner—with your date still in the car—and, of course, housecleaning. "Once I asked a guy at the end of the night if I could come up and use his bathroom," notes Lisa, 33. "He got this panic-stricken look on his face, but, of course, he said yes. When I walked in, it looked like something had exploded in his apartment."

While getting her up to your pad for a midnight rendezvous may not always happen on a first date, you should always be prepared for such a situation. Clear away the three-day-old pizza boxes, and put away the poopie undies and porno mags. If you do hit the jackpot and she comes up for a nightcap, you won't want to have to leave her outside while you run inside to straighten up.

PUTTIN' ON THE SPRITZ

You've done both an eye-crud and bad-breath check, put on the right socks, and even memorized three funny stories before heading out—but there's still room to offend. That's right, she's sizing you up by your scent, too. So don't foul things up. Here are some female impressions of some popular scents:

Your Cologne	What She Thinks
Old Spice	"Ick. He's a cheap-ass."
Patchouli or any hippie-dippie oil	"Awe, he's sensitive—or at least pretends to be."
Nautica	"This guy's cool but not trying too hard."
Obsession	"Who does he think he is, Fabio? He's an operator."
Davidoff Cool Water	"Emmm…sexy."
Bulgari	"He reeks of money along with this pricey cologne that bears a shocking resemblance to the smell of Tanquery—but in a good way."
Not wearing any	"He has a girlfriend—so he doesn't need to try."

IMPRESS HER: 10 STEPS TO MAKING A POSITIVE FIRST IMPRESSION

Now that we've covered the basics of date preparation, it's time to move beyond the purely aesthetic and concentrate on to how to make a memorable first impression. Remember, most women who've been on the dating scene longer than a few minutes are already jaded and quick to relegate a guy to the jerk heap. Scratched your balls for a second? She saw it. Accidentally spit on her while you were talking? She felt it (she's just waiting for you to look away so she can casually wipe off her cheek on the way to scratching her ear).

Confused yet? Don't be. Believe it or not, women want to be impressed—they want you to knock their socks off—not to mention their frilly lace underthings. To ensure success, take a few minutes and review the 10 items on the following list. Some you'll need to accomplish before you head out the door; others you'll have to make an effort to remember while you're turning on the charm. Nail each one and you'll make such a good first impression that you may just earn yourself a shot at a second one—hopefully the next morning.

IMPRESS-HER MOVE #1: SHOW SOME POLISH

You may have dropped serious dough on a new shirt and slicked back your hair to a nice gelatinous crisp, but women will still notice your shoes. That's why the paparazzi shots in celebrity rags are usually full-length—to include the shoes. Yes, they care that much. Paying attention to the details will impress most women, and tells them you are likely a thoughtful and considerate guy.

So if the tips of your leather shoes are worn down to fuzzy nubs or the soles of your boots are falling off, take them to a cobbler for a little TLC. If you're admittedly hopeless on the fashion front, throw on the clothes you plan to wear and go to a real shoe store (no, Kmart doesn't count) and ask the sales guy which shoes go with your outfit.

BASIC TIP: Always match the color of your socks to your pants. "I met a guy a few years ago who was wearing black pants, black shoes—and white socks!" explains Betsy, who's 34…and still in shock.

IMPRESS-HER MOVE #2: SEARCH YOUR MUG FOR STRAYS

If you expect to make like a Close-Up commercial and get a little closer with her, get yourself a little closer to the mirror and check for odd hairs poking out from unexpected places, zits in need of maintenance, or any other unpleasantness that will undoubtedly catch her eye.

"I had dinner with a gorgeous guy who had one little hair sticking out of his nose," says Kristina, 27. "I couldn't look at anything else all evening. I couldn't even bring myself to kiss him; I was afraid he'd put out an eye!" The reason you need to be so well-groomed? Early on, some women, and men, too are looking for the teeniest reason to issue walking papers. A dangling booger will ensure you don't get a second chance unless your date is the forgiving type.

BASIC TIP: Spruce up with a flawless shave job and evenly trimmed sideburns. Right-handed guys tend to shave their left sideburn shorter than their right, because of the reach. You never noticed? Believe us, she will.

IMPRESS-HER MOVE #3: FOOLPROOF YOUR DINNER PLANS

You arrive at the Oyster Bar at eight o'clock, and not only is your table still occupied, but there's a bachelor party convening in your corner, and, oh yeah, she's allergic to shellfish. But because you're so efficient, you also made reservations at the classy little Italian joint down the block for 8:15, just in case. No hassles. No hives. Now she knows you're the type of guy who thinks ahead and will take care of her.

BASIC TIP: Check ahead of time that the restaurant takes credit cards—and which ones. If they do take plastic, call your credit card company (they've all got 24-hour toll-free numbers) to make sure that the $400 tab you ran up at Hannah's House of Hooters last weekend did not put you over your limit. The call only takes two minutes but will spare you that awkward testicle-shrinking moment that occurs when your card is handed back to you—in two pieces.

IMPRESS-HER MOVE #4: DETOX YOUR TOILET

Women can find hairs you didn't know you shed in the first place, and nothing triggers a woman's fight-or-flight re-sponse faster than a scuzzy bathroom. She wants to know early on that she isn't going to resign herself to a lifetime of sitting on wet toilet seats at 3 A.M.

BASIC TIP: All you need is a handful of damp toilet paper. First stop: the yellow misfire scum on the rim of the toilet. (Remember: She doesn't lift the seat, so you only really need to get the goo near the hinge). Then wipe your stubble out of the sink and get rid of the toothpaste globs on the mirror. Don't worry about the mildew in the shower; by the time that becomes an issue, she'll have already fallen for your rakish charms, no?

IMPRESS-HER MOVE #5: DESTROY EVIDENCE OF YOUR EX

Miracles happen. You may get your dream date home for a passionate tumble on the Beautyrest, but if she finds mementos of your past conquests lying around, you're likely out of business. The last thing you want her to think is that you are either a relentless womanizer or one of those sad sacks who can't get over his ex-sweetie.

"After this guy charmingly stole a kiss from me in the photo-booth, I walked into his house to find a shot from a photo booth session with another woman stuck on his fridge!" says Johanna, 23.

In that same vein, never talk about your ex when you're on a date. "If he's talking about her, then he's not interested in getting to know me," points out Sasha, 28. "I mean, if you're really over someone, then you wouldn't be talking about them all the time. Hello, Freud!" If she does happen to ask about your last relationship, keep it simple: "She was a really great woman, and we had a lot of fun, butit just didn't work out."

BASIC TIP: Always ignore the blinking light on the answering machine when you bring her home, unless you're certain it's your mom calling to thank you for those flowers you sent. (Come to think of it, that would be a devious little ruse, wouldn't it?)

PLAN LIKE A PRO

Setting up an extreme date to surprise her? Don't lessen the impact with amateurish execution. Here are some tips to keep things running smoothly:

- **DON'T** pack her bag if you're whisking her away somewhere. It's a rare breed that trusts her man to pick the shoes that go with her boot-cut pants.
- **DO** tell her what to pack. Be specific about whether she'll need hiking boots, a swimsuit, or a sweater for autumn-temperature nights.
- **DON'T** make her a guinea pig. If she's never mentioned her passion for paintball battles, perhaps you shouldn't take the shot.
- **DO** make it a big deal. To psych her up, send her a card, some flowers, or an e-mail containing subtle hints about what you have planned.
- **DON'T** leave errands until the last minute. She'll be pissed if she has to wait in the car while you stop for gas, cash, and condoms.
- **DO** leave clues until the last minute. Stick a drink umbrella in her coffee and hide a travel fan—or a coconut!—in her briefcase.
- **DON'T** tell her coworkers what you're doing. It's been clinically proven that women in an office can't keep secrets; they'll blow it.
- **DO** tell her best friend. Make her an accomplice to help free up your girlfriend's schedule.

IMPRESS-HER MOVE #6: JETTISON THE CELL PHONE

Sure, a few years ago it made you look cool, but now that every housewife in Des Moines has one, it can only detract from your image. "Unless he's a surgeon or a drug dealer, who does he need to talk to at 10 o'clock at night?" asks Katie, 31.

BASIC TIP: There's almost no better way to put distance between you and your date than to be constantly interrupted by your cell phone. It's even worse if you indulge these callers with conversation, which will make your date feel awkward, unimportant, and bored. If you must bring one along, tell the callers you are busy and immediately get off the phone and back to your date. If you've asked a buddy to call to bail you out with a fake emergency, fine. But if all's going well, turn off the ringer. This way she'll know that you are truly interested in her.

IMPRESS-HER MOVE #7: REVIEW YOUR ANECDOTES

By the time you head out the door for your date, you should have three funny stories in the back of your mind. (Note: Not the one about the hookers in Tijuana.) One guy we know even keeps a crib sheet of keywords tucked in his pocket. That might be going a bit overboard, but a guy who can rescue his date from awkward pauses is a guy who can rescue them from other things as well.

BASIC TIP: Keep your facts straight, especially if you've swiped your material from other sources. That feminine instinct women are purported to have is no myth. "Last year I met a man who told me a charming story about his family," notes Amy, 27. "But he blew it when he threw in the more impressive details, like the fact that his grandfather invented the turbine engine (he didn't), and that his mother could play 18 instruments, including both the alto and soprano violin. I checked. They don't exist."

IMPRESS-HER MOVE #8: SIT WITH YOUR BACK TO THE DOOR

If you're facing the door of a restaurant, you'll be like a cat at an aquarium: No matter how hard you try to stop them, your eyes will go up and down every time a woman walks by.

"I called it an early night once because my date was distracted by everything happening around us," says Jana, 24. "It's like I wasn't interesting enough to keep his attention. That made me feel awful."

BASIC TIP: Since you know this about yourself, take away the temptation; have her sit with her back to the wall so she can see all the glamorous people thronging the hip restaurant you chose. And you can see only her. Unless you're expecting an assassination attempt, this is one of the simplest ways to keep from making an ass of yourself.

IMPRESS-HER MOVE #9: LEAVE YOUR EGO AT THE COAT CHECK

Of course she'd love to hear about your cool job, but give it to her easy, hotshot. No one likes an ego boy. Here are some all-time members of this Hall of Shame:

- The guy who "mentioned" his six-figure salary in the first six minutes of a date.
- The one who "brought up" that he works out three hours a day.
- The dork who, at a rock concert, just "happened" to shout that he was a Harvard graduate.

"I was so impressed by my blind date, because he hinted at his great job by talking around things when appropriate and not just blurting out crap," explains Meg, 29. "The fact that he was so low-key made him seem confident—not cocky—which is always a plus."

BASIC TIP: Women would rather hear that you're still clawing your way up the ladder of that cool job, not how you survey all that is beneath you from your lofty perch. Too much perfection will make her nervous—and pretty damned suspicious.

IMPRESS-HER MOVE #10: TREAT OTHERS AS YOU WOULD TREAT HER

When Holly opened the door to his office, she was already impressed. He had a full head of hair, his belt matched his shoes, and in the two minutes she waited for him, five people popped in to touch base, make appointments, and toss around private jokes—just like the perfect Hollywood portrayal of Mr. Popular. Then, as he mounted his white horse, he barked orders at his secretary on the way out.

"Obviously he was trying to show me how powerful he was," relates Holly, 30. But in her eyes, his stock had already plunged below the critical level. Women know they're likely to be the target of this type of behavior once you get to know them better and are no longer on your best Sunday school behavior. So if you're a tempestuous jerk, learn how to cool your jets or you'll never get past date number one.

BASIC TIP: Always exhibit patience, coolness, and generosity in dealing with others when on a date. Here are some examples:

- Bartenders: Be generous and over-tip. (On that note, don't ask your date what you should tip. She'd like to think you've figured that out by now.)
- Hostess: Thank her while looking her in the eyes (as opposed to looking at her more shapely attributes).
- Waiter: Be firm and put your foot down in the face of rudeness, but be polite and thank him or her for the extra service. (Patience is super-attractive.)
- If you run into a few of her friends: Be enthusiastic and pleased to meet them. Think about it—it's fantastic PR. If her friends like you, they'll root for you, too. And at this stage, you should take all the help you can get.

SPICE UP HER NIGHT

Before you get wrapped up in another tedious "I don't know, what do you want to do?" conversation about Saturday night, know this: A five-star, bells-and-whistles, one-for-the-memory-bank kind of date doesn't hinge on a five-star restaurant. What women really want is a man with a plan. So forget about dinner and a movie and give her a date that will really keep her humming.

Since an evening she'll love often means one that will bore you to tears (antiquing, winetasting, anything vaguely involving Gwyneth Paltrow), we present you with some activities that'll not only keep your dating stock at an all-time high but also entertain you as much as they do her.

■ Impress Her With Hot Air

Head for the skies in a hot-air balloon. Soaring Adventures of America, Inc. (800-762-7464) has locations across the country that offer one-hour flights at dawn or dusk for about $160 a person. Lest you think this is all rainbows and guys in top hats. The only thing keeping you from plummeting from the height of a 100-story building is a piece of fabric thinner than your jeans.

■ Do the Macarena

Head to your local wedding factory (i.e., the Hilton) and check the activity board for the next big bash. Bring along a gift-wrapped box of something you don't want anymore—like that punch bowl Aunt Natty gave you or your old ghetto blaster with the broken FM switch—quickly down some shots at the bar, and prepare to tear up the dance floor. Hey, somebody's got to start the conga line.

■ Bet on the Horses

Take her to the track, but hide the wallet (you'll just spend your winnings on her anyway). Instead, place bets on where you'll go on the next few dates. Come up with 10 proposals and match them with horses in each race. If Pretty Woman wins, she drags you to a Celine Dion concert; Trigger in first gets you a Saturday-night Hockey game.

■ Get Housed

Scam snooty real estate agents by touring impossibly expensive apartments. Show up in your best casual clothes and act detached: If the agent mentions money, explain that you don't handle such frivolous financial matters, then remark on how cheap it sounds compared to your place " in the islands." Note: Make sure you're serious about this girl first; you may set off some premature nesting instincts.

day, including a free tank of gas and 100 free miles, unlimited use of a cell phone (but don't forget the cell phone dos and don'ts discussed above), and a satellite navigation system. What the heck, you only go bankrupt once.

■ Take It to Art

Flex your culture muscles at an art auction. Park West Gallery holds auctions three times a year in hotels in over 30 North American cities (800-521-9654). The art falls somewhere between legitimate high-end and the $9.99 schlock you find at a Holiday Inn starving-artist sale. It's free, but you must register with a credit card. You can always use the bidder's paddle to fan away the perfume of the old biddies next to you.

■ Fake Her Out With Takeout

Although your usual Saturday night together involves a four-topping pizza and a bottle of Coke, surprise her by bringing home a four-course dinner and a bottle of vino from a swanky restaurant. Before she arrives, place votive candles around the room and fold a couple of paper towels into little swans (or lame little triangles) to transform your seedy apartment into a four-star ristorante.

■ Build an Erection

Invite her to help you build a fort in your living room. Gather straight-backed chairs for the walls, couch cushions for the floor, dark sheets for the roof, blankets, a flashlight, and a six-

■ Create Your Own Soundtrack

Smooth over the awkward silences on a date by paying a street musician to provide personalized tunes. Ask the next Bob Dylan collecting coins in his hat to follow the two of you from theater to restaurant to bar for a few hours. If your streets don't foster beggars, post a flier at the local college offering easy cash to music majors. On second thought, this could be really annoying. Forget this one.

■ Rent a Jag

When your 1982 Datsun's got you blue, take her cruising in a brand-new Mustang convertible for around $80 a day at Budget Rent-a-Car. Excellence Luxury Car Rental (888-526-0055) rents out Porsche 996 convertibles for $500 a

pack. Remember, the sturdier you make your cushion cathedral, the wilder the activities within it can be.

■ Fork It

Fondue originated in Switzerland in the days where locals would be snowed in with nothing to eat but stale bread, cheese, and wine. These days a snowstorm is not required to enjoy this culinary treat. Grab a spaghetti pot and a couple of shish-kebob skewers and melt four ounces of Gruyère cheese, eight ounces of Swiss, a cup of white wine, and a tablespoon of kirsch over low heat; then drown chunks of French bread in the cheesy mire. Gina Steer's *The Fondue Cookbook* (Contemporary Books) also has recipes for desserts—if you can't figure one out for yourselves.

■ Have Guns of Fun

Practice for your office *Doom* tournament on real moving targets. The National Skeet Shooting Association (800-877-5338) can hook up members with a field in your area that will rent you a gun as well as ear and eye protection; you buy the box of ammunition. With no previous training, you can pop off a round of 25 clay pigeons in less than an hour. Warning: Because this game is about hand-eye coordination and not strength, it's quite possible your girlfriend will whip your ass.

■ Take Two Balls and Call Us in the Morning

Celebrate Naked Day! Call in sick for each other and then strip down. The USFDA's *The Bad Bug Book* can suggest a handy disease (vm.cfsan.fda.gov/~mow/intro.html.) The only rule is that you can't wear clothing, even—and especially—when the Chinese food delivery guy shows up. Just make sure she has a sense of humor before trying as a first date.

■ Boat for Sail

Why should dopey guys in Top-Siders have all the fun? Charter yourself a sailboat for a day. Seacoast Yacht Charters (800-468-1807) in Cape Coral and Tarpon Spring, Florida, for example, provides 20- to 50-foot yachts for $215-$425; and if you don't know your port side from your backside, you can book a Coast Guard–certified captain for an extra $150. Snooty Thurston Howell III voice lessons cost extra.

10 WAYS TO TALK YOURSELF OUT OF SEX:

Because it's hard to kiss a man with his foot in mouth.

Things were going so well: You were sure that tonight this woman was yours. So why are you sitting there alone while she's talking to him? Chances are you've let loose with one of these not-so-fabulous confabulations.

1. "I've never been dumped by a woman. I've always been the dumper."
2. "My mom is my best friend."
3. "All the bartenders down there know me by name."
4. "Can you imagine having sex with just one person for the rest of your life?"
5. "Order whatever you want — it's my dad's credit card."
6. "You don't think I come across as feminine, do you?"
7. "I plan to retire at 40."(Which means she'll be sitting home alone while you work 90 hours a week until then.)
8. "You can only tell the difference between real ones and fake ones by squeezing them."
9. "That area is just full of strip joints. I mean, I've heard…"
10. "I'm my buddy's alibi tonight—he's out with some new babe from work."

FIRST-DATE SEX

OK, you've impressed her to death and spruced up your pecking skills. Now what? Well, unless her name starts with Sister, first-date sex is always a possibility, and an eventuality you should be prepared for. Now, thanks to our idiot-proof guide, you can turn every date into a sure thing.

The truth is that women love first-date sex as much as you do—maybe more. They love meeting a guy who is so overflowing with hot, animal sexuality that they want to jump his bones. Sarah, 24, explains it best: "If I wait until the third date, I'm nervous. By then I know things about his last girlfriend, and I start to worry about how I compare," she says. "First-date sex is better because it's taboo: You feel like a bad, bad girl."

One thing you can bank on: Your dinner companion is not wearing her ratty period underwear on a first date. When she got dressed she more than likely put on her "do-me party panties" in the hope that you'll be worthy of first-date sex. That means you have a shot.

But don't get too confident. There are plenty of opportunities along the way for the clumsy and the inexperienced to blow a golden opportunity. "I may have cleaned my bedroom and gotten a bikini wax thinking I'd want to take him home on the first night," explains Susan, 26. "But even though I'm salivating over him, he still has to show some key things—responsibility and trustworthiness, for example—before I'll feel comfortable doing it on the first date." The good news: You can be that stellar guy. You just need to earn your merit badges. Here's how:

Humble Yourself

Cockiness will blow a night of first-date sex faster than cold sores and a wedding ring combined. Why? Because it's key for a woman to feel that she's giving you a gift; not something she does with just any guy, but a special thing she's green-lighting just for you. "The last guy I had sex with on the first date paid a lot of attention to me, and just me," remarks Caroline, 24. "A guy who checks out the whole room, including my friends—that makes it obvious he only has a sex agenda."

After you've greeted and ingratiated yourself with her (again, minus the swagger), it's time to be all about her. Ask her questions about herself, and keep batting the conversation back to her. ("Colorado Springs is my favorite city—but what is it about Dublin that you dig so much?") Because in a woman's everything-means-something brain, a selfish conversation signals that she's found a man who won't be very concerned with helping her achieve record-setting orgasms. Would you rather boast about outmaneuvering your boss at that staff meeting now—or watch her waving to God and all the angels later?

Show You'll Keep Sex on the Q.T.

A woman can't have you bragging all over town about her easy-access ways, so she needs some proof you'll keep your mouth shut about her little coffee table fetish. So how do you sign her unspoken nondisclosure agreement? As she asks you questions about yourself, wait for the right time to give her this line: "Sorry I'm not talking about myself much. I have a little trouble sharing personal stuff, even with my buddies; I guess that's a male thing, huh?" You've just let her know you're a sexual-information vault. Now don't blow it by talking about your ex-girlfriends, the sex lives of any of your male or female friends, or which Hollywood celebs you've heard are bumping uglies.

Treat Even Non-Dates Like Dates

She won't hook up with you if you don't make your first date feel like a date, even if you just met her for the first time at a party an hour ago. Be a Boy Scout and offer to brave the bar line to get her another gin and tonic, help her with her coat, and generally make her feel special.

TALK HER INTO BED

You know who gets a woman into bed on the first date? A guy who says all the right things. But what exactly are those things? And why isn't "I drive a Beemer" on the list?

1. "I cried like a baby." These five words say worlds about you symbolically: not only that you've used your tear ducts on at least one occasion, but that you're comfortable enough with your masculinity to gush forth with such a fountain of feelings. You earn extra points if your tears are emotional (from watching *The Champ*) rather than pain-related (from getting the crap beat out of you in college). Never mind that if you dump her like yesterday's pork fat, she'll tell everyone that you are a big baby.

2. "You've got the most gorgeous eyes/beautiful collarbone/amazing laugh." Rather than telling the woman you're with that she "looks great," compliment something unique about her. This, by the way, works best when expressed in a revelatory tone, as in, "Wow, I hadn't really noticed until the light hit your face in that certain way" or "...until I saw you smile from across the room." Steer clear of features that get Hooters girls hired, like her breasts, butt, legs, and lips (or at least save those compliments for later, when she's stripping down and wants you to notice all of her 2,000 sexy parts).

3. "Some jackass was trying to start a fight with me." While every woman has had a fantasy about two men fighting to the death over her, in the real world of supermarkets and sports bars, they don't like men who fight. Don't think you're impressing them with your tough-guy speeches. They'd much rather hug the big hairy ape who can calm those ready-to-rumble types down.

4. "It was for charity." Women don't want to date telethon hosts, but they love to hear that every so often you do something that benefits a greater good, however inadvertently. What woman doesn't want a man who spends time on things that don't somehow serve to make him money, earn him more leisure time, or get him into a girl's pants? Well, not directly, anyway.

5. "I'm going home tomorrow to help my mom install her new computer." It warms a woman's heart to hear that a guy is happy to spend time with his family. Getting along with one's family is key in the sexual-selection process. Being close with your family means you can adapt socially to other people you can't choose—like your in-laws. Not to mention that they're thinking if all goes well, she might be spending time with your family, too.

6. "I like to cook." You don't even have to be good at it. If you're whistling while you pour pancake batter into the shape of silver dollars, women don't care that you can't make crepes: Dating you would bring her that much closer to living out one of those scenes in a J. Crew catalog where barefoot men in log cabins crack eggs into cast-iron frying pans.

7. "I'm taking a vacation next week." You'll do whatever it takes to get ahead in your job, you love jetting around the world for business meetings, and you plan on being a CEO by 35. Sounds great—to a PalmPilot. Women want men who love their jobs, but trust us when we tell you that no woman wants a workaholic. So if you tell her you work to live—rather than live to work—she'll sigh with relief. Plus, talk about the warm sand and the tropical breezes you're looking forward to and she'll wonder if you might not want a travel companion.

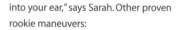

This special treatment helps assuage another of her fears: that you won't respect her afterward. Nip that one in the bud by saying, as she's talking about her career choices, "That's really smart. I really respect women who can [whatever she just said]."

Time It Just Right

In the 21st century it's fairly acceptable for a woman to go back to your place or her place on the first date. But wait for a natural moment or for her to invite you. "My last date took me to a fun party that was still going full-throttle, but at 10 P.M. he asked me if I wanted to go someplace else," says Marlene, 25. " He might as well have asked me to go home and get naked with him—it was so obvious." Always wait for the party to dwindle (but not die) or for the conversation to wane a little (but not collapse) before proposing a change of scene.

Nail the Pre-Foreplay

Now that you've made it to the privacy of the sofa (that's right, most women prefer a little warm-up on the couch before hitting the sex chamber), keep moving slowly, and kiss her for at least 15 minutes before you venture anywhere else. Touch her through her clothes for another 20 minutes before you move on. If she moves your hands away, wait five minutes and try again. Rochelle, 27, explains this dynamic: "If I say no or swat his hands away, I definitely mean no. "But gently moving his hands away means I'm not quite sure and that he can try again in a few minutes."

Unfortunately, some guys blow it simply because they're so close to the finish line. "You can tell a guy is just thinking, *sex, sex, sex* when he puts his tongue too far down your throat or shoves it too far into your ear," says Sarah. Other proven rookie maneuvers:

- Squishing her into an uncomfortable position—always make sure she's comfortable.
- Pulling her clothes off without unbuttoning or unzipping them.
- Reaching inside her bra from underneath instead of from above (that forces the bra to squash her boobs down—very unsexy).

Once clothes are coming off, gently suggest moving to the bedroom. Stand up and lead her from the couch as you say, "Would you be more comfortable in here?" Hold her hand as you walk down the hall. This is a crucial moment, and if you break contact with her, she'll feel abandoned and weird. Move back to kissing for a few minutes, and then, when she's panting as hard as you are, get down to the thing that makes life worth living.

Of course, this all comes with one caveat: There's still a chance you'll end the night alone, playing handyman. That's because you've executed these strategies so brilliantly that she's no longer thinking about whether to have sex with you on the first date. No, she's moved on to planning your wedding, naming your kids, and picking out patio furniture, and she's going to nix the possibility of sex tonight to make sure you keep coming around, the clever vixen. The good news: If you adore her back, soon enough you'll be getting lots and lots of fabulous sex on demand from a woman who truly wants you bad.

KISSING 101

Before we can proceed, there are a few more basics to cover. While you may think yourself the best kisser west (or east) of the Mississippi, it's never too late for a little refresher course. A kiss may seem spontaneous, but the skill required to position your hands, face, and body can make a Jackie Chan action scene look easy. Women know exactly how they like to be kissed, and we've broken it down for you, move by move. Listen to what they say, put it all together, and you'll make her knees weak.

THE APPROACH

"Put your hands on my face, look me square in the eye, glance at my lips, then move in slowly."—Adrian, 29, publicist

"My ex-boyfriend pushed me up against the wall (nonviolently, of course), put his hands around my face, and started kissing me slowly." —Marie, 28, office manager

"It's all about the tease. I love it when a guy gives a couple of sweet pecks, then moves into a full-on tongue, and then disengages by sucking on my lower lip."—Dora, 34, advertising director

THE HANDS

"Run your hands through my hair while you're kissing me." —Karen, writer, 27

"I love kissing while a guy's hands start on my face, then end up around my waist."—Erin, 30, paralegal

"The hands make the kiss, like the bread makes the sandwich. So many guys have great, talented hands but never use them a tenth as much as they should. During a kiss, your hands should be running through my hair, cradling my head, stroking my face." —Lisa, 33, police officer

THE LIPS AND TONGUE

"First lick my lips with only the tip of your tongue. Let me get a taste of you and want it. Then pull away and kiss my cheeks lusciously before going back to my lips."—Karen, 27, writer

"Don't use too much tongue. Pillowy soft lips between tonguing is key. Otherwise, it's invasive and lizardly." —Alicia, 30, lawyer

"I like a slow, wet, long kiss that goes into a passionate, hard one, where you can't stop groping each other." —Michelle, 29, accountant

"The best kisser I ever dated gave me one light kiss, looked me in the eyes, smiled, and moved in again. He kissed me lightly, mouth open slightly, then slowly inserted his tongue. After speeding up his technique and really getting into it, he slowly pulled away from me and slid the tip of his tongue along and around my lips. Not slobbery, though. It made me tingle all over." —Corrine, 29, publicist

"I really like when a guy doesn't hold back when he kisses. When he's really into it and even kind of rough at first. But a controlled tongue is essential—slobber can ruin everything." —Beth, 24, photo assistant

"Sometimes I want to be kissed like a 15-year-old in a parking lot, other times like a grandma. Vary your intensity and keep me guessing."—Janine, 21, student

"I like more lips than tongue, soft lips (not too wet or dry) with tongue dips—defined as a semisoft tongue that enters my mouth but is neither erect and jammed into my mouth nor hidden like a turtle in his. Big tongue action every so often is good. Frequent movement is important, too; don't suction yourself onto my face."—Rachel, 26, stylist

THE FINALE

"After a good kiss, a sweet peck on my nose and forehead will seal the deal."—Rochelle, 27, manager

"A kiss should finish with small, lip-only kisses."—Erin, 30, paralegal

OTHER PEOPLES PLAYS

Your date was a hit, and now she's all over you like (Reggie) White on (Jerry) Rice. Our panel of experts offers several tips on how you can send a typical sex session over the moon.

1. Hit the Showers

"My boyfriend shut off the lights and lit candles in the bathroom; then he lathered up my hair and every inch of my body. Feeling his hands all over me made me so hot, I didn't bother to wait for the soap to rinse off before dropping to my knees to return the favor." —Gisele, 25, intern

2. Be a Tease

"We'll start off a night by fooling around with our clothes on, basically working each other into a sexual frenzy. Then we'll force ourselves to head out for dinner and drinks, whispering about how much we want each other. By the time midnight rolls around, we're ready to tear each other apart." —Sylvie, 32, writer

3. Sweat It Out

"I love working out with him at the gym and then doing it the second we walk through the door, while we're still covered in sweat. Maybe it's the fantasy that we're still at the gym and everyone's watching us get busy on a weight bench." —Anitra, 24, accountant

4. Frighten the Birds

"Having sex outside is my all-time favorite. One guy and I did it under blankets at the beach, behind the reptile house at the zoo, and even in the woods right off a crowded ski slope. The trick is to make it fast and furious." —Pamela, 31, police officer

5. Tell a Story

"I get incredibly turned on when my boyfriend tells me what he's going to do to me as if it's already happened. He'll say, 'And then I pushed you back onto the bed and slid my hand up your skirt, and then I ran my tongue along your collarbone.' When he actually does it a few minutes later, the anticipation is so high, I start to shake." —Nicky, 28, veterinarian

6. Rent *Scream*

"After reading that scary movies put couples in the mood for sex more than any other genre, my boyfriend and I started seeing them more often. When you're scared, your heart beats faster, and you get kind of hot. It puts extra oomph in your bedroom activities." —Janelle, 29, nurse

7. Stop and Start

"For big, big orgasms, we stop intercourse to go down on each other, and then start back up again. We'll do it over and over until we've been making love for more than an hour. When we finally do cum, it's insane." —Sandra, 28, secretary

8. Worship Satin

"On special occasions, my ex would deck his bed out in black satin s heets to let me know we'd be having some seriously intense sex that night. When I'd slip and slide into different positions, the satin felt so sexy against my skin." —Tina, 24, art director

9. Have Fun With Living Room Furniture

"Sex on a bed is boring. I like to be bent over a table or the back of a couch, or on a chair with me on top, facing the same direction and pumping up and down. I only use beds for sleeping." —Theresa, 33, customer service rep

10. Give Yourself a Hand

"Nothing gets me going more than seeing my guy touch himself. I'll straddle his thighs and rub my clitoris while he beats off. Every one of my girlfriends agrees that seeing her man's hand on his penis is a turn-on." —Gloria, 30, fitness instructor

[Only follow this advice when you know it'll go over well. Walking out of the bathroom with your tool in hand while she's still sipping her wine may not have a desirable effect.—Editor]

11. Make Love Blind

"I used to feel too self-conscious to move my hips as quickly as I wanted to when I was on top. My boyfriend knew I was holding back, so he let me blindfold him so I could grind my heart out and not worry about what I looked like."—Kimberlee, 19, model

12. Say Please and Spank You

"One guy I dated would ask me questions like 'Do you want me to pinch your nipples harder?' 'Should I bite your neck?' and 'Would it turn you on if I spanked you softly?' My answer was always yes, but it was hearing him ask the question that drove me crazy." —Rachel, 27, dentist

13. Sixty-Nine to the Finish

"Instead of having sex, we'll 69 until we both come. We start with him on top and do it slowly, and then we'll flip over so I'm on top. It gets crazy, with us squirming and pushing our bodies against the other's mouth pretty hard. But we don't stop until we've each had our orgasm."
—Jacqueline, 28, attorney

14. Create New Hot Spots

"We recently discovered a special kind of lubricant, called Hot Licks, that feels normal at first but then heats up when you blow on it. It feels incredible on my breasts, thighs, and rubbed on the outer lips of my vagina. He likes it front and center: surprise, surprise."
—Angel, 25, dancer

15. Hand It to Her

"I'd bet most women would love to keep one hand on their clitoris at all times during sex, but they don't want the guy they're with to think he's being upstaged. I like it when a guy takes my hand and puts it between my legs. It lets me know I can touch myself without doing damage to his ego."—Danielle, 29, clothing designer

16. Put Your Finger on It

"Men who know how to stimulate the G-spot are few and far between. Just slide your finger in there, try a few things, and ask her what feels best. Trust me, how wet she gets will make it worth the effort."
—Amy, 30, caretaker

17. Lighten Up

"We goof around and do silly stuff in bed, like tickling or wrestling each other in the middle of sex. It's also a way to work in some kinky stuff, like spanking and making ridiculous but kind of sexy comments like 'C'mon, tough guy, I know you can push harder than that!'" —Rosanna, 32, jeweler

18. Keep Her Waiting

"My boyfriend tortures me by refusing to put his penis inside me. He'll suck on my nipples, rub my clitoris, go down on me, do everything but that—and he'll keep torturing me for, like, half an hour. Finally he asks me if I want it in me, and I'll scream, 'Yes! Yes! Yes!'"—Jodi, 23, human resources manager

19. Scream for Ice Cream

"You wouldn't believe the fun we've had going through our freezer. I've given him a blow job with frozen grapes in my mouth. He's dribbled Ben & Jerry's between my legs, then licked it off. We've misused Popsicles, ice cubes, frozen strawberries... you name it." —Ann, 26, real estate agent

20. Stay Suited Up

"Having sex with a guy in a suit is such a turn-on. I'll ask him to leave everything on and just undo his fly and pull his penis out. Feeling the fabric against the insides of my legs and grabbing him by his tie gets me off every time."
—Sharlene, 18, caterer

21. Arouse Her in Her Sleep

"Sometimes my live-in boyfriend caresses my breasts and strokes the outside of my underwear while I'm still half-asleep. Then we make love, and it's like I'm dreaming."
—Joy, 24, seamstress

22. See a Really Bad Movie

"One night we couldn't sleep, so we dragged ourselves to a 1 A.M. movie. The place was empty and the movie sucked, so we took turns going down on each other. The next thing we know, we're half naked and doing it every which way we can without falling off the seat."—Felicia, 28, investment consultant

DEAL-BREAKERS: SUBTLE WAYS TO SCREW UP A SURE THING

As confident as you may feel from our expert advice, one wrong move can set her tides against you, and you may never recover the magic. Avoid these common pitfalls.

Simpering Fealty

Do not simply agree with everything she says; you'll look either spineless or calculating. "A guy who constantly hangs on my every word is such a turn-off," says Gretchen, 32, actress.

Indifferent Hygiene

It's way beyond deodorant: Unshaven, scraggly hair, dirty nails, and other forms of unkempt grooming can kill your chances faster than a three-inch wart growing on your cheek. Shave and get a good haircut; clean and trim your nails; harvest the earwax. This tells her she's worth primping for. But you should know all this already.

Complaining and Confessing

Day sucked? Gobble some happy pills; she's not your therapist. "I don't want to hear how bad your life is on a first date. I'm not going to fix it," says Susan, 19, student

Dirty Jokes

If she tells you one, she's trying to hint that she's just a little naughty (tee-hee). Do not follow up with the one about the donkey, the Girl Scouts, and the condom dispenser.

Showing Off

Unless she complains that it tastes like vinegar, don't send the wine back. And don't flaunt your social calendar or money clip: If you make mad presidents, she'll sense it.

Excessive Touching

"If a guy is constantly touching my arm or thigh when he's talking to me, it's weird and nasty," says Marisa, 26. Wait for her to initiate incidental contact, then follow suit.

Droning On About Other Women

You can't win here. Trash your ex and the one you're with will fear for her own rep; speak fondly of your ex and you'll appear to still be hooked. "Don't talk about an ex in any way, shape, or form. We know you have one or two or a hundred—don't remind us at the time of naked intimacy."—Julia, 25, writer

Your Scuffed Shoes

"If a guy's shoes aren't polished, it tells me he doesn't pay attention to details," reveals Ambika, 26. Sandals that show off hairy toes are similarly lame, Mr. Birkenstock.

Getting Too Mushy Too Fast

"A guy should never say, 'Let's make love,' when we're not in love."—Daria, 27, journalist

Quiet Lovin'

"Quiet ejaculators are a huge turn-off. I hate it when guys make no noise. What? Don't I turn you on?"—Adrian, 29, publicist

Assuming She's Dirty

"This guy once told me that girls should always take showers right before fooling around to eliminate 'the nasty factor' if they expected guys to go down on them. I didn't take it personally (he hadn't gone south on me, so he had no way of knowing if I had a nasty factor to eliminate). But still, bad move."
—Marie, 28, office manager

The Mid-Sex Bathroom Break

"We were about to make love and he said he had to go to the bathroom. How frustrating! Men, relieve yourselves before you come near the bed."—Lisa, 33, police officer

Pick Only-for-You Porn

"He suggested we put on a porno. I love pornography, so that's no problem at all. I flicked the TV on, then he put the tape in the VCR and fast-forwarded to two women making out. I said, 'What am I getting out of this? Nothing.' Then I left."—Jo, 27, human resources manager

■ **Inappropriate Chatter**
"It was my birthday and we were in the thick of it when his cell phone rang. He said, 'That might be my brother,' picked up the phone, and started chatting away. Not about anything important, but about music. When he hung up the phone, he started kissing my neck and wasstill up for it. I told him to drop dead, then kicked him out." —Laura, 27, personnel director

■ **Getting the Whole Partial-Nudity Thing Backwards**
"Please don't walk around in a shirt and no pants." —Rosie, 32, human rights advocate

■ **Passionate Faux Pas**
"Yeah, we know you're not in your right mind, but try not to say anything during sex that you're going to regret later, like 'I love you.'" —Rosa, 34, advertising director

WHY SHE REALLY BLEW YOU OFF

You took her out, had a great time, and did all the right things—pulled out the chair, paid the bill, made her laugh, and walked her to her door. So you follow up the date with a phone call but your gal has suddenly stopped answering the phone. Why the phone-call freeze-out? The reason probably wasn't as arbitrary as your mismatched socks. If women are that superficial, Marilyn Manson would be a lonely man. The truth is, some deal breakers are quite subtle and near undetectable to the male eye. Some things you just can't help—like your nervous twitch—so if that is what she has a problem with, then cut your losses and move on. But many "problems" can be altered with a bit of charm, humor, and tact. Here's a rundown of some brush-off scenarios that she's liable to spring on you, and how you should handle them.

BRUSH-OFF #1: SOMEBODY ELSE

You both had a great time and are looking forward to the second date. But somewhere between the good-night kiss and the follow-up call, she met somebody else. Shit happens.

"I went on a date with this guy John, who was nice, but then I met Larry a few days later. We went out and really hit it off," says Lynn, 29. "I mean, what could I tell John other than I met somebody else?"

Ouch. You can't stop fate. If her chemistry with another man explodes even as you two are starting to sweat it up, don't sit around wondering what this guy has that you don't. Understand there's nothing you could have done and move on.

BRUSH-OFF #2: YOU WERE TOO HONEST

You had a few laughs, tossed back the booze, and in your drunken haze you felt like you could tell her anything, and you did, including all your messy breakups, occasional bad temper, and sexual exploits.

"I was on a first date with a guy who told me that his ex-girlfriend had gotten a restraining order against him," says Maria, 30. "I think he wanted to make fun of it, and let me know *she* was the nutso one. But, of course, I didn't even want to chance it after that."

As a general rule, it's best not to exorcise any demons on a first date. Your intentions may be honorable but you never know how she'll interpret the things you say. It's best to reveal your true self over time, thus preserving some of the mystique that surrounds you.

BRUSH-OFF #3: SHE GOT TOO DRUNK

She got trashed with you, feels she made a fool of herself, and now can't bear to face you again.

"I'd had a crush on Marcus for months," says Jennifer, 26. "He finally asked me out, and I was so nervous that I didn't eat all day. I ended up getting completely sloshed and was hanging my head out the window the entire ride home."

The best way to tackle this one? Feign ignorance. Tell her she didn't say or do anything stupid, and let her believe that you were as drunk as she was. And don't mention that her puke left a greenish-yellow stain on your shoes that you can't get out. In the future, when you sense your date is headed toward a Maker's Mark moment, skip the next round. She'll appreciate that you're looking out for her.

BRUSH-OFF #4: YOU'RE TOO MUCH OF A GENTLEMAN

She digs you and your good manners (for the most part), but making no attempt at physical contact at all (hand on the knee or arm around the shoulders) is read as rejection.

"I was attracted to this guy I was with, but at the end of the night, instead of moving in for the kiss, he darted from the car like he'd left the oven on back home," says Ruth, 28.

This tactic can be especially bad if you're a known player going for legitimacy. She'll wonder why you've slept with everybody else but not her. The solution? Call her up with a manly plan, and tell her you were a flake last time because you were coming down with tonsillitis but want to see her again. Tell her that you're a gentleman, but not *that* much of a gentleman. You dirty dog.

BRUSH-OFF #5: YOU COMMITTED A VERBAL OFFENSE

During dessert you broke out your favorite smut jokes, or worse, made some insensitive remark about women's issues.

"On our first date, he said something about Hillary Clinton needing a real man to put her in her place," says Justine, 30. "It was too early on to tell if he was being sarcastic or serious, but it didn't really matter."

Be extra charming, and keep the humor in the middle of the road, avoiding potentially sensitive issues.

BRUSH-OFF #6: YOU DIDN'T NOTICE SHE WASN'T HAVING FUN

You had a blast, thought you cracked some great one-liners but actually spent the whole evening talking about yourself. In all the excitement, you never once asked her if she liked the food or was enjoying herself.

"Every time there was a lull in the conversation," says Carrie, 24, "he'd talk about people at work. I don't know these friggin' people! Boring!"

Maybe you were nervous or preoccupied that day. Whatever the reason, tell her you're sorry if you bored her to tears talking about your frat buds the whole date. Then ask if she wants to go on a real date sometime. If she agrees, use the following warm-and-fuzzy math equation: Ask her at least two questions about herself for everything you reveal about yourself. Pretty soon she'll be bragging to her friends about what a great listener you are.

SIGNS SHE WANTS YOU

Only in your dreams do unfamiliar babes at parties hold up signs urging you to "Come and get it!" In the waking world, you have to decipher more subtle, unconscious signals, according to Allan Pease's book *Signals: How to Use Body Language for Power, Success, and Love*. Here's the lowdown:

- If she tosses her head... ...or lets her hair fall onto her face and peers out from under her cage o' locks, holding your gaze—you're in.
- If she exposes her wrists... ...it's a subtle come-on. (The bondage imagery won't be lost on the discriminating male.)
- If she spreads her legs... ...or strikes a wide-legged stance, she's either hot for your bones or has a serious thong-wedgie situation.
- If she thrusts her foot... ...or moves her tootsies in and out of her shoe, it's more classic nookie symbolism. (Don't ask her if she's got bunions.)
- If she flashes her neck... ...it's a come-hither sign of passivity. (If she flashes her breasts, you're either at Mardi Gras or your alarm clock is about to go off.)
- If she fondles cylindrical or starts running her fingers up and down objects...the stem of her wineglass, she's—well, what do you think?

One final note: Giving the finger still means go away.

ASK (HER) ANYTHING

The questions you want to ask your girlfriend, but would get slapped if you did. We consulted Linda Yniguez, Ph.D., licensed psychologist and host of *ShrinkRap: A Women's Forum* on www.AdrenalineRadio.com to get you answers to some of the more puzzling mysteries of the female body and mind.

Why do some women smell more than others down there? How do I talk to my girlfriend about her scent without hurting her feelings?

Unless a woman has an infection or doesn't shower once a day, she shouldn't stink. Each woman is different and has her own scent. More likely, you have an aversion to your girl's scent, explains Yniguez.

If it's a new problem, then believe it or not, soap may be to blame. A woman's odor can be thrown off by the slightest thing, like suds that mess with her pH. Or if she eats lots of carbs or takes tons of vitamins, she's going to have a more detectable smell. But if she hasn't gone vegan or healthy on you, then an infection is a likely culprit. If she smells, well, yeasty, she might have a yeast infection. If something smells fishy, that's probably a bacterial one. Bringing it up is tricky because, for the most part, women are self-conscious about odors emanating from down there. To get rid of the problem—especially if you think it's an infection—ask her if she's noticed any changes with her body, says Yniguez. Even offer to go to the doctor with her. The easy way out: When you plan on heading south, suggest showering together first—or better yet, take care of business in the bath. If things don't get better, remember what they say: You can't argue tastes.

My old girlfriend used to gush like Niagara Falls. My new girl doesn't seem to get that wet. I think she's turned on, but could she be faking it?

Not all women were created equal in the wet department, explains Yniguez. Some gush, some barely get lubricated. Hormones are often to blame, not a lack of horniness or, lucky for you, your love handles. Just because she doesn't flow like a fire hydrant doesn't mean your girl isn't turned on. So why not introduce a lube like Astroglide (it's odorless, tasteless, and, many contend, the closest thing on the market to a woman's natural secretions) into sex play. Don't make it seem like there's something wrong with her. Instead, tell her that you really go crazy when you slide right into her. Then ask if she wouldn't mind if you guys tried it with a little lube to make it extra slick. If she's all lubed up and still no cigar, then, buddy, hit the gym. It just may be that spare tire turning her off.

I've seen pornos where the women ejaculate, sometimes spraying huge amounts of liquid over great distances. Can this actually happen?

Yes, Timmy, there is such a thing as female ejaculation. About it traveling great distances, not likely. There can be tons of this clear, milky, thin liquid, explains Yniguez, but since it's released from the urethra (that's where her urine comes out), not the vagina, it's more likely to drip down. Just because it's released from the pee passage doesn't mean it's urine. During an orgasm, it's virtually impossible for a woman to pee, since her PC muscles are tightening. Those are the same muscles that contract when you stop whizzing.

Now, for the real question: How are you going to get your girl as close to a porn star as possible? Stimulate her G-spot, or internal hot button, which coincidentally, is located behind her clit. Use your fingers in a come-hither motion. [See "The Big Ohhh: How to Get Her Off" and "Sex-Machine Maintenance" for details.] If your handy work does the trick, she should arrive.

Can it hurt either partner to have sex while the red tide's in?

Well, let's see, other than the fact that you might get some gross looking stuff on you? The answer is no. It's not dangerous to either partner. In fact, some studies show that having an orgasm actually relieves a woman's cramps.

Most times women think you'll be weirded out by it, so they won't push sex at that time of the month. But if you're not the squeamish sort, tell her you're OK with it. That's usually enough to get her going. After all, a lot of women experience major horniness during their periods as a result of raging hormones. Here's a tip from Yniguez: Entice her into the bath right before sex. The water tends to hold back the flow. And don't forget to grab a towel and put it underneath you so there's no messy cleanup after.

How can I tell the difference between a woman with bad PMS and one who's just in a bad mood?
Your best bet is to look for signs her period is on its way. Are her boobs busting out? Is she dragging around? Is she having a lot of bad hair days? Yes? Chances are her hormones are raging. PMS usually lasts less than a week, so keep tabs on your crab. If her alter ego Sybil rears her screaming head around the same time every month, your girl probably has a bad case of PMS. If it's a lot more often than that, you might have gotten stuck with a crab.

If PMS is to blame, whatever you do, don't mockingly say something like "Are you PMSing again?" unless you want to enjoy a long night on the couch, advises Dr. Yniguez. Instead, try to be understanding, sensitive, blah, blah, blah. How, you wonder? Ask her if she's OK and if there's anything you can do. Sure, it sounds like work, but it's easier than getting into a fight that's sure to outlast the commercial breaks.

How come women don't pass gas with the same power and/or frequency as men?
While it seems like men are the farters, women cut the cheese as often as men do. A recent study out of Australia suggested that men and women fart an average of 15 times per day. (The numbers go up if you've been to Taco Bell.) The difference is girls, are more shy about it, suggests Yniguez. While guys pride themselves on producing big, smelly ones, girls are taught that it's not ladylike to let loose. Instead, women are more likely to head for the bathroom when they're about to blow. And you always wondered what takes women so long in the bathroom. But why do they go in pairs…?

Can I get my girl over the edge using the back door or other nonvaginal means?
Some books say girls can orgasm just by thinking about it. For most women, scoring an O is a lot more work. About 70 percent of women can't even come from intercourse alone. So obviously, women have varying degrees of ease with achieving orgasm, says Yniguez. Mostly, a woman needs to be totally relaxed and absorbed by the sensation for it to happen—and clitoral stimulation is required. As for taking the back door, only a minority of gals can respond orgasmically to anything but a direct hit on their front door.

Is frigidity purely psychological?
Pretty much. Girls aren't hard-wired to *not* want sex. Neither are guys. If your girl seems cold, unresponsive, or unavailable, don't take it personally. A couple of things might be working against you, explains Yniguez. First off, the two of you may just have mismatched libidos. You like your bugle blown in the morning, she likes her love button pushed at night. Or maybe she's just really tired from her stressful job. Since women really respond to romance, why not buy a couple of candles, play some Portishead, and pop open a bottle of Champagne. All this works much better if you actually turn off the TV, rather than leaving the game on mute. Making your girlfriend feel special and sexy is enough to get her sex drive out of neutral.

Should I take a woman who says "I have a headache" at face value?
Unless she suffers from major migraines, a woman who uses the oldest excuse in the book just isn't in the mood. With women, when the sex well starts to dry up and pathetic excuses crop up, it's usually a sign that the relationship is on the rocks. Don't be afraid to ask her to (gulp) talk, says Yniguez. Tell her you've noticed she's been acting differently and you wanted to know what's going on. Ask her lots of questions and listen to what she has to say, painful as it sounds. The benefit: If you figure out what's bugging her (chances are it's something as simple as you to take out the trash more often), you'll see the return of your sex dynamo.

The Big Ohhhh:
How to Get Her Off

Women have it easy. When it comes to pleasuring a man, there is pretty much just one erogenous zone to handle—the ol' schlongola—and the sooner they get there the better as far as we're concerned. Women, on the other hand, much like your father's old AMC Rambler, need to be coddled, stroked, and caressed before they warm up. But once they get going, they've got more hot spots than Miami Beach during spring break, although they're a lot harder to find. And as much as women like to say they're the great communicators, when it comes to sexual techniques that get them humming, they're often struck dumb and expect us to magically know exactly what they like. But don't worry, fellow spelunkers, we're here to let you in on everything you need to know about oral sex, touching, and caressing, so that you'll be able to get any woman to enjoy sex more than she ever has before.

ORAL SEX: HOW TO GO FISHING LIKE A LESBIAN

Some guys might not consider giving a woman oral pleasure real sex, but most women do. In fact, when a woman is on the receiving end of a man's oral attention, she's having more than just real sex: She's having *really amazing* sex. Here's all you need to know to be the Jacques Cousteau of muff diving.

■ A Primer

Believe it or not, inch for inch, the muscle in your mouth holds more potential for a woman's pleasure than the one in your pants. And considering that only about 30 percent of women can climax from vaginal sex alone, it's a good thing if your limber lingua can deftly reach those little spots where your lumber can't go; for in a woman's world, little things mean a lot.

Furthermore, your skilled oral acumen will prove you are enlightened (and generous) in your appreciation of the female body. "In college I had boyfriends who would go down on me, and I was like, I don't get it," recalls Bridget, 27. "So I thought I was the one who had the problem. Then, after college I met a man who went down and things were...different. This man had skills. All of a sudden, the heavens opened up, and I was, like, Holy shit, this is the best thing that's ever happened to me."

As Bridget learned, being a cunning linguist is what separates the men from the boys, and you can be assured, if you can introduce her to the pleasures of dining at the Y, she'll never forget it (even during catty conversations with her girlfriends). Here's how to make the heavens open for your honey.

■ Give Great Lip Service

The first thing your mouth needs to do is properly warm a woman up by pitching a little woo. Before you've undone the last button of her Levi's, let her know how much you love the idea of going down on her. Please, will she let you go down on her? Please?

"When a guy tells me how excited he is to go down on me, it lets me know that he's not just doing it as par for the course," says Felice, 28. "I can relax and get ready to enjoy myself."

The fact is, a lot of women worry that guys go down on them only as a gratuitous offering to move sex along. Thanks also to the "not so fresh" mythology, she might worry that your spending 10 minutes going down on her is like six months on a chain gang to you. Therefore, you must assure her that you don't buy into all that FDS bullshit. When you're with your girlfriend and things are starting to heat up, whisper in her ear how every inch of her turns you on and how it would be like Christmas morning to give her a big kiss down there.

■ Get the Lay of the Land

In a matter of minutes, you're going to be dispatched on a pleasure mission with no flashlight, no map, and a 50 percent decrease in oxygen because there's probably a blanket over your head. So it's a good idea to brush up on her anatomy by studying Chapter Two so you are as familiar with her privates as you are with the palm of your hand. While you're going down to appreciate her fruits, you don't want to be flailing around like a blind man with Parkinson's disease.

While you're kissing her neck and cooing in her ear, slowly slide your fingers down her body. Pause at her chest and take a few languid laps around each breast. Be lazy. Take your time. A series of pit stops that tickle and tease will get her plenty buttered up before you even get there, and with each breath she'll let herself relax into the trusted hands (and soon the mouth) of a pro.

Now that your fingers have reached the Promised Land, you must understand that a woman's private bits are carefully tucked away beneath those lace undies for a reason: They're delicate. So don't go rooting around like she's a bowl of change and you're trying to dig out quarters for laundry. Better to approach her precious parts as a blind millionaire reads his Braille bank statement. Lightly, carefully, gingerly, slide your fingers across the outside, uh, petals. Using your index and middle fingers, gently—and we mean gently—stroke her; gradually (gently and gradually—get it?) work your way inside the petals, making sure you glide around—not on—her hot button (i.e., her clitoris). Circle your two fingers softly, stimulating her while you survey the area, getting a sense of where she likes to be touched and how. Be sure to ask her how she likes it (but not in a "how does the painting look hanging here" voice—go with a sexier "How does that feel?"). This will get her vocalizing her pleasure, plus it lets you in on exactly what turns her on. Inevitably, if you're tender enough, her clitoris might appear like those turkey roaster readers, kind of popping out. That's her body's way of playing *The Price Is Right*—and yelling for contestant number one to come on down.

■ Going Downtown

Now that you've mapped the territory with your fingers, let your mouth follow the same scenic route. Kiss, lick, and nibble the places you touched before, as a way of saying "Allow me to reintroduce myself." Don't rush, but don't dawdle, either.

Before you plant your face in there like you're bobbing for apples, let's reflect a moment on the Zen principle of oral pleasure: You can't see pleasure in a woman, but you can feel it. With this in mind, begin by using your tongue to trace her contours inside and out, just as you did with your fingers. Then move inside with your tongue and lips. Now give her a light smooch. Then a long, lingering kiss, then a swirly doopity-doop with your tongue. Feel familiar? That's right, you're kissing her, with all the sensuality of your lips and the seductive probing with your tongue that you use on her mouth. And again, easy does it. Think of licking an ice cream cone, tracing her name in cursive, or catching a snowflake on the tip of your tongue.

Give her a selection to choose from. But stay away from rapid "hummingbird" action and deep lunges into any orifices. Remember, your tongue is not a smaller, pinker, inferior version of your manly tool, so keep the mining to a minimum. As she gets more into it, you can gently slide a finger or two in there—but keep your mouth up around the clitoris.

■ Love Her...Don't Leave Her

Sometimes when a guy is focused on going down on a woman, she starts to feel like the magician's assistant who's been put in a box and sawed in half. She's lying there, looking around, wiggling her fingers and toes, and as the audience oohs and aahs, it's as though every part of her above her navel has vanished. "I've had guys go down on me and it's like they've left the building," says Marina, 26. "You want to say, 'Hello? Are you OK down there?'" It can get a little cold and lonely when you're gone, so quell her Bermuda Triangle phobia by giving her a three-minute demo of your work—then paying a 30-second visit upstairs to check quality control. Smile and say, "I'm

TASTER'S CHOICE: WHAT MAKES A WOMAN?

As with fine wine, taste, of course, is in the mouth of the sampler: Some men prefer a light, sweet flavor, while others enjoy a more heady, complex bouquet. And what a woman ingests affects the "taste" of her body. Saturated fats like meat and cheese, for example, are metabolized and then partially secreted through sweat glands, so a cheeseburger lover will have a particularly pungent zest, says Alan Hirsch, M.D., author of *Scentsational Sex*. Vegetarians, however, eat less saturated fat than meat eaters and may therefore have a subtler flavor. More important is the amount of hot chili a woman sprinkles on her chow. "Spices have the most effect on a woman's taste," says sex therapist and educator Patti Britton, Ph.D. If she loves garlic or uses a lot of soy or steak sauce, that will most likely contribute to a more potent flavor. Similarly, alcohol and cigarettes, whose essences are also secreted through sweat glands, may contribute to a tangier zip. For more on the taste of a man's marinade, see Chapter 8.

really enjoying this. Is there something you like that I'm doing or not doing?" This gives her the chance to put in a special request for a tongue ripple, or perhaps she wants to feel your fingers inside her. And when you head south again, don't hold back your excitement. Moan in pleasure, caress her belly and breasts, and kiss the insides of her thighs. "And don't forget to look up at us while your head is down there," says Elise, 25. "That's key."

■ Read Her Hips

If she's enjoying what you're doing, she may run her hands through your hair or start chanting like a Gregorian monk. Or maybe she'll just lie there with her arms over her head in a pleasure coma, a big gooey grin on her face. But you can't see much right now, so you'll have to rely on what's in front of you to know if she likes what you're doing. Start by keeping your head still and observing her pelvic "platform" as she moves her body around. If she's pushing forward into your face, she wants more pressure from your tongue; if she's inching backward, that means it might be too much and you should ease up. If she's sliding from side to side, it's possible you're off target and she's helping you locate her bull's-eye.

Whatever it is, she wants to let you know what feels good (and what doesn't) without having to spell it out for you, so pay close attention and let her body be your guide.

■ Play to Have Fun—Not to Win

Like we said, women suspect that most guys approach oral sex like they do eating their vegetables, a necessary evil if you want to reap healthy rewards (full-blown sex). But you should look at it as a complex adventure game filled with mysterious objects that reveal the next clue. Instead of a gun-and-run video game, you need to have patience and a willingness to explore and play for hours—with the understanding that what worked the past three (or 300) times you played may not work on this round. All women are different: What's fab for one ain't necessarily so for another—or even for the same woman on a different day.

That being said, the approximate amount of "down time" the average woman will expect you to put in is a good 10 to 15 minutes—20 max. "Maybe I'll want to wait and climax during intercourse," explains Cheryl, 27. "Or maybe I'm enjoying his ministrations, but I just can't seem to get there that way." Whatever is going on, after you've hit that 15-minute mark, head back up and ask if there's anything else she would enjoy you doing or if you should continue. She'll let you know what to do next. And maybe what she'll want to do next is you.

18 EXPERT ORAL-SEX TECHNIQUES AND POINTERS

The most important thing you can remember when it comes to oral sex is that every woman is different, and while it's possible to give general guidelines, what has one woman climbing the walls with pleasure may send another woman up the walls with annoyance. But here are a few tricks you can try out to see what works and what doesn't.

1. THE ALPHABET

Simply use your tongue to spell the alphabet on her clitoris. If done right, you won't reach "O" before she does.

2. GIVE HER THE MINT TREATMENT

Ever since Monica Lewinsky talked about popping those "curiously strong" mints to give the president a curiously strong hummer, breath mints have become an oral-sex staple. But you've got news for her; mints work even better on women, because the vulva has more nooks and crannies for the menthol to get to than does your penis. So dissolve one in your mouth, then head south. *Surgeon General's Warning*: Women have different levels of sensitivity to menthol, and some may experience a burning sensation if you use too much (that's also why you should avoid the cinnamon flavor). To be safe, start with one candy and wait five minutes; if she doesn't feel it, pop another and repeat. Hope you're hungry. She may want a tin's worth.

3. LET YOUR FINGERS DO THE WALKING

Sex can be a lot like quitting smoking: You just don't know what to do with your hands. But while enjoying her sweet petals, be sure to use both your fingers and tongue to send her over the edge. The labia and the entrance to the vagina are the most sensitive, so try focusing your efforts there, while continuing to apply pressure with your tongue. If your partner is on her back and you slide your finger in fairly shallow and curl it upward, you may be able to reach the famed G-spot on the inside of her vagina [See Chapter 6]. But be careful you don't start off too hard, because that's a very delicate area as well.

4. DON'T...STOP...COMPLETELY

Sure, changing up your method and execution is fine and even desirable, up until you find the magic movement that has her grabbing the bedsheets, and then the more repetitive the better. When she says, "right there, don't stop," she really means it. Your tongue may be killing you, but unless you want a kick to the head, press on. Which leads us to our next point...

5. STAY COMFORTABLE

Anyone who's spent some time camping out in the dark forest knows how important this one is. The minute you get a crick in your neck or your legs fall asleep from sitting on them, there's a chance you'll throw in the towel before delivering that knock out punch. Once you've made sure she's comfy, then get yourself set up, too. If you have to change it around to stay relaxed, do so; get a pillow or have her move to a chair that you can access while sitting on the floor. Get in the 69 position and take turns on top. If your tongue gets tired, take a break and continue to stimulate her with your hands (or even chin) until you can carry on.

6. FLICK HER BIC

After you've got her firing on all cylinders, gently flick her clitoris. They may say the clitoris is a female penis, but don't make the mistake of treating it as aggressively as you've been known to grope your love handle. Women want just the opposite. In fact, generally, the more you tease, the better; just keep in mind that some women's hot buttons need to be pressed more firmly than others'.

7. SUCK THE CLIT

Obviously, not too hard. Anyone who's tried this knows it's no small task, especially considering that clitorises come in all shapes and sizes. Here's where some experimentation comes in handy, as depending on the size, it might be a tough task to pull off. Try sucking it gently into your mouth and holding it there with your lips.

8. COMBINE THE TWO

If you can manage it, while you're sucking on her clitoris, flick it with your tongue. She will think you're a god.

9. EXPERIMENT WITH TONGUE SURFACE

Don't think of your tongue as just one size like a finger. It can fold, widen, and narrow at a moment's notice, so experiment with licking long like the dirty dog you are and licking as if you were signing your name.

10. TAKE A DIP

An excellent technique is to stiffen your tongue and dip it every minute or so into her vagina. Don't worry about not being able to deep-thrust her like you can with your penis; her most sensitive areas are around the opening anyway.

11. USE YOUR HANDS

While going downtown, don't be afraid to let your hands roam. Reach up and massage her breasts, stroke her sides, tummy, and legs. Women love to be touched, so let her know you appreciate her body through the gentle yet firm movements of your hands.

12. PENETRATE WITH YOUR OTHER DIGITS

Multiple sensations are incredible, so while you're sucking on her clit, penetrate her with your fingers. While we've already discussed caressing her G-spot with your fingers, thrust your fingers in and out, especially as she's coming.

13. DON'T SHY FROM ANAL PLAY

While many people might have a problem with the Devil's Onion Ring, some women find anal stimulation wonderful. While you're busy lecturing her, use her natural lubricants and some store-bought, water-based lube as well, to thoroughly (and we mean thoroughly) coat your fingers and gently rub around the opening to the anus. Of course, if she doesn't like this, don't try and force anything.

14. TELL HER HOW MUCH YOU'RE ENJOYING YOURSELF

For women words are more of a turn-on than almost anything else. And considering that most women have heard all the same fish jokes we have, many are undoubtedly self-conscious about a man roaming about in their garden. So be sure to let her know how wonderful she tastes and how beautiful she is. This will help her relax and enjoy what you're doing, which in turn will enhance your experience as well.

15. TRIM YOUR NAILS

There's a reason your penis doesn't come with any hard pointed edges, so you should carry that same thought over to your fingers. If you know you're going to have an evening of lovin', file your fingernail edges smooth, or, ideally cut them all the way down to where they connect to your skin. No matter how careful you are, your nails can cause her soreness inside, or even hurt her more seriously if you're not careful.

16. ICE IS NICE

But don't just reach for any old ice cube unless you want the cold shoulder. The ice should be relatively warm on the outside, with no sharp edges and a gentle layer of water from where it's slowly melting. The best way to ensure this is to put it in your mouth first. Keep the ice in either the palm of your hand or in your mouth. You can stimulate her with your fingers or tongue, then gradually work the ice inside her, or you can simply cool your fingers and tongue with the cube, so she can feel the different temperature when you lick and touch her.

17. WARM HER BACK UP

In fact, you can switch back and forth between cooling your tongue with ice, and warming it with hot (not overly hot) coffee or tea (or even hot water). The changes in temperature may be very stimulating.

18. HO, HO, HO

When Christmas time rolls around, some stores sell a kind of candy cane that's over an inch thick and six or eight inches long at the straight part (kinda like you, huh?). Take one end, suck or lick it until it is more rounded and smooth, slap a condom on it, and proceed as you can imagine.

WOMEN GET ORAL ON ORAL

Everyone knows women are usually more touchy-feely than men, but few know that each and every woman likes to be touched and felt in her own preferred way. Instead of relying on our own years of field experience, we decided to find out what oral ministrations really have women seeing God.

"Start slow. Nibble the inside of my thighs, then eventually involve one then two fingers, gliding in and out. When I'm about to cum, I want those fingers moving faster and faster. Don't just stay on the clit and move your tongue up and down over and over."—Becka, 27, flight attendant

"I don't like it when guys tease. It seems just when I'm about to cum, they change the play, and then I have to start all over again. Think of it as a plane taking off down a runway: You're building up speed, building up speed, then bam, you're off. I don't like it when guys want to jam more than two digits in there. That's my personal thing."—Adrian, 30, actress

"Guys need to pull back the lips to reveal the clitoris so it's standing at attention. For some reason some guys think they can just flick away when the hood's still on. Note: If the skin is pulled back, it heightens the sensitivity."—Rhonda, 25, model

"I really like it when a guy slides one finger in while giving head."—Delia, 28, office manager

"Get us to the point of no return with your tongue, then hit the G note! And make sure you wet your fingers (two) before entering."—Sara, 36, artist

"A guy needs to not tease. I hate it when they know how to get me off but try to do some whole 'I'm going to drag this out' kind of deal. They've hit the spot, they're on the right track, and then they pull some tongue twist thing and pull away. It's OK once or twice to build the anticipation, but not a bunch of times."—Rita, 31, supervisor

"Guys should take their time and keep up some kind of rhythm. I'm not gonna go nuts just because he pokes around with his fingers and tongue a little."—Shaylyn, 25, executive assistant

CUNNILINGUS CATCH PHRASES

Use the following guide to make sure you're never at a loss for words when cunnilingus is part of the conversation:

Phrase: Yodel down the valley
Proper Usage: Gunter was too tired to talk, having spent most of the day yodeling down the valley.

Phrase: Dine at the Y
Proper Usage: Jen didn't care for fancy dates; she preferred guys who liked to dine at the Y.

Phrase: Go pearl fishing
Proper Usage: Gorton refused to go pearl fishing, saying he didn't like oysters.

Phrase: Eat mutton
Proper Usage: "He accidentally bit his tongue while eating mutton," Gwen told the surgeon as blood poured from Jim's mouth.

Phrase: Talk to the canoe driver
Proper Usage: "I wanted to explore Venice," Jarrod said forlornly, "but I spent most of the trip just talking to the canoe driver."

Phrase: Sneeze in the basket
Proper Usage: "I didn't mind that he was a midget," said Mrs. Kersten, "because he could sneeze in the basket without bending down.

STROKES OF GENIUS: NEW WAYS TO TOUCH YOUR WOMAN

The lights are dimmed, the wine has delivered its inhibition-weakening whammy, and you've both shucked down to your tan lines. Of course, you and your heat-seeking stinger can't wait to zero in on the classic targets, but because *Maxim* has schooled you in the following ancient Eastern ways of awakening your woman's sexual energy, you will hang fire. Instead of heading for the obvious anatomical hot spots, you head straight for...her nose.

What? Waste precious real-sex time on some Tantric acupressure pseudospiritual yogurt sex mojo crap? Patience, young grasshopper. Anyone can make the mattress springs sing. But if you want your woman hitting the high C, these millennia-old tricks will warm up her vocal cords...not to mention the rest of her body.

Please note, you don't have to do all the techniques listed here at one sitting. Try a couple and see how they go. You can do them as foreplay or during play. Alternate sensations every 30 to 60 seconds: Touch with your fingertips, kiss, vary the pressure. This helps build the sexual charge. Oh, and by the way, you need to be naked. Get ready for sexual godhood, you lucky bastard.

■ HOT SPOT

The tip of the nose

Your Move Starting at the nose, lightly trace a path with your fingertip down the right side of her body: down her neck, armpit, breast (resist the urge to stop here, you perv), stomach, genitals (yeah, that's right, keep going, buddy), and back up the left side of her body to her nose.

What It Does to Her The tip of the nose is at one end of the meridian, or channel of energy, that connects to the sexual chakra, the center of erotic energy, which resides at the base of the spine. No, you can't just dive straight for her sexual chakra, you Western dog; you have to create this circuit of energy to awaken her sexual desires.

■ HOT SPOT

The frenulum, or little piece of tissue inside the mouth that connects the upper lip and gums

Your Move Gently suck her upper lip between your lips (please, plead our test subjects, no teeth) so that your lower lip lightly rubs her frenulum.

What It Does to Her Ancient masters tell us the frenulum is directly connected to the clitoris, not in those knee-bone's-connected-to-the-ankle-bone terms (which would explain why men are so hard-pressed to find it), but via a meridian. Women have been known to have orgasms from this. Write us if you manage to pull this one off.

■ HOT SPOT

The four- or five-inch circle between the base of the skull and the tops of the shoulders, smack in the middle of the neck.

Your Move Alternating between gently grasping, squeezing, biting, and sucking (and not necessarily in that order), move up the back of the neck to the base of the skull.

What It Does to Her Releases energy trapped at these notoriously tense points. This is key, because they are also on the meridian that connects to the lower back and the pelvis, two focal areas for sexual awakening.

■ HOT SPOT

Between the shoulder blades

Your Move Facing her, reach around her and lightly rub the area to warm and stimulate it. Slowly move closer to her until your chest is pressed against hers (hey, *now* we're talkin'), massaging deeper and deeper between her shoulder blades while holding her in your arms.

What It Does to Her The contact of your chest in front and your hands in back opens a channel through her heart—the seat of passion, caring, and love. She'll feel nurtured and want to nurture you back—and maybe even play nurse.

■ HOT SPOT

The lower back, right above the tailbone

Your Move Apply light, then increasingly firm, pressure. Watch for movement in other parts of her body accompanied by more rapid breathing to see which she responds to best. You can also scrape your nails against the lower back or grasp the soft flesh there, gently tugging the skin away from the spine, then releasing it.

What It Does to Her Touching the lower back increases the amount of energy that flows into the pelvic organs, including the genitals, uterus, and ovaries. She'll either be sexually aroused or turn into a hula girl.

■ HOT SPOT

The yoni, or external female genitalia (us Westerners call it a vulva)

Your Move Place your right hand on the woman's yoni, palm to pelvic bone, with your fingers either covering her love triangle or resting between her legs—you make the call. At the same time, put your left palm on her heart. You thereby create a circuit of passion that runs from her heart through you and back into her yoni.

What It Does to Her Do we really have to explain this?

HOW TO SPOT A FAKE ORGASM

It looked real. It sounded real. It felt real. But did she…really? Five telltale signs that her bliss is bo-oh-oh-gus.

1. There's No Flush

During orgasm blood flow increases and becomes more apparent below the skin's surface. So look for a light, rashlike crimson glow creeping across your honey's cheeks and chest immediately after she goes all wobbly. It's easy to detect—in the light, at least—and according to Bernie Zilbergeld, Ph.D. author of *The New Male Sexuality*, "The sex flush is the only sign a woman who's faking it can't reproduce."

2. She's Too Dramatic

Be skeptical of the big-screen effort. But don't interrupt the performance: Sex therapist Barbara Keesling, Ph.D., author of *The Good Girls' Guide to bad Girl Sex*, warns, "She may be exciting herself with her own sound effects."

3. She Doesn't Look Stoned

At the big moment, "…her sympathetic nervous system is activated, which increases pupil diameter," says Beverly Whipple, a professor at Rutgers University and an expert on the female orgasm. "You can probably see a difference just from looking in her eyes."

4. There's No Clench

When she's really coming, the vaginal muscles rapidly clench and relax, clench and relax; sexperts Masters and Johnson have estimated that the contractions are 0.8 seconds apart.

5. Her Timing's Exquisite

If you two are always in perfect orgasm sync, be wary. The Hite Report's sex survey of 3,000 women says only 30 percent climax regularly during intercourse.

■ HOT SPOT

A few inches below the navel, in the area just above the pubic bone (also known as the "elixir field")

Your Move You can use soft, light touches with your fingers or whole hand, or just gently rest your palm there, letting the energy flow from your hand into her body.

What It Does to Her Get this: Touching here stimulates the sacred spot (what we call the G-spot) from the outside. Press lightly and she'll feel her breath moving into that area and experience enhanced arousal, and the more enhanced the arousal, we say, the better.

■ HOT SPOT

The hollows between the Achilles tendon and the ankle bone

Your Move Using two hands, massage the hollows on both sides of the ankle at once. Then do the same to the other ankle.

What It Does to Her This point is on the kidney meridian. The kidneys house a type of chi (pronounced chee, meaning energy) that controls will, constitution, and sexuality. Low kidney chi equals low libido. This massage restores this key energy and creates full-body (it doesn't get much better than that) arousal.

■ HOT SPOT

The crease of the wrist. To find it, flip her hand palm-up, then run your finger down the pinky side to the fleshy groove where her hand meets her wrist.

Your Move Massage gently.

What It Does to Her If she's tense or distracted, this will relax her and drain her of sexual anxiety, the worst kind of anxiety to have when you're trying to have sex.

■ HOT SPOT

Her feet and toes

Your Move Starting between her first two toes, slide your fingers up a couple of inches from the web to where the bones join. You may kiss her on the beak while you're doing this. Massage that area on both of her feet.

What It Does to Her This is a point on the liver meridian, which encircles all the genitalia from the cervix out, including, of course, the vagina. Rubbing this spot on her foot balances the energy in the genitals, draining tension and relaxing that area. She will open to you like a lotus blossom.

THE PRIME MOVES

Jerry's had something to do with a counterclockwise swirl. Puddy stole it to use on Elaine. George had trouble mastering it. We're talking, of course, about a Seinfeld story line (make the sign of the cross) involving a surefire gal-pleasing sex move. Let's advance the discussion: Most men have a signature sex move—a John Hancock, if you will, that they can always fall back on. It might be a position, a movement, or some flourish that prompts women to say, "Thank you, sir! May I have another?"

What's this? You don't have a signature move? Zoinks! OK, stop quivering, Shaggy— all is not lost. Because we like you, we've called friends, friends of friends, estranged brothers-in-law of friends—basically, anybody we could get to confide their sex secrets to us—and compiled a list of completely authentic, original, you-heard-it-here-first sex moves. (Think it was easy asking longshoremen at Dick's Last Resort about sex technique? Nuff said.) Of course, we'd never pass on a random bunch of moves without field-testing them on real live women first (because the blow-up kind can't talk). So we enlisted nine of our wives and girlfriends and told them to unplug the phone. Here are their observations on our best efforts. (Note: You may have more success with some of these sexual twists and turns than we did.) Read on and prepare to become a man—or at least act like one in bed.

MOVE#1: The Postman Always Rings Once

"In the riding position on top, lick your left thumb like it was a stamp and place it on the top of your girlfriend's private spot. Continue to put pressure on the "stamp" with your thumb while you put your 'special delivery' in her envelope."—Joel, 34

Results:

Erica, 23: "You call that a move? That's not a move—that's boring. At least move it around a little bit. Don't just press on it like it's an elevator button."

Danielle, 22: "I waited for something to happen, but nothing. Finally I said, 'Try massaging it downward firmly, in rhythm with your strokes.' That worked a little better. You know what women always say: It helps to be hard, but it's hard to be good."

MOVE #2: The Standing O

"Stand on the floor. She's lying on her back on the bed with her butt barely hanging off the side. Hold her bottom and really lean into her when you thrust. This position will get you as deep inside her as you are long." —James, 26

Results:

Caroline, 32: "We had to go slow because I could feel him hitting my cervix. But what was really cool was when he would slowly pull all the way

out, then push all the way in. That felt really, really big. Mm-m-m."
Erica: "No, no! There are vital organs in there!"

MOVE #3: Closer to Her Head
"While on top shift your weight forward so your hips are directly above hers. This lets you directly stimulate her clitoris and puts your penis in direct contact with her pelvic bone, giving her something hard and rigid to grind against."—Joe, 33
Results:
Jeri, 25: "At first this was awkward. His penis kept slipping out of me, and he was supporting himself with one arm, which kept shaking from the effort. Finally he lay down on top of me, scooped one arm under my butt to help keep us in contact, and started grinding. Guys, that is something you should use!"
Caroline: "Absolute orgasm frenzy."

MOVE #4: Shaft!
"During lovemaking, pull your penis out, grasp it by the shaft, and manipulate the head against her clit—like you're tonguing it with your penis. Fast, slow, medium—it's all good. And it keeps her going while you take a short breather."—Mark, 32
Results:
Carmella, 31: "That was a hot tease. I loved being able to look down and see him rubbing against me."
Danielle: "It felt good, but it's more like foreplay. I wanted him back in right away."

MOVE#5: How Do You Do?
"Nobody ever thinks of this, but it's so easy. Hold her hands while you make love. Stretch her arms out above her head, or hold them out to the sides, forming a human letter T. Every now and then, kiss her hands. It's really intimate."—Ralph, 26
Results:
Denise, 24: "My last boyfriend did that the first time we made love; I'll never forget it. All girls like this, especially right before we come."
Celia, 30: "That and looking right into my eyes when you come will make me your love slave. I came again just from the excitement of watching him come and being so intimate about it."

MOVE #6: When You Don't Know the Words
"While performing oral sex, you have to kinda hum. Don't be obnoxiously loud, and don't turn her into a karaoke machine. But hum softly, like you're blowing into a wet harmonica."—Tim, 38
Results:
Denise: "This was the weirdest thing any guy has done to me. I tried to get into it, but we both started laughing. Hearing him make noises down there is too weird. Maybe save this one for when you're both drunk."
Caroline: "It felt good, but to come I need some heavy-duty tongue pressure. This was more of a light warmup."

MOVE #7: Ben Dover
"Not all girls like it from behind, but here's my way of making it more intimate. Enter her vagina, but put your legs outside hers. Gently lower her to the bed so only her pelvis and butt are slightly raised. Lie down on her back and kiss her neck or whisper into her ear. You can't really do full thrusts from this position, but it feels great for both of you."—Bob, 29
Results:
Denise: "Fucking awesome. When he got on top of me, I held his hands above my head and told him not to move, and just ground away under him for 10 minutes. Wow. Then I asked him to reach under me and finish me off. It felt like I was dreaming."
Carmella: "I can feel him against my G-spot, but there's not a lot of thrusting going on. I'd rather he just bend me over and have at it."

MOVE #8: Cyrano Lives
"Even if your nose isn't long like mine, you can use it to full advantage while your head is between her legs. Move your nose in and out of her, up and down. Try to breathe normally. If she gets up on top to ride your nose, be careful not to inhale her juices."—Diego, 22
Results:
Erica: "I'm, like, 'What the hell is that?' He told me, and I was, like, 'That feels good, now get your tongue working, too.'"
Celia: "It wasn't anything to write home about. I prefer tongues."

MOVE #9: Toe That Line
"Start from the bottom and work your way up to her pink heaven. Rub her toes and kiss the soles of her feet. Lightly caress her thighs. Let your fin-

gertips glide up near her area, but don't touch her there. Be a big tease, until she begs you to put it in."—Barry, 33

Results:

Leslie, 28: "This wasn't new to me, but I've always loved it. After about five minutes, I was begging for him to hit the spot, even grabbing the back of his head. It's all about the anticipation: I keep thinking that it's finally the moment, but then it's not. Eventually, I can't stand it anymore and I'll do anything for release."

Carmella: "I tend to be too impatient for this sort of thing. Though, once my boyfriend tied me up first and did this: That I won't forget."

MOVE #10: Rock the Boat

"During intercourse, don't just concentrate on in-and-out. While it's in there deep, slowly move your hips side to side. Speed up for a minute. Slow down for a minute. But keep putting pressure on her pelvic bone in a side-to-side motion."—Don, 35

Results:

Maura, 27: "It hurt. It just hurt."

Caroline: "I liked it a lot; it did help me get closer to orgasm. But I could see how it would hurt if, you know…I mean, I wax it off, but, yeah, with pubic hair that would hurt."

MOVE #11: Bull's-Eye

"Too many guys grab the whole breast with their hand or just suck on the end of the nipple. Instead use your tongue to slowly draw circles around the areola. Make your circles smaller and smaller, and faster and faster. Watch her breathing get shorter and faster too."—Raoul, 24

Results:

Leslie: "Absolutely. It makes every nerve in my body catch on fire."

Celia: "Great for foreplay, but when we're having intercourse, I like them treated a little rougher."

MOVE #12: Knockin' on Heaven's Door

"While you're doing it missionary-style, reach around behind her and gently rub her back door with your index finger. Go slowly at first. Moisten your finger with her juices. The more she moans, the more pressure you should apply."—Bradley, 30

Results:

Maura: "I said to him, 'Ew—what are you doing?' He'd read in a magazine this would drive me crazy. Ah…no."

Caroline: "I liked the sensation, but it definitely didn't blow my mind. I'd rather he squeezed my cheeks hard, like he was really excited. That's a turn-on."

MOVE #13: Double-Breasted Pursuit

"This is especially good when she's on top. Grab both her melons and squeeze them together. Put both her nipples in your mouth. It drives women nuts. Even if the girl you're with has small boobs, it will work if she has long nipples."—Gordon, 37

Results:

Denise: "Ouch. It really hurt to be squeezed together like that. I don't know why a woman would be into this."

Celia: "I love to have my breasts touched during sex, but that was too much of a good thing. I felt like I was being sexed up by a giant leech."

MOVE #14: Inside Out

"When you're on top, instead of having your legs inside hers, put yours on the outside. With her legs together, she gets even more stimulation from you than normal. You can still thrust the usual way. But a circular motion—like you're stirring a drink with your penis—will really send her."—Gavin, 40

Results:

Carmella: "That was one of the first times I ever had an orgasm from intercourse alone. I told him, 'Buddy, this is now officially in your repertoire.'"

MOVE #15: The Flank Spank

"Both of you are lying on your side.Enter her vagina from behind. She can curl her legs up, and you rotate your body away from her so you're almost perpendicular. A good wake-up call—especially helpful against morning-breath."—Fergus, 27

Results:

Maura: "I'd never had that done to me before. At first it was a little uncomfortable, but after we got going, I got really into it. I liked that I could control how spread apart my legs were and I could get more stimulation by bringing my legs closer together."

Celia: "My new favorite position. When he was lying beside me, it was nice, but then he sorta sat up and gripped my hip, with my bottom leg between his. He was just pounding my G-spot from that position. Oh, Jesus."

DO NOT ENTER!

They may have sounded good, but these moves were recipes for disaster.

"My boyfriend apparently watched an S/M video before he pulled out two clothespins and told me there was a move he wanted to try: So he clipped them onto my nipples! I'm open-minded, so I let him try, but it was only about two seconds before I was shrieking with pain."—Erika, 30

"I had a guy tell me to close my eyes so he could suck on my eyelids while he was rubbing my breasts. But he sucked so hard, it felt like my eyeball was going to come out. It was gross."
—Natalie, 29

"I was with a guy who was really into my feet. When he was licking my toes, it felt great. But then he moved upside down on top of me, like an almost-69, and put his feet onto my chest so he could stimulate my nipples with the tops of his feet. I didn't appreciate having his dogs practically in my face."—Tracy, 26

"I had sex with this guy who was really into teasing. His big move was licking around my nipples but never actually getting to the target. It was a turn-on at first, but then he spent about 20 minutes roaming around my clitoris but never actually coming in contact with it. That's like trying to start a fire with two sticks by waving them around next to each other."—Jenna, 32

BE BETTER THAN HER LAST LOVER

Is she still thinking of him—even when she's with you? That bastard! Well, don't worry: Here are the sex moves that'll erase her glorified memories of that chump from her sexual databank forever.

Any guy who wants to nab the number one slot on his woman's hot-lover list should boink away the memory of every boyfriend she's ever had. Pay close attention to the following. Here, more than twenty women describe their ex-boyfriends' tantalizing techniques—the ones they still can't shake from their overheated minds. Read them slowly, take notes, then try 'em on your babe one by one. When her back arches so high you can't see her head and her hips pop an involuntary wheelie, you'll know that her recollection of old what's-his-name just got Bobbittized.

PRE-PENETRATION PRIMERS

Yes, yes, your penis is the most powerful force in the universe, it is monarch of all it surveys—whatever, we're all really impressed. But most of the women I spoke with said the sex moves that made the biggest impact on them (figuratively speaking) were made before a penis even entered the picture.

"My biggest turn-on was when my high school boyfriend would feel me up over my bra and panties. Now that I'm dating older guys, they almost always go straight for skin after just a few seconds. If they would just stroke me through the fabric a little bit longer, I'd be soaking wet. I'll grab a guy's hands to stop him from unhooking my bra or pulling down my underwear, but he'll usually stop altogether because he thinks something's wrong. If a guy doesn't get it after a while, I just give up on him."
—Nadine, 32, currency trader

"A neighbor and I had been flirting pretty fiercely when finally he made the first move. He pressed his body up against me from behind and reached around to touch my breasts. He circled my nipples with the tips of his fingers, then worked his way down. He never even turned me around—just unbuttoned my pants, pulled them down, and made love to me standing up. I can still remember every little detail."
—Cheryl, 23, grad student

"My ex-boyfriend would get down on his knees in the shower and eat me out until I was as wet on the inside as I was on the outside. It's been over a year and I still fantasize about it: I have to fantasize about it, because the guy I'm going out with now doesn't get the hint when I drop the soap."—Maria, 29, systems analyst

"A lot of guys either rub your clitoris or put a finger inside you to rub your G-spot; I've only been with one man who figured out that if you do both at once, you get the best results. We slept together a few times, but things didn't really work out, and now I'm seeing one of his friends. I wish the two of them would get together and swap sex tips so my boyfriend would figure it out."—Bethany, 20, student

"The most amazing night of my life was when a guy I was dating visited me late at work. He propped me up on my desk, sat down in the chair so that his face was between my legs, and just went to town."—Pam, 26, advertising executive

"Mark made me a huge fan of 69. With a hand on each butt cheek, he moved them in an inward circular motion so my labia were being pushed together and pulled apart while he was tonguing me. He was a natural. I'll tell my boyfriend to put his hands on my ass, but he still hasn't gotten the motion right. He's a learner, not a natural."—Anya, 29, singer and dancer

"My most amazing sex was with a guy 15 years older than me. I was about 20 and I didn't even know I had a G-spot until he pressed it and I almost died. I'm praying my husband will be that good in five years."—Sandra, 30, circulation manager

CREATIVE—AND KINKY

As the old saying goes, To a man with a hammer, everything looks like a nail. But there's a lot more you can do than just bang away. Drill, press, pry, saw—screw. When it comes down to actual sex, these handymen knew a few secrets to getting the job done:

"He would push his penis so that just the tip was inside me; then he would pull out and let it drag up across my clitoris, and then back down and in another quarter of an inch. He'd keep doing it until I begged him to put it all the way in. I haven't been able to get another guy to do that without spelling it out, which kills the mood."—Jennifer, 23, photographer's assistant

"Right now I'm with Evan, a bedroom-only kind of guy. Jason, on the other hand, used to slip his hand up my dress every chance he got—under the table at a restaurant, or in an empty aisle at the grocery store. We would end up having sex in the car because we just couldn't wait to get home. Evan seems boring by comparison." —Elizabeth, 28, dental hygienist

"When I'm masturbating, I imagine the time my ex Tony bent me over the hood of his red Lotus and did me from behind. My boyfriend Rich is more practical: He'd never blow a lot of money on a sports car—he'd think the whole thing was tacky. He'd better hope Tony doesn't move back to town."—Ruth, 31, mutual fund manager

"During sex he pushed my breasts together and licked up and down my cleavage. It's so simple, I can't under-

PRISONERS OF LOVE: CARELESS SEXTHLETES GET PINCHED

In 1993, Ronald Shawn Ryan, 23, of Edmonds, Washington, was found guilty of twice breaking into a funeral home and molesting the remains of four elderly women. "We all agree this is a deplorable situation," said Ryan's lawyer, Richard Tassano; but he argued that at least his client "is not going out and attacking live people."

A British couple was charged with public indecency after allegedly refusing to stop engaging in sex acts on an international flight. Amanda Holt, 37, and David Machin, 40, had been drinking heavily and cuddling underneath a blanket when apparently they became "a little over-familiar." "A steward saw what they were doing and asked them to stop," explained an airline employee. "They did not stop." Machin and Holt are married—though not to each other. The two were complete strangers prior to the incident.

stand why more guys don't do it."—Ann, 20, student

"Carey, a coworker I dated a few years ago, was the king of quickies. He would seduce me in the supply closet during our lunch hour, in the dressing room of a clothing store, anywhere. I stopped wearing underwear and started carrying a tube of K-Y jelly in my purse."—Jamie, 27, aerobics instructor

"I'd be lying on my side, and Pete would be between my legs. He'd use one hand to massage my butt and the other to rub my clit. He made me explode. Now I'll place a guy's hands in all the right spots, but it's never as sexy when I have to walk them through it."—Lucinda, 25, publicist

"I was an anal virgin before he gently inserted a finger, then his penis, as far as it would go. I was shocked at how much I loved it. Whenever I bring up anal sex around my new boyfriend, he acts all disgusted."—Felicia, 22, copywriter

"Matt would wake up in the middle of the night and start making slow, sweet love to me when I was half asleep. It was like something out of a dream. I'll always remember him because of it. I've tried seducing my boyfriend in the middle of the night. He just grunts and elbows me back to my side of the bed."—Megan, 25, photo studio manager

"He'd cover me in vanilla massage oil, ice cream, or champagne, and we'd roll all over from room to room. He made sex feel like the most exciting event of the day. If I dripped maple syrup onto my current boyfriend, he'd freak out about getting it on the sheets."—Laura, 24, nurse

"HE'D COVER ME IN VANILLA MASSAGE OIL OR ICE CREAM, AND WE'D ROLL FROM ROOM TO ROOM."

CLIMAX CLINCHERS

If you really want to make the memory of her ex fade, you've got to be a clitoral connoisseur—and that means putting in more hours under the hood than Mr. Goodwrench. Seventy percent of women need clitoral stimulation to climax, according to *The Hite Report on Female Sexuality* pulished in 1976. Here's how other men hit women's hot buttons:

"He'd put his thigh between my legs and move it back and forth against me until I was within seconds of an orgasm. Then he would pull away just long enough for me to come back from the edge before he started all over again."—Karen, 32, graphic designer

"Robert would always find a way to get his hand on the spot above my clitoris and work it in a circular motion. When we were doing it doggy style, he'd reach around with both hands at once."—Tracey, 28, teacher

"The only guy who has made me come was a one-night stand. With my legs pressed as tightly together as possible, he would thrust into the space between my vagina and the tops of my thighs. A couple of times I've put my boyfriend's penis between my legs, but he won't stop trying to get inside me."—Brianna, 20, student

"He took me into the bathroom and had me straddle the side of the tub while he saddled up behind me. He pumped away while I ground my heart out. I can't even look at a bathtub without thinking about him."—Nichole, 27, researcher

"One fling used a vibrator on me—on my breasts, my clitoris, inside my vagina, all over my butt and thighs. When my boyfriend's away, I close my eyes and relive the whole experience with a little help from my multi-speed massager."—Heidi, 24, accessories designer

HOW TO BE A MASTER IN THE SACK

Sex is a game of give-and-take—and you'll get more out of it if you play your partner right. So forget all the complicated techniques, weird yoga positions, and obscure anatomy lessons. The truth is, making a gal happy in bed is simpler than you think. And if she's happy, not only do you get to feel like a decent, compassionate, and accomplished human being—you'll get more, way more, sex. Here are 10 no-fail, gal-friendly moves guaranteed to make her melt.

MOVE #1: Slow It Down

Sex is goal-oriented, but lovemaking means savoring every delicious moment, enjoying the process. You know you've got a serious affair on your hands when you and your partner spend hours rolling around, mauling each other with clothes on.

Gradually loosen belts and untuck shirts and blouses, and spend lots of time groping under each other's clothes. And when you do start peeling down, do it like an old-fashioned striptease: button by button, layer by layer.

Quickies are fine—once in a while. But most of the time, if you tear off her pants and immediately try to get to business while she's still zipped into her parka and carrying the groceries, she's going to feel silly and used.

MOVE #2: Kiss Her, You Fool

Not just while you're tumbling around during foreplay—throughout the main event, too. Kisses are the ultimate expression of affection and convey an enormous amount of passion. Beseech her to kiss you, too: If she's on top, and you suddenly whisper, "Kiss me," your words will go through her heart like Cupid's arrow; and she'll fall upon your lips like a woman stranded in the desert who's discovered Evian burbling out of the sand.

Handholding is another little gesture that takes on enormous emotional import in bed: "Some sort of bio-rhythmic-Zen-tantric connection is made when a guy suddenly intertwines his fingers in mine and presses my palms to his, right in the middle of making love. It's breathtaking," says Shelly, 25.

MOVE #3: Say Her Name

Women appreciate how tough it is to utter anything coherent out of a lust-choked throat. So when the actual sound is our name, it'll pack a real wallop.

"When I'm in bed with a guy I'm starting to get tight with and he says my name in the heat of passion, it reassures me that he's really there, with me and no one else. No *Playboy* bunny fantasy, no really hot girl he saw on the bus, and no ex he hasn't gotten over."—Julia, 28

A bit of dirty talking can also be great—but you'd better not start spouting filth unless she lets you know she's really into it. (Clue: If she laughs, she's not into it. If she laughs in a strange, derisive, snorty way, she's really not into it.)

MOVE # 4: Press the Flesh

In porn movies the only body parts making contact are the actual genitalia. In the real world women love it when you maximize the skin-on-skin contact.

"Embrace me in your arms, press my chest against yours, and entwine your arms and legs around me like a pretzel."—Giselle, 30

Never push your girl's head down, even if that's the direction you want her to go. And when she is going down, for Pete's sake, don't lie there with your arms folded behind your head like some sleazy Hollywood executive. Run your fingers through her hair, stroke her face, and say something nice, like "Oooohh."

MOVE #5: Communicate With Her

Lovemaking really ought to be full of murmurs and sighs and laughter and gentle questions and answers.

Women are deathly afraid of sounding like drill sergeants in bed, so give her an easy out by asking (in a whisper, big fella) if she likes what you're doing. Don't break her mood with essay questions—try simple yes-or-no, "Do you want me to do this harder?" queries instead.

Likewise, if she's doing something that feels really great, let her know with a word or an unambiguous moan. That being said, nothing's more fun for a woman than asking a lover "You like it like this?" and finding him unable to respond because she is doing it right and she's completely incapacitated him.

MOVE #6: Make Her Glad She Has Boobs

Having breasts is no picnic. Women don't get to feel the sun and breeze on their chests at the beach like you do, and bras cost a ton. But in the right man's hands, a woman's boobs can bring her so much pleasure that all the years of lugging them around suddenly seem worthwhile.

"Don't rush to tear my bra off: Caress and lift my breasts through the material. This feels particularly sexy and warm from behind, a sort of "Here, let me carry these for a while" goodwill gesture that's greatly enhanced by kisses on the back of my neck."—Daphne, 26

Always handle bare naked breasts with care. If she's lying on her back, you should palm them with not much more pressure than the natural weight of your hand. When you kiss her breasts, work your way slowly toward her nipples. While she's actually dying for you to get there, the teasing is an excruciating pleasure. After a short visit, go back to kissing her mouth. Message: I love you, not just for your boobs. Sue us if she doesn't involuntarily arch her back in delicious agony.

MOVE #7: Look Her in the Eyes

Outside the bedroom, staring unwaveringly into someone's eyes is usually seen as a sign of insanity or hostility. (Try it on your dog sometime.) In bed it can help you determine how your lover really feels about you. If she quickly looks away, she's not ready to let you get really close. (And if she says, "What the fuck are you looking at?" that's pretty self-explanatory.) But if she locks you in her gaze and continues rock steady, you'll know she's willing to face and share the terror of getting deep into each other. And since you could be ogling her nudity but are opting instead to look into the windows of her soul, she'll know you're crazy about her, in every sense.

MOVE #8: Objectify Her

While most women don't care to hear "Nice ass!" comments from strange men on the streets, they aren't die-hard Women's Issues 101 students either. Within the context of an intimate exchange, it's OK for you to tell her something like, "Oh, man, that bra is so sexy it's killing me," because chances are she put it on that morning hoping for just such a response from you.

And remember, women are known to feel self-conscious in the nude, so say something encouraging. Telling her she has a sexy body is a great start, but be as specific as possible, since it will show her you are really tuned in to her body and aren't just telling her something you think she wants to hear.

MOVE #9: Ladies First

Most women understand that guys can get so excited during intercourse that they can't keep from climaxing rather quickly. Some women even find it flattering as long as the man is sensitive to her needs after he's finished. But if you can manage it, do whatever it takes to help her orgasm first. Since it often takes longer for a woman to reach her climax, it's harder for her to stay in the groove if the guy has already come and she feels his attentions are fueled by politeness rather than lust. Besides, patience builds intensity, so in the end you'll probably enjoy your orgasm more if you've satisfied her first. Also, unlike men, who often wilt and go to sleep after orgasm, a woman is often ready to do it again right after she's climaxed. So once you've gotten her to that point, she'll be primed for a long, inhibition-free romp.

How can you give her the winning edge? Engage in lots of foreplay to bring her close to the brink before you commence the main event. Set up a system so your lover can signal you just before she blows (a tap on the shoulder or an ardent "now!" ought to do it), and when you get the sign, shift into high gear. This greatly increases the odds she'll climax during intercourse—for our money the best in-bed bonding experience.

MOVE #10: Be a Gentleman
It slays a woman to be pampered and taken care of in bed. If you notice that your gal's head is getting precariously close to the headboard, slip your brawny arm under her and slide her down to safety—then retrieve a pillow and put it under her head. If the covers have fallen off in a chilly bedroom, get on your knees between her legs, pull the blankets up around her shoulders, then gently fall on her, keeping the covers with you. It's a killer combination.

And after the lovin', do not jump up and throw on your pants or roll over to catch a few winks. That'll just send her the message that you got what you wanted and that's all you care about. (Try to hang around for at least one sunrise, even if the sex started at noon.) When bodies are suddenly still after all that rocking and rolling, a girl can get chilly, so after you've finished the ground-crew cleanup, tuck her in, paying attention to her feet, and slip in next to her. Then settle for some snuggling and a postgame wrap-up. Tell her how much you enjoyed being with her and you'll be on the road to bliss, dude...if you're not already there.

FULL-BODY DEBAUCHERY

Sure, there's a handful (or a mouthful) of female erogenous zones every guy knows about. But to play her to perfection, you have to use all the keys. Here's what you need to know to earn the title "*maestro*":

■ **Toes** Suck them and you may reap rewards. In 25-year-old Darlene's words: "If a blow job feels better than slipping a toe into someone's hot, wet mouth, I understand why guys would do anything for one." Sure, you risk athlete's mouth, but think of the payoff.

■ **Fingers** Gobble them like fries. "When I'm touching myself and he licks the wetness off my fingers, it lets me know he's planning on going down on me," says Alison, 22. "It also makes me want to go down on him."

■ **Neck** The way you kiss her neck sets the sexual mood—either slow and deep or wild and passionate. "Getting kissed on the neck sends tingles through my body and straight between my legs," says Jen, 26.

■ **Breasts** "Most men focus on nipples or grab your entire breast at once," says Cassandra, 25. "They should pay attention to the tops, the outsides, and around the nipples, licking and touching them softly." Any objections?

■ **Face** Run your fingertips over her lips and cheeks, and allow her to do the same to you. "Letting her touch your face shows you want to be with no one else," says Liza, 27. (Try it with all your girlfriends.)

■ **Wrists** Slide an ice cube over them or heat them up with your tongue. "Lick them with long, thick strokes," suggests 23-year-old Sharon. "It feels great and makes us think about your tongue in other places."

■ **Legs** Weird erogenous zones: her upper thighs, behind her knees, even her ankles. "My ankles are real hot spots," confesses Raquelle, 28. "If a man puts his mouth anywhere near them, it drives me wild."

■ **Abdomen** Zero in on the area below her navel and above her pubic hair. "Try licking from her bellybutton to the tip of her pubic bone and then back," advises Kristen, 24. (Then discreetly discard the lint.)

■ **Sides** Softly run your hands d own her sides, from her underarms to her hips. "Paying attention to uncharted places on her body shows you're more willing to explore," says Sharice, 32.

Getting What You Want

Bookstores and magazine racks are brimming with material that purportedly instructs men in the finer points of pleasing their women. But few, if any, of these "guides" tell us selfless men how to go about getting a little of what we want. None tell you how to get her to play your skin flute without asking, or to talk dirty to you and then engage you in a wet and wild threesome with her better-looking best friend. But fret no more, amigos! This chapter is devoted to dropping the necessary hints at just the right time to get her to do a little bit of giving—and not just receiving.

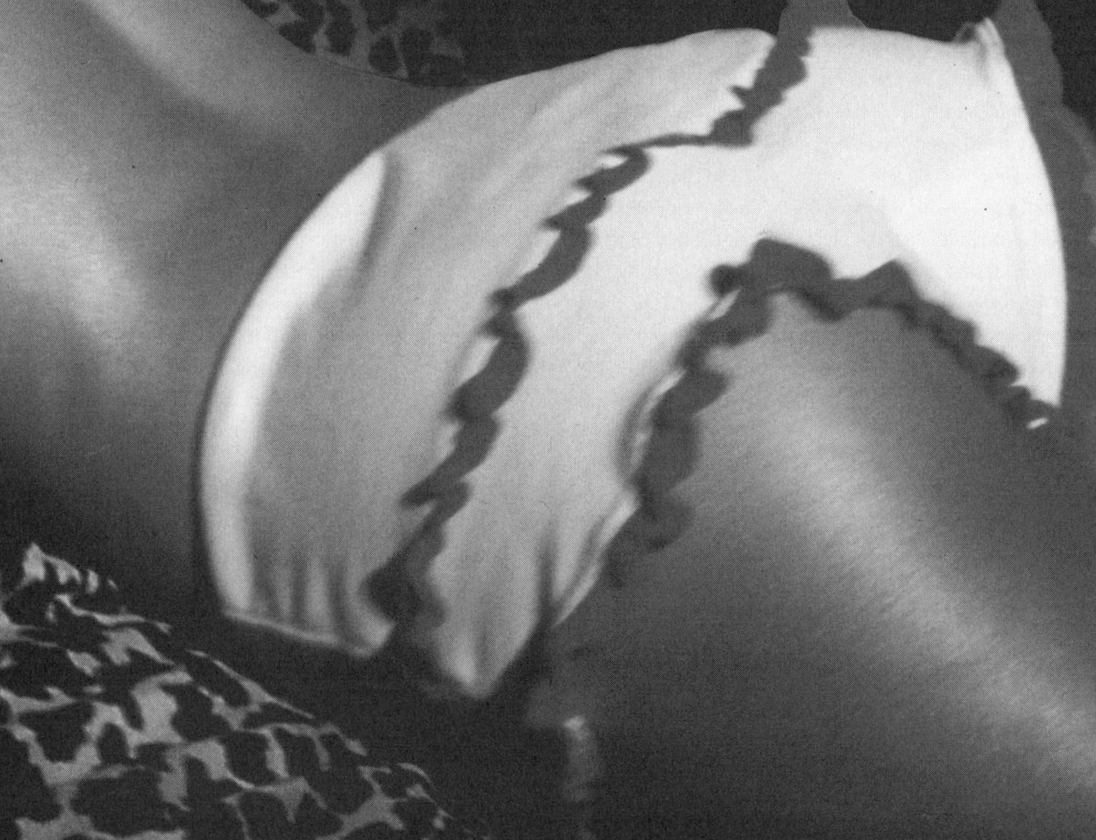

A GUIDE TO GETTING A-HEAD

Expecting great oral sex from a woman the first time out is like hitting a hockey game and expecting eight brawls and a hat trick in the first period. The odds just aren't with you. But this is not reason enough for you to lose hope. If you're willing to put in a little effort (very little effort, considering), you can make sure she'll want to go down on you the next time. Ya see, the more she enjoys it, the more she'll want to do it in the future. And the more she does it...well, we're sure you get the picture.

■ Fear of Flying

For many girls, their disdain for going down got its start way back in high school when they heard horrifying tales of giving head. "You have to retract your teeth, deep-throat him, and pump your head up and down faster than a president's yes-man," they were told. And where does the blowing come in? Is that some sort Swedish secret? After a few times of heading south, women start to fall into three different categories: Some love it, a few hate it, the rest do it because they know you like it.

The only way you'll find out is by asking. "I used to hate blow jobs until I went down on this one guy who told me I didn't have to swallow," says Beth, 28. "I realized that it wasn't giving head I didn't like—it was having guys come in my mouth that was uncomfortable." In other words, she may say she doesn't like Big Macs when it's just the special sauce she could do without. No surprise to most men, but there's no sense in throwing out the baby with the bathwater. Just let her know ahead of time that you don't expect her to swallow.

■ Don't Ask, Don't Tell

Your best bet? Don't ask for it. If you don't know a woman well, there's really no way to ask for head without sounding like the pizza guy in a cheesy porno. "I was making out with this guy in his car on our first date when he said, 'Suck my cock,'" says Kim, 35. "I was so repulsed I didn't go out with him again." In general, telling a date things like "Blow me" and "Lick my dick" or pushing her head down forcefully is about as big a turn-on for her as a 60-year-old naked guy lying on a red shag carpet with a cowboy hat hanging from his schlong. Sure, this type of play might fly when you've been in a relationship for a while, but if things are still in their infancy, doing any of the above is a ticket to being dumped (and don't think she won't tell all her friends what a perverted creep you are, either). Plus, putting in a request takes the fun out of it, kind of like having to ask your friends to get you a stripper at your own bachelor party. What you can do is tell her how hot she makes you and how amazing it would be to have her warm, wet mouth around you.

■ After You

Here's a novel idea: Go down on her first. To cite a little biblical wisdom, do unto others as you would have others do unto you. Basic, sure, but it works. Your willingness to take the plunge tells her you're a team player who has no intention of leaving her unsatisfied after you've had your kicks.

"Basically, if he goes down on me first, I find it inspirational," says Sue, 26. "I will be his slave after that." It's the rare man who'll camp down south for no reason other than for her pleasure, and if you do, you can be assured that she'll want to return the favor.

■ Baby, Remember My Name

Sure, the beauty of the blow job is that you don't have to do any work: You can hang up the hip action, free your forearms, and save your sweat for the StairMaster. But tuning out and folding your hands behind your head like you're in an ad for a Jamaican resort is not going to make the Popsicle practice pleasurable for her at all.

One thing you can try is touching her. And we don't mean sticking your fingers into all the orifices. While that can be a turn-on for some, most women say they can't concentrate on the task at hand if they're being stimulated at the same time. Touch her tenderly: Run your fingers softly over her back and shoulders, stroke her face, and play with her hair, all of which will make her feel more special and less like a blowup doll. Advice for those with John Wayne Bobbitt nightmares: Don't ever grab her head and drive it like a jackhammer on your piece of work. As one resentful woman put it, "That's the best way to get it bitten off."

Also, make it clear it's her you like, not just her technique. You can start by saying her name: Whisper it, groan it, or stutter it if that's all you can muster. "One guy I was dating actually chanted my name when he got really hot," says Beth. "Then he'd reach down and move the hair out of my face, saying he wanted to see me while I blew him. I loved that—I felt like his personal porn star."

If she's making your bacon fry, tell her how great it feels and that this is the best you've ever felt (leave out the "...in the last 10 minutes" part) and let loose with an occasional "OhmyGodohmyGodohmyGod."

"I love it when they start telling you what they want to do to you while you're pleasing them," says Clio, 25. "Like, 'I want to make you feel as good as you're making me feel.' That's always a winner."

■ Houston, We Have a Problem

But what if it's just not working? What if you've gotten a better performance from a raw rib-eye? Then you have to tell her what you like. She doesn't have her nose nuzzled in your 'nads for nothin': She wants to make it work. If you feel comfortable enough, tell her exactly what you want her to do ("Grab that part with your hand"), and once she's on course, encourage her with simple directives ("A little lower, yeah; a little faster; yeah, just like that"). Or disguise your desires in fantasy: Tell her to pretend she's licking an ice-cream cone or sucking on a straw. She knows what it's like to have a guy feverishly rubbing her an inch off her clit, so she'll appreciate knowing what makes you melt.

If giving explicit directions makes you self-conscious, at least acknowledge when she's doing something right, as in the hotter/colder game you played as a kid: The closer she gets to lip-launching your missile, the hotter you tell her—in words, moans, or Morse code—she is. But watch how you say it. "One guy I went down on talked to me like a sports coach," remembers Catherine, 27. "He actually patted me on the head and said, 'That's right, baby, keep it up, you're doin' good.' I mean, encouragement is nice, but save the 'way to go' crap for your baseball buddies!"

And by all means, if she's hurting you, tell her right away. There's nothing worse for a woman than hearing that her nails have been scratching you...for the past 20 minutes. A simple "Oooh, I'm a little sensitive there" or "Just a bit lighter" can make all the difference. Take it from Jen, 29: "I was dating this guy for four months before he told me that my teeth were rubbing him raw every time I gave him head. I was so embarassed!"

■ The Big Gulp

So you want to believe that a woman thinks your semen is the most delicious thing she's ever tasted and that she'll feel empty inside if she doesn't lick up every last drop? Guys, if your jam was that good, it'd be on the shelf next to the Smucker's. We haven't met too many women who actually look forward to consuming it. Many can live with the taste, but that's quite a bit different than living for it, which is why you should let her know when you're about to come and let her decide what she's going to do. She may prefer to finish you off with a hand job and watch your geyser go from afar. Whatever her preference, respecting her wish will only work in your favor.

"This one girl I know," says Clio, "told me about a guy who didn't tell her he was coming. When he ejaculated in her mouth, she was so surprised she spit it in his face."

Once your gal actually starts to enjoy these oral sessions, she may decide some adventurous (and probably drunk) night to bring you to blow-job bliss by swallowing. Until then, don't pressure her. "This one guy kept telling me how much sexier it would be if I could swallow it," says Betsy, 31. "But when I tried I ended up gagging, running to the bathroom, and dry-heaving over the toilet. I mean, how sexy is that?"

■ It Ain't Over

We probably don't have to tell you this, but it ain't kosher to pass out right after the blast. Pull her up to you, cuddle with her, stroke her hair (can't stress that hair thing enough), and kiss her (this tells her you don't mind swapping fluids).

"Keep something around for me to clean up with, like a towel or a box of tissues," says Megan, 26. "And have a glass of water on the nightstand—or better yet, offer to get me one!" Then, whether she really rocked your world or not, tell her how amazing it was. Tell her again before you both fall asleep. Thank her in the morning, and call her at work the next day to tell her you can't stop thinking about it. Because any woman who feels she's made an impression like that will want to come back for an encore.

HOW TO GET HER TO SWALLOW

What's the difference between like and love? Spit and swallow. Ha! But seriously, guys know that even the most committed girl may instantly gag at the thought of taking it all in like a cheap porn star. So why is it that some women seem to revel in the idea, while others would, roll in a pile of horse manure before dousing their tonsils with your love juice? Well, it probably has a lot to do with the thick texture that makes it stick in her throat and the accompanying bitter aftertaste. But to find out what they really think, we asked a bunch of women about the best ways to convince her to take it all in.

SOUND THE ALARM

"I'll swallow if I've been with a guy for a while, but certainly not in the first few months. Also, if he doesn't give me warning the first time that he's going to come, I deem him an inconsiderate sod. Overall, the taste isn't all that great most of the time, but each guy, believe it or not, tastes different."—Hannah, 25, receptionist

EAT RIGHT

"Whether I swallow or not has a lot to do with the man and his taste, and I don't know if you can alter the way you taste."—Emily, 29, attorney

DECLARE YOUR LOVE

"It tastes disgusting; it's as simple as that. But if you're in love, you should be willing to swallow if he wants you to?"—Elizabeth, 23, musician

WATER HER DOWN

"It's kind of gross to swallow, but if he makes sure there's water close by, that helps get the goo out afterward."
—Taylor, 33, office supervisor

FAKE IT

"The whole swallowing thing is tricky because it really is gross to have that goo in our throats. I don't think you guys really care so much about the swallowing as the illusion of swallowing. So if you want the sensation that bad talk to your girl. Tell her you want her to keep her mouth on as you come and that she should sort of start releasing it from her mouth as you're coming. I've noticed some men's semen has more of a bleach smell and flavor than others."
—Lauren, 25, marketing coordinator

SHARE THE STUFF

"I would be more willing to swallow if he would be more willing to kiss me after I've pleased him. That's the measuring stick—it's only fair. Then I'll keep going without interruption. The taste is not pleasing."—Ashley, 28, Web Designer

THREE'S COMPANY: THE MÉNAGE-À-TROIS

The threesome (you and two girls—no other combos allowed) may be the ultimate male fantasy. Most men rank the threesome at or near the top of their sexual wish lists. Yes, if you want to attain true sex-god status, you gotta wrangle your way into the ultra-exclusive Threesome Club. But your chances of having a ménage-à-trois are probably only slightly better than being abducted by aliens. Let's try and cut the odds down to a more manageable size. First of all, the good news is that many of the girls we've talked with have at least entertained notions of forming a human triangle. The bad news? Even if your woman is 100 percent into a trio, one or two insensitive moves on your part can guarantee she'll hold off until she's found a man who is more tactful. Rule number one: You have to play this very cool.

■ Don't Push It

The thought of a threesome may make you randier than a three-peckered billy goat, but just because you think you're going to explode unless you can enjoy two girls at once, it's best to keep your emotions in check. Merely being sly with your intentions about the three-way will up your ménage potential tenfold.

"Personally, I like a man who tells me, 'If it happens, it happens. . .but if it doesn't, it's no big deal,'" says Marie, a 27-year-old single girl who, though intrigued by the idea of sex with women, is wary of ménage hounds. "The guy who pushes the three-way comes off as creepy, whereas the guy who's nonchalant is the one I am more likely to go along with."

So why is forcing it such a bad idea? Simple. Even if your woman is sexually adventurous, if you suggest an addition to your coupling—especially on more than one occasion—she'll instantly suspect that you're trying to tell her you're not satisfied with her. And that kind of talk will put out any raging fires of experimental passion faster than a whole platoon of Smokey Bears.

Monica recalls her perfect ménage experience, with her boyfriend, Jeff, and her best friend, Karen: "We were all at my mother's beach house, enjoying a little too much wine. Then Karen and I got naked and jumped into the hot tub. There was definite sexual tension between us, and when my boyfriend jumped in, I reached over to both of them, and it was, like, Hello. Pretty soon we were all just touching each other, never minding who was who."

The situation was perfect for Monica, because there were no expectations heaped on her by Jeff. "I knew I didn't have to do anything I didn't want to do," she relates. "Because Jeff hadn't nagged me about it, I didn't feel I had to go for it with Karen or be forced to listen to his whining about how we missed our big chance."

■ The Importance of Spontaneity

For all the reasons stated above, even the most inquisitive females' ménage fantasies usually require one tricky condition: "I only want it if it's spontaneous." To you that's like expecting to win the lottery without buying a ticket. But that's the way it is. Though you may be dying to grab your girlfriend's address book and start plowing into possibilities, your girlfriend most likely will prefer that you leave it alone and wait it out until a potential situation arrives. And when the beautiful constellation comes together, which it can, if you are patient... let her make the first move. Witness Greg's blissful backseat ride:

"My girlfriend and I were drinking screwdrivers in the back of my Chevy Impala with her best friend, waiting on my friend Peter, who was supposed to double-date with us. He never showed, but while we waited, my girlfriend and I started kissing and fooling around a little. At one point my girlfriend, who felt bad for her friend, started kind of caressing her, and then I started kind of caressing her. The next thing I knew, they were getting undressed together, and I was sitting there in amazement, drinking and watching them. At first I'm thinking, This is the best show I've ever seen. Then I'm thinking, if I don't get in there quick, they're gonna kick me out and send me home. So I joined them."

"I wanted to, um, stay with it as long as possible, so I spent a lot of time concentrating on foreplay. But when we did get around to actual intercourse, they started to get a little catty."

■ Make Your Woman Girl Number One

Trying to please two women simultaneously is like being a DJ spinning two tables—and if one of those tables is your main squeeze, you'd better make sure that she knows it.

"Making the girlfriend of primary importance is crucial to most successful ménages," explains Ted McIlvenna, Ph.D., who heads the Institute for Advanced Study of Human Sexuality in San Francisco. The first time the three of you meet, sex experts suggest, try to hold back when the other woman and your girlfriend are becoming sexually acquainted; and it's better not to have intercourse with the other woman this first time. There'll be less chance that emotions like jealousy and possessiveness will rear their ugly heads and make things weird the morning after.

Says Justin, who, with his girlfriend and a friend, wound up in a 12-hour round of sexual indulgence: "We spent that night, until the late morning rolling around, then watching TV, then eating cold pizza, then rolling around." Justin didn't have straight-up sex with the friend—nor with his girlfriend—that night but says that wasn't the point. "Fooling around and having two women rub their naked bodies all over me while we jerked each other off for hours and hours was more than satisfying for all involved."

UNLEASH HER WILDCAT SIDE

Nothing beats a roll in the hay—except maybe a roll in a Jacuzzi full of green Jell-O with two women in wigs. Unfortunately, most of you have probably experienced the former more than the latter. You may blame it on the fact that your current relationship is past that shag-till-sunrise honeymoon period, or that your girlfriend's about as receptive to new sexual experiences as she would be to an alien implant, but life's too short for excuses. Since she'll probably say "No way in hell am I doing that" when you first pop the question, we've devised ways to warm her up to the idea, so you can have a night of risqué sex without the risk of being labeled a complete pervert.

AURAL SEX

The Payoff: Dirty talk encourages porno-style sex without the god-awful '70s Muzak soundtrack.

The Risk: She'll think you're Johnny Wadd's younger (and smaller) brother.

How To Pull It Off: Start with a G-rated vocabulary, then build toward XXX. Instead of murmuring incoherently while she's polishing your torpedo, start by telling her how warm and wet her mouth feels. If she doesn't trade your bologna for a cigarette in disgust, push it further, gradually bringing her up to speed on your depraved thoughts. By the time you get to twisted, it'll seem, well, almost normal. Of course, you want her to get into it, too. To achieve this, ask her simple unimposing questions, such as "How does that feel?" or "What do you like better, this position or that one?" That's how Julie, 26, got her start. "At first I was too shy to respond with much more than 'That feels good,'" she says. "But after a while, my words got wilder. The next time I said, 'That feels really good,' which eventually became 'That feels really fucking good.'"

Another tactic is to ask her "What do you want me to do to you?" and make her request sexual favors by name—an I-dare-you-to-say-it strategy that got Celeste, 26, swearing like a sailor: "He knew I wanted him to go down on me, but he wouldn't do it until I told him to. I kept my lips zipped for a while, but eventually I wanted it so bad I started screaming 'Eat me out!' in a number of ways. The more graphic my language was, the more he got into it."

THE MILE-HIGH CLUB

The Payoff: The possibility that you two will be caught sharing more than toothpaste does wonders for the libido.

The Risk: You'll get caught by a nun, be kicked off the plane by an uptight stewardess, or suffer possibly fatal "turbulence torque."

How To Pull It Off: The lower your odds of getting busted, the more willing your girl will be to become a mile-high member. Get a red-eye flight so most of the passengers and flight attendants will be too groggy to hear—or care—you're hot-dogging in the john.

First, place some blankets over her lap, and give her some covert manual foreplay. (She should dress appropriately: A skirt's better than a one-piece prison jumpsuit, for example.) Once she starts to get into it, whisper in her ear, "I want you so bad...should we try it?" Hopefully she'll take the bait, like Michelle, 28: "I've never had any desire to have sex on a plane, but my boyfriend had me so riled up in my seat that I'd have done it anywhere. I told him I was going to the bathroom and that he should follow me in 20 seconds so as not to look conspicuous. I was so turned on that we both orgasmed in less time than it takes most people to brush their teeth."

If you have the urge to have high-altitude sex but can't talk her into it, you can always cheat via a custom sex plane: Log on to www.milehighclub.com or www.fantasiesaloft.com, which offer featherbed mattresses on their one-hour flights. Just leave out that little detail when you're bragging about being in the club, wouldja?

THE SPYING GAME

The Payoff: Spying on your girl getting naked—or getting off—fulfills a healthy fantasy you've had since age 15.

The Risk: Your girlfriend will worry

you're also sneaking peeks at the big-busted divorcée next door.
How To Pull It Off: To calm her fears that you're a habitual Peeping Tom, convince her that you want to watch only her. Start up close and personal. Ask her to masturbate in bed while you watch, side by side. If she pulls that off successfully, tell her you want to see her do it again—this time from a distance. "Once I got comfortable masturbating in front of my guy, he said he'd always wanted to watch me from the window," says Abby, 27. "He loved thinking I was so horny that I had to get myself off without him. He got so excited talking about it that I got excited. Next thing I know, I'm standing near the first-floor window touching myself as he's peering in from outside. When neither of us could stand it anymore, I opened the window, he climbed in, and we had amazing sex."

BACK-DOOR DELIVERY

The Payoff: Besides the tightness thing, anal sex is more taboo—and titillating—than shouting "Satan lives!" during a church service.
The Risk: Even if you have a quart of 10W30 on your dipstick, she knows she'll be waddling the next day.
How To Pull It Off: Erase her fear that anal sex is just one big, painful practical joke on womankind: Let her be on top. "I'd had bad experiences with guys entering me too fast in the past . So when my current boyfriend asked about it, I said I would only if I could control the action," says Mara, 29. "So he lay on his back, and I took my time easing onto him. After a while it felt so good, I allowed him to take over thrusting duties."

If she does allow you to take the reins from the start, lay on the lube as if your life depended on it. And make sure to test the waters with one, then two fingers before you let little Johnny jump in. Says Patti, 27: "Once my boyfriend showed me with his hand how good it feels to be stroked down there, I was raring for more. I really thought it would be a one-time thing, but I was so pleasantly surprised, we've both become anal-sex connoisseurs."

TYING THINGS UP

The Payoff: It's the ultimate carte blanche: She can't push you away, smack you, or—don't forget the ball gag—say "No thanks" to any activity.
The Risk: When she's tied up, you'll brandish a meat cleaver and say, "Dinner time!"
How To Pull It Off: Before she'll let you render her helpless, you've got to establish not only that you're not a psycho but that you can read her sexual cues more accurately than a Geiger counter. Recounts Larissa, 31: "He was so in tune with my sexuality, I knew he could turn me on without my guidance. We had dated six months before I let him handcuff me to the bed. It was worth the wait."

To awaken her submissive urges, first try a little tie-me-up without the strings. Hold her wrists above her head when you kiss her, or pull her toward you by grabbing on to her shirt or skirt. If you do graduate to real ropes, tie them loosely so she can get out if she panics when she realizes she's missing *Oprah*. "One time my boyfriend loosely tied me up with my pantyhose, then teased me for hours," says Sophie, 24. "I could have undone my bonds anytime, but it was enough of a suggestion of force to give sex that night an edgy, erotic feel."

WIG OUT

The Payoff: A different appearance can encourage her to act like a different person, feeding your biological jonesing for sex with more females.
The Risk: She'll think it's a half-assed way of cheating on her.
How To Pull It Off: Steer her toward the wig section of a department store. Once she dons a do you like, say, "Excuse me, do I know you?" If she's game, she'll fabricate a new name. Then ask her if she'd like to come over for "coffee."

Focus on how cool and sexy she is for taking on a new persona—not the new persona. Says Katrina, 26: "He called me a new name—Bambi or something tarty like that. But at the end, he said, 'Sorry, Bambi, I miss Katrina. I can't see you anymore.' That convinced me, in a roundabout way, that no girl compared to me. It was so sweet, I took off the wig and jumped him again."

PLAYING SCHOOL

The Payoff: Mutual perversion leads to frank, no-holds-barred gruntfests.
The Risk: She'll think you're a closet pedophile.

How To Pull It Off: To avoid being labeled with a Lolita complex, discuss your lust in age-neutral terms. Don't tell her you sport wood when she acts like a 14-year-old—she'll have a right to get skeeved. Instead, tell her you find it a turn-on when she acts innocent (a mindset that can occur at any age), and you just want to show her some new tricks. *Capiche*?

Also, she'll see the time you invest in your fantasy as time invested in the relationship, which is always a good thing. "My boyfriend went all out during our role-playing," says Candace, 26. "He bought me a schoolgirl-style short plaid skirt, white blouse, brown Mary Janes with heels, and a lollipop. I was so psyched he took the time that I really got into it.

FILM THE ACT

The Payoff: She may put on a better show once she's on camera; plus, the experience may soften her up for watching pornos regularly.

The Risk: She thinks you'll share it with a pool room full o' frat brothers or accidentally return it to the video store.

How To Pull It Off: The only way to calm her fears that her performance won't become famous throughout town is to let her keep the evidence. "After he told me I could keep the tape, I was much more comfortable with going on film," swears Jenna, 27. "I don't even tell him where I hide it. It's so cute to see him beg for it when he's over at my place."

So the tape is hers. But then she may start wondering. Doesn't a camera add 10 pounds? Assure her that the very reason you want her to go on tape is that she's the hottest girl you've ever been with. In case this isn't 100 percent true, lower your lighting or use candlelight, like the boyfriend of Amy, 27, did during their porno shoot. "The light from a few candles made our skin look smooth and sexy, and also made our bodies sleeker," she said. It will also keep you from saying to yourself later, "Sheesh, who knew my ass was so damn hairy?"

SHAVING GRACE

The Payoff: A crystal-clear view of muff central—and no more short 'n' curlies between your teeth.

The Risk: Blades and blood. Also that Lolita thing again.

How To Pull It Off: Plant the idea in her head days before, while in bed. Since it's fantasy at that stage, she won't feel pressured to make a split-second decision with a sharp object near her hedges. "Sometimes sexual things I wouldn't do grow on me over time," says Chandra, 25. "When he talked about it...the idea got to me."

Then sexify the process to the point of distraction. Molly, 28, was wooed into smooth sailing this way. "My boyfriend lit candles, propped me on the sink, spread my legs wide, and took his time applying shaving cream," she says. "As he teased and shaved me clean, he talked to me in a low, slow, sexy voice, saying he was going to give me the best oral sex of my life. He was so right."

YOUR KEYS TO THE KINGDOM

Don't beg. Don't grovel. It ain't manly. Besides, it ain't necessary. Sex has become as predictable as your morning commute? Beverly Hills relationship therapist and lecturer Sharyn Hillyer gives you a few shortcuts to getting way laid.

Stick to the rules. If you tell her, "I just want to tie up your hands," and as soon as she's obliged, you secure her feet, too, she'll never play pirates with you again. Game over, you fool. You've lost her trust.

Talk her through it. Silent sex is creepy. And if you get all quiet while you're doing something out of the ordinary, she'll truly feel weirded out. Try saying: "Is this OK for you?" and "Can I keep going?" and "This feels so great."

Don't be a bigmouth. Women live in dread that they'll get a reputation as that kind of girl. Tell her this is just between you two so she knows you won't be bragging later to the guys out on the golf course.

Do a postgame analysis. Comments like "Was that fun?" and "Could I have made it better for you?" will show that you really care and appreciate her taking a chance. She's more likely to let herself go next time, too.

WHAT DOES SHE REALLY THINK **OF YOUR KINK?**

One intrepid female writer (and a startling survey of females) reveals the odds of getting what you really, really want: Guys, let me clue you in to a small fact about your fantasies: We women know exactly what's on your horny little minds. We know just how badly you want to take porno Polaroids, dress us up in Catholic school girl uniforms, or watch us ride our vibrators to nirvana. You can tell us almost any kinky thoughts you want and chances are we won't be shocked. We may even have fantasized about those same things ourselves.

But that doesn't mean we're going to let you do them for real. Unless…

Unless you earn our confidence and can bring up in just the right way the topic of taking the back-door route, or of inviting our cute roommates over for a game of topless touch football, or of pulling out the camcorder and recording every last move for posterity. Because fantasies are fun when they're in your head, but they can get a little scary when push comes to shove.

So to find out precisely what it would take to get us to act on your every desire, we hacked into the *Cosmopolitan* Web site and begged, cajoled, and flattered the mag's readers until they confessed what they required (or would require) to live out their men's fantasies. More than 300 live ones responded. Then we broke the results down with some statistical analysis that will (we hope) tell you at a glance what your chances are. Good luck. And, hey, let's be careful out there.

OF HUMAN BONDAGE

Chances she'll tie you up: 8 in 10
Chances she'll let you tie her up (eventually): 7 in 10
Chances she'll let you tie her up on the second date: virtually nil

According to the fit-to-be-tied females we surveyed, a little light bondage is no big deal—as long as it's in the context of a serious relationship. Only a brave (and probably not too bright) few said they'd let a guy tether them to the bedposts after just a few dates. Here's why: "I once let a random hookup tie down my wrists and ankles, and woke up the next morning to find him gone and his Irish wolfhound licking my feet," said a 24-year-old who refused to divulge even her first name.

Still, an eager 8 out of 10 said they'd be more than happy to bind their boyfriends if asked to, and about half would "tease, tickle, and torture" them once they were where they wanted to be. "My boyfriend whispered in my ear that watching me take off my clothes drove him wild," said Gina, 27. "So a few nights later, I tied him to a chair and then did a striptease followed by a lap dance." For best results, skip scratchy twine and scary ropes and opt for girl-friendly materials, like scarves, neckties, and old nylons.

ON A ROLE

Chances she'll dress up like a cheerleader and let you play with her pompoms: 1 in 2
Chances she'll surprise you by dressing up in an outfit: 1 in 7
Chances it'll be the Phillie Phanatic costume: 0

Sexy lingerie is one thing, but if you're dying to see your girlfriend decked out as Little Bo-peep—frilly bloomers and all—you may be asking too much. Seven out of 10 women confessed they thought elaborate role-playing was "a little weird," but most admitted they'd "try it once or twice." "This guy I was seeing kept buying me costumes to wear to bed," said Elissa, 25. "I thought it was cute the first time, when he presented me with a little nurse's outfit from Frederick's of Hollywood, but when he rented a Cinderella dress from a Halloween shop, it freaked me out." If you're lucky, your girlfriend falls into the smallish 15 percent or so who like to surprise their significant others with kinky clothes. "Dressing up like a Girl Scout, complete with sash, kneesocks, plaid skirt, and buckle shoes, was my

idea," confessed Melissa, 32. "Then he asked me what I was willing to do to earn some badges."

To put the idea into action, mention in a flirty, fawning way (preferably over a romantic dinner) that having her play dress-up would turn you on. "My boyfriend was constantly telling me how sexy I would look in a dominatrix outfit, how it would show off my body and how [we think this is key, folks] he'd never done anything like that with anyone else," said Anne, 30. "It got to the point where I couldn't wait to try it because the thought of him worshiping my body got me really hot." That's step one. Step two is to actually go out and purchase said outfit. While most of the women reported they'd try a costumed ball, few would be willing to fork over the cash for an outfit themselves.

SHAVING POINTS

Chances she'll be willing to shave off her pubic hair: 1 in 2
Chances she wants you to shave off yours: 0

Every woman I've ever known who's gone bare down there swears by it. So why don't more of us make the move to pube-free privates? A simple lack of impetus, it seems. About 8 in 10 hairless hotties claimed that the first time they took it all off was at the persistent urging of a man. "He kept telling me how good he thought it would look and feel if there was nothing but smooth, sexy skin," said Janine, 28. "But it wasn't until he asked if he could do the shaving that I really got into it." The truth is, your enthusiasm—and participation—is a huge turn-on. Just be sure to offer lots of oral sex in return, and keep your comments positive. "Mark was giving me oral sex when he poked his head up and said, 'You're so hairy. Every time I go down on you, I get a mouthful of hair,'" remembered Bridget, 26. "I eventually ended up shaving all the way, but Mark wasn't around to enjoy it." About half the women who had never done so said they'd consider baring all.

GIRLS ON FILM

Chances she'll let you take porno pictures of her: 1 in 2
Chances she's afraid they'll wind up on nipplebandits.com: 10 in 10

When you propose breaking out your Vivid Video amateur kit and making your very own video nasty, the more body-conscious gender immediately thinks one thing: Will I look fat? About half the women said they shy away from being shot because they fear they won't look foxy on tape.

To help her get over her naked-photo phobia, start by telling her she has a drop-dead gorgeous body—over and over again. "When he asked to take pictures of me in the buff, I hesitated at first, but he kept saying I had the best body and that I was so hot he wished he could see me naked more often," said Erin, 22. "What can I say? Flattery got him everywhere." A healthy dose of feigned spontaneity/stupidity (as in "Oh, hey, a Polaroid camera! Gee, I wonder what we could do with this?") will score you points. One in three chicks *Maxim* polled would feel better about a frisky photo session if it was a spur-of-the-moment thing, not some perverted plan.

LOCATION, LOCATION, LOCATION

Chances she'll make love to you in a public place: 3 in 5
Chances she'll ever make love to you again after spending a night in jail for public indecency: 1 in 10

Guys aren't the only ones who fantasize about doing the deed on a desk at work, in an apartment-building elevator, or on a picnic table in the park; you're just the only ones who'll admit it. Three out of four women we talked to confessed to having dirty daydreams set in odd locales. And a little more than half said they'd risk it in real life.

The best way to get lucky in the location of your choice? Drop a heavy-handed hint. "My boyfriend told me about a dream he had that we were making love in the music room where he teaches," said Kristen, 29. "One night while he was practicing late, I came in wearing a very short skirt minus my panties. Before he even realized what I had in mind, I was all over him." If the dream thing doesn't work, try a flat-out request. "He would go on and on about how amazing it would be to do it in the rain," explained Carrie, 19. "He was so sincerely passionate about it that I decided to make his fantasy come true."

PORN TO RUN

Chances she'll watch a porno you "picked up on the way home": 4 in 5
Chances she'll watch a porno you pulled from your extensive collection: 1 in 8

The problem with trying to make pornography part of your romantic routine is we're bound to think you're burnin'-hot for those bleached-blonde bimbos with breasts the size of basketballs. Numberswise, about a fourth of our tell-all group said they'd worry you're more turned on by a two-dimensional tart than by the flesh-and-blood babe in your arms. Fact is, you are. Now what?

Convince her that this is far from the truth and things may play out in your favor. "I definitely needed convincing," said Colleen, 23. "But he won me over by saying he wanted to reenact it scene by scene so we could try different positions and discover new ways to make each other feel good. When he put it that way, it sounded kind of sweet." But be sure to pretend you actually had to make a shopping trip to procure a porno, as opposed to simply picking one from your enormous library. Eight out of 10 women said they wouldn't date a guy with a creepy smut habit.

HOW TO START A HAREM

When it's time to sheik your booty and chase some veil.

Sure, we all know monogamy's the way to go. But haven't you ever wondered what it might be like to have a few dozen ladies on the side? Heed the advice of Alev Lytle Croutier, author of *Harem: The World Behind the Veil* and at least your fantasies will be historically accurate.

1. ***Pick a Spot to Hang Your Hookah***
Simply moving to Utah ain't gonna cut it. You'll have to head for the Middle East. Almost any nation there will do (except Turkey, where harems have been banned since 1909). If the political climate makes you nervous, you can also opt for northern Africa, Southeast Asia, or India. If you move to a Muslim nation, have the decency to convert to Islam—nothing ruins a good harem like a fatwa of death on your head.

2. ***Become the Man of the House***
It's traditional harem protocol to ice all your existing male relatives so there won't be any disputes over the order of succession. Can't stomach fratricide? There is an alternative. "In the 17th century, it became acceptable to simply banish princes into secluded apartments known as golden cages," says Croutier. Set 'em up with ESPN and a couple of concubines of their own and they won't put up a fight.

3. ***Court your courtesans***
Though this would seem creepy in any other culture besides Italy's, you'll need your mom's help to recruit your harlots. As Croutier explains, your mother assumes the title of *valide* and is responsible for rounding up your fillies. "The *valide* decides which girls to present to the sultan and gets rid of girls she doesn't like," he says. Also, get yourself a team of eunuchs to oversee day-to-day operations—you'll never have to worry about them dipping their pens in company ink.

4. ***Manage Your Assets***
When you see a harem girl you like, simply drop a handkerchief in front of her. Your head eunuch knows this is the signal to groom her for the evening's festivities. He'll also record the event in a Day-Timer called the *Book of Couching* "to avoid the slightest doubt of paternity," says Croutier. This also eliminates all spontaneity as well as any chance for group action. Hey, just what kind of fantasy is this?

BLOWN OFF KILTER

As if wearing a condom during actual sex weren't bad enough (but again we stress that unless you want to keep your penis the healthy pup it wants to be, use caution), now we're going to tell you that you should also seriously consider wearing one during oral sex (yours, not hers, numb-nuts). But why, dear God, why?

First of all, there's Herpes: An estimated one of every four Americans has it, and no one talks about it. Worse, 30 percent of all new cases of genital herpes are caused by a partner with oral herpes (cold sores) giving head to the previously uninfected partner. Oh, and by the way, there's no known cure.

Secondly, more and more evidence seems to be pointing to the fact that unprotected fellatio significantly increases your partner's risk for contracting HIV due to the swallowing of sperm, which isn't exactly the kind of negative reinforcement you want to be giving your partner. Of course as with most initial scientific reports, further studies are needed, but do you really want your girlfriend to take that kind of chance?

GET HER TO SEXPERIMENT

Six women reveal the ways their guys got them to go from uptight to up for anything.

You and your woman have been using the missionary position so long, you're convinced you could convert a synagogue. But how can you introduce your mate to the thrill of sexploration when she seems perfectly happy with—or afraid to stray from—the well-traveled terrain of your ho-hum love life?

Pick up some pointers from the following testimonials by women whose bedmates won them over to the virtue of variety. Not only will your woman be willing to try your ideas on for size, we guarantee that she'll start improvising on her own, faster than you can say "I'll go get the wet suits."

■ Turning Her On To Toys

"I had never used a vibrator in my life, although my boyfriend and I had joked about it. Then one night he pulled one out of our bedside drawer. He grinned and turned it on, and I freaked because I thought my roommates would hear it buzzing. Plus it seemed so unnatural—it was blue! He held me and apologized. He said he thought I'd like it because I enjoy being touched fast and sort of rhythmically. He also said he felt like a failure because it takes me a lot longer to climax than it takes him. Then he asked me why I didn't want to try it. I told him the thought of some blue thing inside me seemed, well, slutty. A week later he returned it and got a quieter, off-white model. The fact that he'd gone back to the sex shop to get the one that I'd like better made me realize he cared about making me happy. We tried it that night, and although I felt strange at first, he kept whispering how he wanted to make me feel good, so I let him keep going. He started by just moving it across my breasts and thighs and then heading, uh, home. He was right. It was amazing. I orgasmed a lot faster, too. These days it's usually me who gets it out of the drawer when I'm feeling a little crazy."—Joanne, 22

■ Selling Her on 69

"I like giving oral sex, and I love it when guys go down on me, but when you do sixty-nine, the guy's face—his eyes, his nose—are positioned much more right in there. Plus, I didn't think I could relax enough to climax if I had him in my mouth at the same time. One night at my place, my boyfriend kept saying how much he wanted to experience sixty-nine with me because he loved my body. He asked me what I was afraid of, and I told him how all those women-smell-like-fish jokes had made me uptight. I said the

only way I would try it was if I had just taken a bath. He jumped up and said, 'Well, let's take a bath together.' When we got back into bed, he started kissing me from my lips down to my thighs, and then he positioned us head-to-toes. I hadn't realized we could do it lying on our sides; I'd always pictured me on top, with some guy suffocating between my legs. So I put him in my mouth, and he moved my legs apart, and suddenly we were doing it. He kept saying how great it was and asking if he should keep going, which was reassuring. I've happily been in that position—post-shower—many, many times since."
—Anne, 33

■ Bonding With Bondage

"My current boyfriend casually mentioned after two months of dating that he wanted to tie me to the bed. I was horrified, because all I could picture was handcuffs ripping into my flesh or him having a heart attack and dying with me attached to the bedpost. One night when he was going down on me, he reached up and held my wrists so that I couldn't move. I started to struggle a bit, but he moved up next to me and pleaded, 'Why can't you just relax and let me please you?' My unwillingness to try new things was making him feel threatened by my old boyfriend, as if by clinging to old routines I was clinging to my ex's memory. I was touched by this admission, so I said I'd think about it. The next time we were together, he got a silk scarf off my shelf and placed it on the bed. I liked that, because he was letting it be my call. I left the scarf there while we were making out and then let him move my arms above my head and tie my wrists

together without tying me to the bed. He then made love to me really slowly, talking to me as he touched me, which was a relief, because although the 'taboo' feeling was exciting, I felt vulnerable being constrained. But I trust him completely now, and we do it—with me tied to the bed—about once a month."—Stephanie, 26

■ Talking Her Into Talking Dirty

"I'd gone on a few dates with my current guy, and one night it was pretty obvious that we were going to have sex. As we were making out and taking each other's clothes off, he started describing what he was doing to me in very specific—and spicy—language. He'd say things like 'I love kissing your tits.' But he never used degrading words, like bitch—I'd have kicked him out. Suddenly he whispered in my ear, 'Talk to me. Just tell me how you feel, what you want.' I was nervous that I'd sound silly, but after dating so many guys who just wanted a quick screw or didn't listen to me, here was a guy who was urging me to express myself. I tentatively chimed in with 'I love it when you run your hands across my ass like that.' We took turns saying what we liked or wanted. Every time I said something, he held me tighter or moaned, reinforcing how crazy excited it was making him. Afterward he asked if I'd minded talking to him like that. To be honest, it didn't feel totally natural, but it gets him so hot that I get excited, so I'm learning to like it more and more." — Sarah, 25

■ Knocking at the Back Door

"During college I was living with a guy who could usually get me to try new things simply because he always gave me what most women really want: oral sex. He'd go down on me for an hour, literally, and make me climax two or three times, until I felt sort of stoned and in love. He'd say things while he did it that made it clear he really enjoyed it. When he mentioned that he wanted to be inside every part of me, I knew he meant, uh, back there, but I was glad he phrased it in a sexy way. One night after he'd gone down on me for about an hour and I'd had two orgasms, we were in the shower, kissing, and he slowly turned me around, rubbed the wetness from my front to my behind, and put it in. It was really emotional—I almost cried—and it felt like everything below my stomach was floating. He kept whispering my name and making it clear how amazing it was for him. He climaxed inside me, and we finished showering. I was in pain from the penetration, but he dried me off and made me a cup of tea, the whole princess treatment. It isn't something I do with every guy—only the ones who put me first and make me feel sexy and desirable." — Heidi, 26

■ Getting Her to Get Messy

"One night my husband of four years told me he wanted to try to liven up our sex life. I sarcastically told him that if we didn't work a million hours a week and if I didn't feel so unattractive (I'd gained a little weight), that sure, I'd be up for that. The next Friday he showed up at my workplace and said he was taking me away for a stress-free weekend. He'd even arranged for his mom to watch the baby and packed my bag. We got to our room, and he unwrapped this crazy lingerie outfit with garters. (I'm a cotton underwear kind of gal), but he held me and assured me that he liked my body better now because my breasts were fuller and sexier, and he kept having fantasies at work about me in a red bra and him ejaculating on my chest (something we'd never done before). I was surprised that he'd been thinking about me in such a sexy, pornographic way, but it was a turn-on hearing him verbalize what he wanted. I put on the outfit after he agreed to turn the lights off, and he kept telling me how sexy I looked. He went down on me, and I had an orgasm; then he asked whether I wanted him inside me or if he could rub himself between my breasts. The way he asked—sweetly, softly, earnestly—and the fact that he'd gone to so much trouble so we could get away from the daily grind clinched the deal. But soon my chest was getting red and sore, so I got some lotion out of my bag. We were both giggling. We knew we were going to be making 'Get the lotion, honey' jokes for weeks. I was a sticky mess at the end, so we jumped in the shower But I must admit that afterward, we felt closer and more bonded."—Olivia, 34

The Ins and Outs of Sex

At this point, you've no doubt at least stumbled your way through your first sexual experience and know all about inserting Tab A into Slot B (and maybe even Slot C–see Chapter 7). But being that Sex Ed was pretty much limited to snickering and exchanging dirty notes with your classmates, there are some finer points of the mattress mambo that you've always wondered about but could never get an authoritative answer on. This chapter will help you graduate into sex-authority territory.

HOW LONG SHOULD "IT" LAST

Thrusters are engaged and we have liftoff; and you're currently initiating the docking sequence. While you're probably hoping to go on forever, your wife is probably wondering just how long this whole thing is supposed to take. And we're not talking about foreplay (which, despite popular belief, is not so named for the number of minutes one is supposed to engage in it), but actual intercourse.

Alas, your worst fears are allayed. Contrary to what Sting leads you to believe, the average session, from actual introitus (it's what is sounds like) to ejaculation is between three and five minutes, depending on how long you've been at sea. And believe it or not, the general consensus among the experts is that anything over that is gravy.

You're operating just as nature intended. After all, when we had sloped foreheads and women had more body hair than Robin Williams, we'd be dino chow if we took too long bumping uglies. We need to get in and get out, so to speak, so the faster we came the better. So by trying to last longer, we're actually trying to buck millions of years of evolution.

The real question is: How long do you need? One couple's 'too short' is another couple's marathon. Of course, if you're happy but the little lady's continually left high and dry, there's obviously a problem. There are a couple of quickie solutions you can do to rectify this particular situation:

HOW TO MAKE IT LAST LONGER

Force the Foreplay

Instead of jumping the gun and going for the gusto within 30 seconds of being naked, slowly work up to it. Start with a nice long massage, lots and lots of kissing, caressing, and of course, oral sex. In fact, shoot for making her come at least once before you even enter her. If not, see just how wound up she can get until she's literally begging for it.

Double-Bag Her

For some, wearing a condom works wonders in deadening the senses, especially if you've been together for awhile. So why not simply use that to your advantage? If this is your first time (or first time in a long time), then a condom (or maybe even two) may be the way to save your day. Just tell her it's your new method for adding girth to your gherkin.

Beat It Just Before

There's something to be said for *There's Something About Mary*, that is, how Ben Stiller's character prepared for his date: relieving a little pressure so to speak. Unless you're a porn star, it's unlikely your second round, no matter how much time has elapsed in between, will go quite so quickly as your first at bat. So while you're getting set for the evening, why not set aside a little quiet time to shake hands with your best friend?

Whack it Weekly

It's been proven that those who masturbate frequently (like, once a day) come all too quickly during the real thing. Reasons for those are many: fear of getting caught teaches a person to hurry things along quickly; you aren't exactly concerning yourself with foreplay and just want to reach your goal ASAP. Ease up, lefty, and let nature return things back to normal.

Fake It

Long the realm of womenfolk, faking it is, believe it or not, a very viable alternative. The secret is that you need to calm down for a little bit and allow a bit of loss of erection. Then when you regain your erection, you'll be able to go even longer, plus she'll be impressed that you were able to rise to the occasion again so quickly. Obviously, this is far easier to pull off if you're wearing a condom, but we've heard of plenty of people who have faked it sans cover and the women were none the wiser.

Add on Afterplay

If you finished before you really wanted to, finish her off by either masturbating her or with oral sex. Of course, there could be a couple of problems. Some women just can't climax unless they're engaged in intercourse.

MARATHON MAN

Don't punish yourself with damaging visualizations of Janet Reno to last longer in bed. In America we have drugs. We're talking desensitizers: those magical sprays and creams that claim to turn a minute man into a long-distance runner. Always up for easy ways to look good in bed, we had a couple road-test some formulas. We handed them the elixirs and a stopwatch and told 'em to go at it like epileptic poodles ("Anything for science," said the guy) and report back in a week. Using nothing the first time, our man took an embarrassingly speedy 59 seconds to fire his weapon. Here's how he did with the help of America's top scientific minds:

STUD 100 DESENSITIZING SPRAY FOR MEN ($15)

Secret Ingredient: Lidocaine, also used in nasal sprays

Directions: Mist your fern with a few sprays. Wait no more than 10 minutes, then jump in. Wash off after or…shit, it doesn't say what happens!

Sensation: "After waiting five minutes," said our tester, "I got a warm, tingly feeling." Inspired, he got to it, but the harder he revved his engines, "the more numb Mr. Happy got." After 12 minutes, "a trickle of feeling came back," he said. Five more minutes turned the tide.

Shot fired in: 17 min., 31 sec.

Buy it at: HardAid.com

IRON WOOD ($28)

Secret Ingredient: Radix asari, a Chinese herb. Also cures headaches, but probably not the kind she has.

Directions: Just like Right Guard, Iron Wood comes with a roll-on applicator. Rub its speed stick over yours, wait 40 minutes, wash off, and hop in the saddle.

Sensation: The label says to expect a "slight burning sensation" right after application. "It should have read 'Your cock will burn like a lit match,'" said our tester. The pain left after five minutes. "In the sack I felt only slightly less than normal."

Shot fired in: 5 min., 47 sec.

Buy it at: HardAid.com

INDIAN GOD LOTION ($10)

Secret Ingredient: Isopropyl alcohol. Conveniently, it's also a substance used in wart removers.

Directions: Spray the soldier's helmet, wait a half-hour, then rinse and deploy.

Sensation: A cold, numbing, tingling sensation in minutes after application. "It felt like I had visited a dick dentist," the guy complained. "And in the sack I felt like a pick swinger in a coal mine."

Shot fired in: Didn't happen. After 30 minutes of continuous motion, he rolled over and fell asleep. "But for once I had an excuse," he reported happily.

Buy it at: Winghopfung.com

WHEN YOU THINK YOU'RE DONE...ADD FIVE MORE MINUTES

Never want to hear the words "Oh, baby, I was so close!" again? Master these sure-fire techniques and we guarantee that your phone number will be scrawled on women's room walls across the country.

It takes about five minutes for light to travel halfway from the sun, for Crayola to manufacture 60,000 crayons, and for Bill Gates to make $195,000. It also takes the average woman about five minutes longer to reach orgasm than it takes most of us. Every poll since the Crimean War has shown that one of women's main beefs is that men decant too soon. Experts say most guys reach orgasm in under three minutes (after 30 to 60 thrusts). Most gals require at least seven minutes. Do the math, and give her a few seconds for good measure. But if you'd rather be doing something besides math...and doing it longer...continue reading. Our experts swear that by following their advice, you'll last at least an extra fiver. Hell, if you want, you'll remain hard so long that your erection will need to be carbon-dated.

MIND OVER MANHOOD

In every movie where a nuclear generator is involved, there's a moment when the sirens start screaming, the meters start moving into the red, and everyone near the reactor starts yelling, "It's gonna blow!" And then someone pulls the emergency cutoff switch. Here are a few switches of your own to pull when critical mass is imminent.

Bring It to the Brink

The practice most frequently suggested by sex therapists is called the stop-start method, says Mark Schoen, Ph.D., a sex educator and producer of the instructional video *You Can Last Longer: Solutions for Ejaculatory Control* (Sinclair Institute). You basically rock along until you feel an orgasm rushing on. At that point you freeze, either inside your lover or after you withdraw (she'll probably feel less bereft if you stay inside). Gain control of your senses. Ask yourself what day it is. Give your sausage a moment to cool. Start again. Repeat as needed. Nothing could be simpler. An orgasm, you see, is one part lust, two parts friction. Stop the friction, stop the orgasm.

Fine-Tune the Technique

To get the most out of the stop-start method, you should endeavor to bring yourself closer to the detonation point each time you employ the maneuver. That way, you'll learn to read your body's signals, to monitor your level of excitement, and to nail the exact millisecond you need to stop. Over time, experts say, you'll be able to cum so darn close to ejaculation without actually spilling any seed that you'll almost think you have. Yet you'll be able to stay erect and keep on going and going with only an occasional moment's hesitation—perpetually blissful, like some kind of sexual legend.

But will Betty Lou see you as a Casanova or as a cad whose constant stopping and starting makes her feel like your sparring partner? "Most women are very supportive. Why wouldn't they be? The key is to make sure that the two of you talk about what you're doing and why," says Rohn Friedman, M.D., director of the human sexuality program at Boston's Beth Israel Deaconess Medical Center.

One gal we interviewed indicated that his stopping and starting actually helped her get off. "I often feel uptight about how long it takes me to climax," says Jennifer. "For my part, alleviating the pressure to orgasm far outweighs the interruption in stimulation, because it's not like every time my boyfriend stops, I go back to square one. In fact, it's a lot sexier, because he leaves me hanging—begging, if you want to be honest, which ironically makes me climax faster."

Of course, your teammate doesn't always have to be present for you to practice. Sex experts heartily advise you to take advantage of those tender moments when you're making love to yourself (doesn't sound quite as

pathetic as "masturbating," does it?) to practice the stop-start technique.

Press the Million-Dollar Point

You can't see it, but there's an ejaculatory duct down at that low-profile soft spot between the scrotum and the anus (closer to the anus). Press on it as you feel yourself almost ready to spout (firmly for at least three or four seconds), and you will stop the ejaculation. The pressure can be applied with your fingers or hers, or, if you're flexible enough, just about anything—your heel, for example. (Sit cross-legged atop one heel, then have your sweetheart straddle you, facing in or out.)

Taoism (pronounced *dow*-ism), begun as a pro-sex consciousness-raising movement in China thousands of years ago, calls this down-under spot the million-dollar point (alluding to its magnificent value). Ancient Taoist sexual practices direct men to make great use of their million-dollar point to delay ejaculation for long periods. By doing so, the Taoists believed, a man will improve his health and live a long life.

Robert Jaffe, Ph.D., says he's not sure about the long life, but he confirms that pressing on the right point will delay ejaculation. "Although," adds Jaffe, a family therapist and sex counselor in Encino, California, "most men find the manipulation somewhat annoying." Tony, one guy who experimented with digging his heel in, complains that his leg went to sleep in the middle of lovemaking. "But it was a small price to pay for becoming one woman's idol," he modestly confesses.

WE'RE NUMBER ONE !

Though they're skinny, they talk funny, and they refuse to admit that their movies blow, French and Italian guys, bizarrely, are still assumed to be great lovers by most of the world's women. Well, not anymore: According to the 1998 Durex Global Sex Survey, American men take a back seat to nobody. Groping for the pulse of 10,000 sexually active men and women around the world, the survey found that the Yankee male gives his partner a world-record 28.1-minute bout, on average—head and shoulders above the universal norm of 17.2 minutes. Our friends to the north, those randy Canadians, come in (so to speak) at 22.7 minutes, but our European chums Henri and Paolo peter out at a high-school-freshman-like 16.1 minutes and 14.2 minutes, respectively. (What's the country with the stingiest lovers? Sex-tour capital Thailand, which puts its collective boxers back on after a scant, sailor-on-shore-leave 10.4 minutes.)

DISCOVER YOUR PC MUSCLE

The penis can be trained without the hassle of starting and stopping or pressing your fingers anywhere, says sex therapist and former sex surrogate Anita Banker-Riskin, co-author (with her husband, Michael Riskin Ph.D.) of *Simultaneous Orgasm & Other Joys of Sexual Intimacy*. But first you must make the effort to develop your pubococcygeus (PC) muscle, which you're now sitting on. The PC muscle involuntarily contracts as you ejaculate, causing semen to fly. But if you purposely contract it during the peak of sex, the PC muscle, says Banker-Riskin, acts like the brakes on a car and can bring an ejaculation to a halt.

PRACTICE PELVIC CRUNCHES

(a.k.a. Penile Push-ups)

"Like any other muscle, you need to exercise the PC," says Banker-Riskin. But first you need to identify it. Take a leak and stop the flow without using your hands. Now do that same trick (without actually urinating), and squeeze hard. You just flexed your PC muscle. Hold for one second. Now relax. Repeat. Do a set of 10 once every day. After a week, add another set per day. Build up until you're doing five sets of 10 every day. By that stage, says Banker-Riskin, you will likely notice your new power. Proceed with your sex life, halting ejaculation as you would with the stop-start or press technique, but using your newly developed mighty PC muscle instead.

Among sex experts, the PC muscle maneuver is a little controversial. James Barada, M.D., director of the Center for Male Sexual Health in Albany, New York, and psychotherapist Jaffe say the Riskin couple may be onto something. Friedman, however, feels some men find squeezing the PC muscle stimulating and, by squeezing it, wind up popping quicker. You'll just have to try it and see.

EXPANDED REPERTOIRE

Don't worry, we're not suggesting triple half gainers with a twist. But there are simple ways to move, groove, and think that can delay the money shot long enough for it to earn interest. Try different strokes. As any Cub Scout who has ever rubbed two sticks together knows, speed and friction make heat. So to turn down the heat, sometimes all you need to do is slow down. "If you want to climax more slowly, move slowly," says sex coach and surrogate Paul Gethard (yes, that's his real name), of Fountain Valley, California. "No heavy thrusting. Just slow, erotic movements."

The ancient Taoists recommended slow, shallow, circular movements to speed up her orgasms while slowing his down. "Going around and around offers maximum stimulation to a woman, because it rubs both her clitoris and the sensitive outer rim of the vagina," says George Schiffer, director of the Singing Wind Healing Tao Center in Arlington, Virginia. "It also keeps the man's mind engaged in his gyrations, and this minor distraction helps him last longer." Think of it like scraping the last bit of mayo out of a jar. The old Tao masters, says modern Taoist Schiffer, also suggested rhythmically alternating between deep and shallow thrusts. They particularly savored nine shallow followed by one deep.

"The actual rhythm doesn't matter," says Barada. "As long as you thrust in an alternating fashion, you'll likely slow your ejaculation." And don't worry about boring her with shallow shoves, adds Barada. He agrees with Schiffer that the outer rim is the place to be. "Most sensation in the vagina is at the entrance, where there is a higher density of nerve endings, not the rear," he says.

One office administrator, Candice, 27, emphatically concurs. "The combination of short and long thrusts is what good sex is all about. The short give the best stimulation, but the long offer an incredibly intimate feeling of being deeply connected. Almost any woman would prefer this thoughtful type of intercourse to mindless pile-driving."

■ Change Your Mount

Gethard says that the missionary position may build strong triceps, but it often leads to rapid ejaculations. "You get to the point where you're so tired, you just need to ejaculate and collapse," says Gethard. Try a more relaxed position, he suggests, such as spooning—both of you are lying on your sides, with her in front. Or flop onto your back and allow her to straddle you and do all the work.

Friedman agrees that the female-superior position often works better than the missionary, largely because it allows her to do the driving and the male to relax his muscles, giving him better control over his ejaculation. "But," he cautions, "all guys are different." For some men, the grand view that a woman on top proves can be dangerously exciting.

■ Keep Your Eyes Off the Prize

Don't focus on your honey's choicest parts, suggests Banker-Riskin. If, for example, your most coveted vision is that of Betty Lou's breasts keeping time with the bouncing mattress, try looking directly into her lovely eyes. If the sight of her dark nether triangle drives you wild, raise your sights north of the waistline. If every part of the female anatomy, even Betty Lou's nostrils, drives you wild with lust, then try closing your eyes.

AVERAGE SEX SESSION:
America: **28.1 minutes**
Canada: **22.7 minutes**
Australia: **22.6 minutes**
Britian: **21.1 minutes**
South Africa: **18.5 minutes**
Mexico: **17.4 minutes**
Global average: **17.2 minutes**
Germany: **17.2 minutes**
France: **16.1 minutes**
Spain: **14.7 minutes**
Poland: **14.5 minutes**
Italy: **14.2 minutes**
Hong Kong: **12.6 minutes**
Russia: **11.7 minutes**
Thailand: **10.4 minutes**

DRUGSTORE TAO-BOY

Two very effective orgasm-control aids the venerable Tao masters couldn't buy at the pharmacy but that you can are condoms and desensitizing creams.

■ Dress the Bishop

Covering Mr. Sunshine in latex is a backseat-proven way of lessening penile sensation and prolonging the enjoyably inevitable. But different condoms provide different levels of help, so you'll want to experiment. Dry might be less stimulating than lubricated. Ribbed condoms tend to be thicker (and less stimulating to you) than smooth ones. Thicker yet are the industrial-strength condoms, such as Ramses Extra and Trojan Extra Strength brands. Natural skins are the thinnest of condoms and will slow you down the least. They are also porous and won't protect you against disease.

■ See Dr. Sex

On the off chance that nothing we've said here slows your Donald down, medical doctors can prescribe a cream called EMLA, which is much like the nonprescription desensitizing creams but possibly more effective. "Most doctors will give it to you simply for asking," Barada says.

And then there are pills. "We've found that certain antidepressant medications, like Zoloft, can prolong erections," says Barada. The medications are given in small doses, and they're given intermittently, not long-term. The main side effect of these drugs is drowsiness, and typically they would be prescribed for men suffering from premature ejaculation and not for mattress cowboys looking to improve their already respectable saddle times. But it can't hurt to ask. Class dismissed. Prepare to be worshipped.

HOW TO FIND HER FRIGGIN' G-SPOT

Dr. Gräfenberg didn't do us any favors when he made "discovery" that bears his initials. While we won't promise sex so good the neighbor's need a cigarette, we will give you the map to where G marks the spot.

■ Assume the Position

Have her lie on her back with a pillows under her hips, with her legs comfortably spread and her bottom slightly up. Now take your well-trimmed (the importance of which cannot be overemphasized according to the women we talked to), well-lubricated index and middle finger and gently ease them in, palm up. About two to three inches up on her frontal vaginal wall, you should feel a patch of flesh rougher than the surrounding skin about the size of a bean or two.

■ Before You Dress, Caress

Once found, you should stroke it gently by making the "come hither" gesture with your fingers. If you've hit pay dirt, the spot should begin to swell in size, anywhere from a dime to a half dollar (the loud moanings from your partner should also be a solid clue). To really send her over the edge, use your thumb to stimulate her clitoris.

■ Wait for the Heavens to Open (Or Not)

Though some warn that proper G-spot stimulation could have her exploding with ecstasy and gushing fluids, there's a good chance the earth won't move; you might not even get a groan of pleasure. While reports tell of those who hit 9.1 on the Richter scale, all some women have felt was an urge to pee. No less a sexpert than Dr. Ruth doubts the G-spot's very existence. It could just simply be that some women have them and some women don't. But considering you have nothing to lose and everything to gain, even the most pessimistic should be willing to give this particular lottery a try.

HOW TO MAKE HER MULTI-ORGASMIC

You've seen the porn: women who could come all night long with nary a break; worse: guys who could make women come all night long with nary a break. The ancient Greeks referred to these men as Gods. Today, the aforementioned women refer to these men the same way. You may think you're pressing your luck getting a woman to climax once, but don't fret; you don't need to be hung like Dirk Diggler or have the stamina of a triathlete to get her to see lightning strike twice in one night.

Those oversexed researchers Masters and Johnson actually found women who were able to reach 50 consecutive orgasms using a vibrator, so we know it can be done. Your particular gal pal may not be able to reach such levels of superwomanhood, but you don't need to have a dick that vibrates either to hit her sweet spot. The reason most women haven't been on the multiple orgasm roller coaster isn't because there bodies aren't capable it's that thier lovers' aren't. Sure, we all now where the clitoris is (or you should by the time you've reached this chapter), yet most women (and even more men) haven't a clue about her G-spot, such as who, what, when, where, and sometimes even why.

AIN'T NOTHIN' BUT A "G" THANG

When you hear world sexual records regarding multiple orgasms, invariably you're talking about orgasms that happen as a result of stimulating the G-spot. Sure, clitoral orgasms are the most common, but most women find it tough to hit the high notes more than once with clitoral stimulation alone, and in fact, like us guys, women typically need a breather after a clitoral orgasm.

Despite rumors to the contrary, an orgasm isn't an orgasm isn't an orgasm. There's a difference between orgasms from vaginal, clitoral, anal, and even breast stimulation (for those women who are so lucky). Sure they might all feel about the same, but a G-spot orgasm not only feels different (when it works–not all women seem to have them), it also gets her body to react differently.

KEEP HER COMIN'

First, it causes what those who study sex for a living (regretting that career decision now?) call a "push out" orgasm. What happens is the area around the G-spot, and those further inside, seem to swell up or to contract toward the opening of her vagina. Now here's sex wizard tip numero uno: If you can discover the right combination of pushing back when this happens and slacking off to let it push out, you can cause her orgasm (as well as her sheer adoration for everything about you) to

99 EUPHEMISMS FOR HAVING SEX

How fast wouldja have been elected class president if you'd have had your mitts on this list in junior high? Faster than Macaulay Culkin chucked his custard the first time he ever saw a pink velvet sausage wallet.

- administer an ad hoc pelvic exam
- apply ointment to her ax wound
- ask the most "probing" question of all
- beat her with an ugly stick
- beating around the bush
- bob for apples
- bump uglies
- bury the hobbit
- bury the sausage
- buzz the brillo
- check her oil
- chuck the muck
- clear the custard
- dance the matrimonial polka
- deionize her antimatter
- dip the wick
- disappear up the wizard's sleeve
- discharge one's porridge gun
- do dirty work at the crossroads
- do front-door work
- do the four-legged frolic
- do the horizontal bop
- do the wild thing
- drain the spuds
- dunk the cruller
- empty the nads
- enjoy a flesh session
- feed the kitty

99 EUPHEMISMS FOR HAVING SEX CONT...

- **fluff her pillows**
- free Willy
- **get a bit of cauliflower**
- get a leg over
- **get into the nappy dugout**
- get one's swerve on
- **get sucked into the black hole**
- get the giddie
- **get your canoe shellacked**
- get your jollies
- **get your leather stretched**
- give her a portion of tube-steak
- **give her the high hard one**
- glaze the doughnut
- **go digging for truffles**
- go for a poke in the whiskers
- **go in through the double doors**
- go like a rat up a rhododendron
- **go spelunking**
- go trick-or-treating
- **have a navel engagement**
- hoe on the pink allotments
- **horizontal jogging**
- infiltrate enemy lines
- **initiate the docking sequence**
- invade the tuna Slinky
- **lay pipe**
- lose the match and pocket the stake

continue happening for a considerably extended period of time.

Some women are even able to be kept at a raised level of sexual excitement, kinda like a prolonged orgasm, afterward, building up to an even bigger climax. In fact, it's entirely possible to keep this pattern of build up, orgasm, plateau, orgasm, build up, orgasm for over four freakin' hours (and no, we definitely shit you not). As if things couldn't get any better, usually there's a pyramid effect that happens with multiple G-spot orgasms; each one makes the next one feel better and makes almost anything else sexual feel better, too. Pull this one off and not only will she vow to be your sexual slave for life, but she will probably offer up her friends and family as collateral.

PLEASE...DON'T...STOP...

Once you've got her in the throws of her first G-spot orgasm, don't wait until her contractions die down to start in on the next one. The outer third of her vagina and her inner labia are still engorged and ripe for another climax. Unless the first one left her spent and virtually anaesthetized, the second will come easier, faster and might even be more intense.

Of course, if she's not quite ready for another orgasm, the best thing to do is to give her nongenital stimulation, plenty of caresses and kisses, and work slowly towards achieving another variety of orgasm, like clitoral, vaginal or (if you're so lucky) anal (see Chapter 7).

To help her along with the more difficult varieties of orgasm – such as the vaginal orgasm – can be had by simply using a bit of imagination. During actual intercourse, either of you should be stroking her clitoris with their fingers. The moment she feels she's getting close to coming, stop the finger flicking completely and have her intensify her pelvic movements and work on vaginal muscle contractions to create extra friction. The contractions should be repeated as fast and as often as possible, held as long as possible, and coupled with the most stimulating pelvic thrusts.

STRANGE SEX LAWS

Before you go traveling, it's important to know the local penile code.

■ In California, not only is it illegal for any animal to mate within 1,500 feet of a tavern, school, or place of worship, but in San Francisco, there's a law stating that the giving or receiving of oral sex is strictly prohibited.

■ Some of the stranger sex laws in Florida are: having sexual relations with a porcupine is illegal; the only lawful sex position is the missionary position; and, San Francisco, oral sex is considered criminal. Oh, yeah, and you also aren't allowed to kiss your wife's breasts.

■ Long before Mississippi considered making it illegal for men to be aroused in public, Indiana already had a law on the books that considers a man guilty of indecent exposure with his "showing covered male genitals in a discernibly turgid state."

■ North Carolina has some wacky sex laws. First, if you're having sex, you must stay in the missionary position and have the shades pulled. Of course, don't even think about having oral sex; it's considered a crime against nature. Also, if a couple is staying in a motel for the night, state law mandates that they stay in a room with twin beds, kept a minimum of two feet apart, with making love on the floor between the beds strictly forbidden.

■ In Louisiana, a prostitute can get up to five years for giving oral sex (a "crime against nature") for money, but will only get a maximum of six months if it's actual intercourse.

■ In Singapore it's illegal to walk around in your house naked, as it's considered pornography, which is also illegal. Just for the record, oral sex is also against the law "unless it's used as a form of foreplay."

■ Tasmanian widows as well as aboriginal women in Gippsland, Australia are required by law to wear their recently dead husband's penis around their neck.

■ Apparently, unlawful sex with llamas was such a problem that the Incas actually passed a law requiring that llama drivers be escorted by chaperones at all times to keep them from copulating with their animals.

99 EUPHEMISMS FOR HAVING SEX CONT...

- make a deposit in her sperm bank
- make a protein shake
- make salad dressing
- make tadpole yogurt
- make tapioca
- oil her springs
- open her passion flaps
- pack the barrel
- part the roast beef curtains
- perform genetic engineering
- play hide-the-salami
- play the naked fun game
- play Where's Waldo?
- poke in the whiskers
- put four quarters on the spit
- ride the bologna pony
- rumpy-pumpy
- shampoo the rug
- sink the soldier
- slap and tickle
- slip her the H.B.I. (hot beef injection)
- slip her the pig
- slip her the weasel
- spear the bearded clam
- splash one's population paste
- split the beard
- spread the gospel
- sweep out her chimney
- take a trip to Hairyfordshire
- take a turn on shooter's hill
- take the old skin boat to tuna town
- tenderize the V-bone steak
- test out the big bang theory
- the 2-minute freestyle floor exercise

HOW TO HAVE SEX IN SPACE

One small step for man… one giant notch for your bedpost.

Really want to go where no man has gone before? Then be the first to officially get your rocks off in space. NASA won't confirm whether members of U.S. shuttle crews have ever gotten astro-naughty, but "we've been flying coed missions since the early '80s," notes aerospace consultant and former NASA flight surgeon Patricia Santy. "If nothing's happened up there, astronauts are less imaginative than I expected." Should you somehow manage to make it into orbit with an agreeable docking target, here's how to rendezvous.

■ We Have Liftoff!

Though the rush of a nine-minute, 18,000-mile-an-hour launch may be the ultimate aphrodisiac, you'll want to wait at least three days into your mission before making the first move; it'll take that long for your body to fully recover. "Besides, there are bigger priorities during the first 72 hours," says Santy, "like not throwing up." Need a good opening line? Tell her that watching a sunrise always gets you hot: Once you're in orbit, there's one every 90 minutes.

■ May the Force Be With You

If pushing off with a finger can send an astronaut flying, imagine what all that buck-naked rogering can do. As you prepare for the final frontier, make a quick inspection of your cabin. Watch for any stray probes or protrusions; in zero-G, any surface is a potential headboard. While futuristic contraptions like elastic harnesses and Velcro suits make for good science fiction, they aren't necessary for landing the *Eagle*. "All you have to do," says Santy, "is just hang on."

■ Space Oddities

Before you engage in exoatmospheric foreplay, you'll discover that your fluids have begun to pool in your upper body, and as these fluids are redistributed your stomach may appear flatter and your chest more ripped. Bonus: You may notice a similarly enticing effect on women. Sadly, the lack of gravity also makes your kidneys work overtime, so make a trip to the head before you get close to her O-ring. Otherwise, Houston, you'll have a problem.

■ Shields Up!

Don't want to end up with a little *Sputnik* of your own? "NASA hasn't studied the effectiveness of birth control in outer space," cautions Santy. You'll have to rely on barrier methods: condoms, diaphragms, lunar-sample baggies—whatever. And as you splash down, remember: The loss of cohesion in zero gravity reduces liquids to millions of individual droplets; that applies to bodily fluids too. Like in *Apollo 13*, withdrawal is not an option.

HOW TO FENG SHUI YOUR BEDROOM

Forget jewelry and expensive dinners: If you want surefire action, just redecorate.

"What's on the walls, the color of the sheets, right down to where you put your toothbrush, affect and reflect you because you put it there," says Karen Rauch Carter, author of *Move Your Stuff, Change Your Life*. While the Chinese art of feng shui may sound like the equivalent of a wet T-shirt contest in Appalachia—in other words, hogwash—chances are your girl thinks it's the best thing since *Oprah*. Even if she's not into it, you'll come across as wise in the secret ways of the East, which definitely won't hurt your chances in bed.

TAKE THE SNIFF TEST

Send your dirty sweat socks and shorts to the Laundromat and open the window to air the room out. You're going to have to spend a little time cleaning, and that includes all those hidden spots where you normally shove everything. "Clutter under the bed suggests there's clutter in the bed," says Carter. "And a door that doesn't open all the way communicates you're stuck in your ways." (See how logical all this is? And the Chinese had to smoke opium to figure this out!) Spray the room lightly with a citrus scent. Cut some fresh flowers from your neighbor's garden and stick them in a vase on the bookshelf.

LOSE THE NEGATIVE IMAGES

You want the room to feel warm and inviting, so dim the lights: Harsh fluorescents give your sexual encounter all the romance of a gynecological exam. A computer or television in the room means you're a workaholic or a couch potato. Move 'em out. Toss all pictures of women (especially the one of Mom), as well as any images of volcanic eruptions (too violent), winter scenes (frigid), and sports figures (juvenile). Replace them with landscape posters of warm sunsets or grassy fields. Invest in flesh-colored lampshades or curtains—one word you want her thinking in your bedroom is *naked*.

LOOK LIKE RELATIONSHIP MATERIAL

Now it's time to focus your attention on the part of the room where all the action will take place Push the head of the bed against the wall so both of you can get in without a struggle—cutting off one side screams selfish bastard. "Trade in the twin bed for a double," says Carter. "If you can't afford to upgrade, at least invest in two pillows." Put a few plants by the window (but not the kind that grow in Phototrons) to show you've got the maturity to maintain life.

THINK HEAT

Strategically place two red candles, symbolic of the two of you, in the far right-hand corner opposite the door. According to feng shui, this is the sex-and-relationship corner. "If you heat up this corner, you heat up your sex life," says Carter. Since red is both the color of love and an energy stimulator, she'll be very impressed by your attention to detail. Leave sensual foods, like champagne and chocolate, within reach of the bed. Now that she's hotter than South Hades in July, put the book away and get down to business.

ROLLING OFF: YOUR GUIDE TO POST-COITAL ETIQUETTE

The number of books that've been written on how to get from horny with no solid leads to bathing in the afterglow could fill the Library of Congress, but nary a word has been written about what the hell you're supposed to do once you've seen the show and just want to get some sleep. But then again, we're not like most sex books (we're the one with the naked-Mark-Twain jokes). From that first postcoital smoke to promising "I'll Call You," we got you covered.

THE MOURNING AFTER

One-night stands can be hot, harmless, ego-boosting romps. But you've got to master the simple rules of disengagement.

This is the story of how a man named Bob came to be sitting in the middle of an important business meeting covered from head to toe in amaretto sour. It isn't a pretty story. But it's a story that may save you from the same fate.

See, one night Bob went with some friends to a nice nightspot not far from his office. There he met a girl—he doesn't remember her name. But after buying her several amaretto sours, he convinced her to show him her pretty new Laura Ashley sheets. Bob saw the sheets. Bob soiled the sheets. And then, when the girl had fallen asleep, Bob got the hell out of Dodge.

A clean escape—no muss, no fuss. But what Bob didn't figure on was that he might run into the lady in question again. Weeks later, when he took a gaggle of Internet entrepreneurs out for dinner, she spotted him from across the bar. She took revenge. Bob took a bath. And the entrepreneurs took their very valuable IPO business elsewhere. Hence our little lesson for this month:

If you're going to make a one-night-only appearance in somebody's bed, you'd better know how to make a graceful disappearance. Here's your at-a-glance guide to sex exit etiquette.

ESCAPE PLAN #1: THE SOCIAL CIRCLE HOOKUP

Sarah met Harry at a friend's party. In the hallway, just by the door, they started talking about rock climbing. When they ducked out for a "cigarette," no one saw them leave. And when he slithered out of Sarah's apartment a few hours later, she never saw him leave. "I woke up and he was gone. No note, no business card. I had to call my friend to make sure I didn't make him up!" The party's hostess was just as pissed about his behavior, which is why Sarah didn't feel so bad telling her about what she thought were cold sores on his lower extremities. Soon Harry became "Herpes Harry," and needless to say, he had some trouble getting dates among their circle of friends.

Be it at a party, a work conference, or your favorite bar, this kind of hookup is fraught with danger. Here's how to exit with your rep intact:

■ Please her. This is your one chance to prove to her—and everyone the two of you know—that you can play a clitoris like a clarinet. So make sure your pleasure is reciprocated, whether that involves extended aerobics, contortionist positioning, or donning scuba gear.

■ Check for "get lost" signals. Bolting too early—or hanging around too long—can turn a perfectly good romp into an awkward ordeal. To gauge where she stands, watch for split signals such as these: "I usually say something about having to get up early," offers Grace, 28. Jeanine, 31, is more proactive: "I put on my pj's. That usually kills any hope of an encore." And then there's Jessica's surefire boot: "I once went to the kitchen and brought back a Coke. Nothing like a nice jolt of caffeine to make sure he wouldn't pass out in my bed!"

■ Don't apologize. "I went home with this guy I'd met at a party, just to get myself one layer past my ex-boyfriend," says Fran. "The guy was still taking the gooey condom off when he started apologizing to me about the 'big mistake' he had just made, how he 'really couldn't go down this road right now.' I just started laughing. I barely knew the guy. What road did he think I was on?" To avoid hearing chuckles while pulling a wet rubber off a deflated penis, try a compliment instead. "A simple 'You really got me excited' or 'That was out of control' usually works," offers Fran.

■ Don't make promises. One thing all women agree on: Never, ever ask for her number if you don't plan to use it. "I think guys do this out of guilt," says Meg, whose "holiday hookup" once invited her to go ice-skating before disappearing without a trace. "All they are doing is setting a woman up for an

99 EUPHEMISMS FOR HAVING SEX CONT...

- the horizontal hula
- thread the needle
- throw a rod
- tie a true lover's knot
- tip one's concrete
- to be up to one's nuts in guts
- uncover the flower of her secret
- varnish your cane
- wear a fish mitten

insult." Instead, mention the next time you might run into each other. A simple " So I guess I'll see you in the broom closet" will do.

ESCAPE PLAN #2: THE FIX-UP HOOKUP

Before Fran even met Kevin, she was convinced he was "it." Her friend Janie spent four months talking about how perfect they'd be together. Of course, no one could live up to the hype, and Kevin and Fran fell flat—on her bed. "I thought maybe if we had sex, the chemistry would kick in," says Fran. "Ha! Nice try." When it was over, they were suddenly left with two disasters: bad date and bad sex.

To avoid disappointing your matchmakers—and keep them eager to introduce you to beddable women—you need to get your postcoital story straight.

■ Keep it honest. When friends are involved, keep in mind that everything is on the record. And keep in mind that anything you say ("I'm moving to Hong Kong") can be fact-checked with the matchmaker. Telling her that you're not over your ex, while effective for most types of hookups, can backfire with the fix-up: She will resent her friend for setting her up with someone who 'just wasn't ready.'

■ Agree on what happened. Whether you confirm or deny the swapping of bodily fluids, you and your one-time partner will wind up reporting back—so your stories had better match. "Before Kevin left," Fran explains, "we agreed on our story, which was basically 'We kissed, but nothing else happened.' It allowed us to rewrite the evening." After all, if two people have sex and no one hears about it, did it really happen?

ESCAPE PLAN #3: THE COWORKER HOOKUP

You and she have enjoyed one of those fun, flirty office relationships. But after you watched her limbo at the office holiday party, the two of you debriefed each other in a whole new way.

Steady, Dr. Evil. Colleague sex requires some limber after-moves, since it is governed by the rules of the workplace. Don't even think about bolting without a closing remark. If you have to go to work the very next day, you have the perfect out: You don't want to show up at work wearing a repeat tie, smelling of cube-next-door perfume.

■ Leave it ambiguous. You need to know exactly what her expectations are before you make any drastic declarations. Maybe she feels terribly guilty and just wants to forget the whole thing. Or maybe she's got a cousin who's a lawyer, and she fell asleep in your arms dreaming of big sexual-harassment bucks. So leave your parting shot open-ended, as Grace's coworker did: "He kissed me good-bye, quickly, and said, 'Thanks for a fun evening; I had a good time.' It was a nice ambiguous ending."

■ Follow-up is inevitable, so get it over with. E-mail is a nice detached way to address the issue, if you keep it clean and cryptic. Address the event, and reassure her it'll go "in the vault." n Stop the insanity. If you find her lingering by your water cooler a week later, you may need to take additional steps. Grace E-mailed I-had-a-good-time man the following week to invite him out for drinks. "He sent back an invitation to a group happy hour, and I got the idea."

ESCAPE PLAN #4: THE EX-GIRLFRIEND HOOKUP

Two months after Dave broke it off with Annie, he had one of those inevitable drunken moments: Lonely and buzzed late at night, he called her. Moments after ejaculation, Dave realized that breaking up with Annie was the best thing he'd ever done—and that Annie now thought they were an item again. How can you keep a moment of weakness from turning into six more months of a lousy relationship?

■ Admit you screwed up. "I think it's best when they try the we're-in-this-mistake-together approach," explains Grace. Something along the lines of "That was kind of foolish of us" is a reliable fail-safe.

■ Don't rehash the relationship. You'll be tempted to explain all the reasons why the two of you aren't compatible. Don't. In the end, remember that women have one-night stands for the same reasons men do: because they're lonely, they're horny, or they want to sample as many dishes as possible before deciding which one to commit to. So don't punish her for the grave error of finding you attractive. The world is small, and you don't want your penile code dissuading others who might fear meeting the same fate.

HOW TO MAKE HER SHUT UP AND GO TO SLEEP

The best weapon you've got against her pointless yappin'…is your own pointless yappin'.

1. Recite dialogue from *Caddyshack*.

2. Show her your high school yearbook and point out your friends, point out your enemies, point out your enemies who used to be your friends, etc. Describe an incident that took place on a Saturday night long ago and involved a few of the people you've mentioned. Refer to them by first name, and act as if she knows them and cares.

3. Explain what *MLB, NCAA, NBA, WWF, NHL, NFC, AFC, Navy SEALs, radar, scuba*, and *NASDAQ* stand for.

4. Exhaustively describe your weightlifting history (e.g., "When I was 14, I could only bench the bar—but now I'm huge. I can bench two plates on each side. And I've done even better on the decline bench…").

5. Show her your baseball card collection and describe to her the monetary as well as the spiritual value of a Wade Boggs rookie card. Explain the various functions of the protective plastic sheath and those of other storage options you may someday employ.

6. Tell her a "really funny" story about something that happened to you—one you've told her before. As you relate it, pause several times to crack up at your own hilarious insights. Halfway through, go back and start again, telling it in exactly the same way with exactly the same inflections.

7. Pop *Larry Bird: A Basketball Legend* into the VCR. Keep shouting, "He's the greatest white man ever to play the game!"

8. Tell her your great screenplay idea.

9. Show her how you can make the hockey video game players "bleed."

10. Tell her about a problem you're having with your boss. Begin with "I'd really like your advice…," then forget you said that and continue to deconstruct the situation down to its minutiae until you figure out the solution on your own.

11. Talk about the episode of *The Dukes of Hazzard* that made you want to move to Hazzard County and get a car like the General Lee. Explain how Cooter went on to become a congressman and how his eventual loss to Newt Gingrich was the beginning of the downfall of American politics.

12. Chat about music or golf.

SHE'S TALKING ABOUT YOU

The way a woman replays a night with you makes men's locker-room talk sound like five year olds describing how babies are made. Nancy Miller invites you to eavesdrop.

When a guy describes sex with a woman to his buddies, he'll most likely say it was "good" or "real good." Meanwhile, a woman's post-sex play-by-play can get so detailed, she'll plug in the overhead projector and reenact the encounter with finger puppets (hopefully not the pinkie) to describe it to her friends. What is your woman spilling about you? Well, that depends on who you are, what you did, and how she feels about you. (And how many beers she's had–many a woman, after she's downed three bottles of Truth Serum Lite, will sing like a Japanese businessman in a karaoke bar.) Here are five major postcoital scenarios that will have her either leaking only little details, or serving up sex stories like mac and cheese at a church potluck.

SCENARIO #1: YOU HAD A ONE-NIGHT STAND

You met. You had sex. You spent the night. The next morning, 10 seconds after you hit the bricks, you better believe she dialed up her best friend and said, "Yeah, baby! I got lucky last night. Let's meet for brunch." Then, over egg-white omelets and coffee, they talk about your dick. Hey, she didn't plan on giving an inch-by-inch rundown of your love fest, but most likely she's aided and abetted in her post-sex recap by a few good friends who like to ask questions—and won't settle for "It was…nice." And, of course, because she knows them a lot better than she knows you, she's obliged to answer.

"My friends expect me to tell them all the details—and I mean all. Especially if it's just a cheesy one-night stand," says Julie, 26. "I had sworn off one-night stands because they always make me feel like shit the next day, but this guy was totally worth it. I met him at a friend's party, and after we hung out for three hours, I asked him back to my place. He was a total rock star in bed. We screwed five times, the sun came up, and then we passed out. When I saw my friends the next day (who had seen me the night before, drunk and making out with this man at the party), they asked, 'How's the no-sex mandate holding up?' And I said, 'Not that well. I got the shit shagged out of me last night by a guy hung like Tommy Lee.' And my friends were like, 'Wow. Was he cut or uncut? What did his ass look like? Did he have finesse or was he just a pile driver? Did he get you off, or was it all about him?' And I told it all."

Like men, women dish about one-night stands because of the conquest factor, but on the other hand, women also reveal sexploits as a way to absolve each other. See, now that the night is over and the sexual hangover is kicking in, she's starting to feel guilty that she got buck nekkid and beyond with a complete stranger, so she needs the support of her friends to convince her there's not a corner on West 42nd Street with her name on it. "When the Tommy Lee guy left, I wasn't sorry it happened," says Julie, "but I felt like he thought I was easy, so I quickly called the friend I knew would say 'Good for you! You got what you wanted!'" Which she did. "And I felt less slutty."

The most important thing for you to remember here is that despite the wham-bam nature of your liaison, in fact because of it, there is no town big enough for you if you botch your one-shot escapades by being selfish in the sack. Even if neither of you plans on seeing the other again, your one-night-only behavior counts if you ever want to sleep with anyone even remotely part of her social circle.

SCENARIO #2: YOU HAD SEX TOGETHER FOR THE FIRST TIME

Unlike the one-night stand, you two actually made an effort, went out on a few dates, found out each other's last names, and watched each other eat before you went at it like greased weasels. What you two have now is the beginnings of a relationship, so this isn't one-night sex, it's opening-night sex. She's sleeping with you presumably because she also likes you as a person. As a result, if you break a sweat in an attempt to make her happy, she's willing to be a pretty forgiving critic.

"The first time I have sex with a guy that I'm dating, if we just totally clicked and it was indeed great, I will offer up to my friends, 'This new guy I'm dating is one good fuck,'" says Diana, 29. "But I'm not expecting miracles the first time around, because great sex can take time to develop. So if I really dig him, I may not even mention that we had sex to my friends. If they ask me directly, though, I'll say it was good even if it wasn't, because I'm optimistic that it will be in the future." In other words, unless you are a complete jerk in bed, she won't sell you out.

SCENARIO #3: WHOA–YOU TWO DID SOMETHING SERIOUSLY KINKY LAST NIGHT

Once the hood's off and the handcuffs are back in the sock drawer, the tale of your late-night leather party will be out before her whip marks fade. "You will never believe what I did last night..." is how a woman starts this conversation— completely unprompted, but totally welcomed, by her friends. "It's hard to resist telling your girlfriends about sex that's out of the ordinary," says Gina, 30. "My friend loved telling me about how she and her boyfriend used one of those coin booths with a real woman behind the glass who does what you tell her. He would tell the woman to touch herself and then whisper to my friend how he wanted to go home and do all those things to her. It sounded really cool."

This is a case in which loose lips can be a boon to you. Call it perv peer pressure, but for a lot of women, trying kinky sex seems more, well, normal if their friends are doing it: "I'm a million times more likely to try something fetish-indulging if I've spoken to my friends who have tried it," says Gina. "Once I hear that someone else dressed up in rubber or bought a harness or whatever, it seems more acceptable. Just watching porn actresses do it is not enough."

SCENARIO #4: YOU DID SOMETHING REALLY EMBARRASSING—AND HILARIOUS—IN BED

The good news is, she's talking about you. The bad news is, it's punctuated by the hysterical laughter of five of her friends. But let's face it: Funny shit happens during sex. We're naked, vulnerable, aiming to please, aiming to get pleased. The average woman will share a story that's amusing not to embarrass you, but because it's genuinely entertaining as slapstick.

"My boyfriend once tried to surprise me with these extra-sexy satin sheets," recalls Chandra, 32. "When I walked into the room, he was standing there naked, excitedly pointing to the bed. 'Look what I got!' he said as he jumped on the bed and proceeded to slide all the way across the sheets, slamming his head into the headboard. He was actually knocked unconscious for a few seconds. After I knew he was OK, we couldn't stop laughing. I had to share that one with my friends."

SCENARIO # 5: YOU BOUNCED HER—BAD.

Yes, he dumped me, but I will always remember him as the best lover I ever had.

Wouldn't it be great if women thought like that? Dream on. If there is any time a woman will talk about the worth of your girth, it's after she's been canned. The general rule: The size of your penis is inversely proportional to the way you treated her—the bigger a dick you were in the relationship, the smaller your dick gets when she talks about you after it's over. And if you dumped her, it's no holds barred—especially if your breakup was particularly ugly.

"My boyfriend of two years dumped me to be with someone else, and it really stung," remembers Mavis, 28. "So I went out with my friends, and I was ticking off all the things that pissed me off , including his behavior in the sack. I imitated his 'cum face,' and I also revealed that when he came, it was 'game over,' like a pinball machine. The last thing I said was 'Oh, I don't care. His package smelled like sweat socks anyway.' And all of my friends laughed and were like, 'Really?' and then I said, 'Yeah, and he had a wiener the size of a champagne cork.' I wouldn't have done that if we had parted friends." So keep breakups clean .Not only because it's the right thing to do, but also because your sexual rep depends on it, Slick.

Think Kink

The same old same old ain't exactly floating your boat? Not sure how exactly to get your girl to don the gas mask? Well, don't think you're trapped in a sex rut. Upping the ante is easier than you think. This chapter will help you figure out how you and the little missus can incorporate toys, fantasy role-play, porn, anal sex, phone sex, and other antics into your erotic life, and that's just the foreplay.

THIRD-PARTY SUPPLIES

And we're not talking about an extra woman…yet.)

For those who are worried that letting their lady pick up a "joy buzzer" (if you know what we mean) will completely eliminate their usefulness (you should've never taught her how to parallel park, either), fuhgeddaboutit. "These little machines are not terrific by themselves," reassures Taryn, 25. "A piece of motorized plastic will never be able to replace a lover's touch." And stop worrying that you're just not enough man for her. "I never feel like I have to resort to using props for sex," says Marisabel, 24. "Toys simply add a little occasional variety." In other words, they just let you have more fun in bed.

Sex toys are also a perfect way for her to show you exactly what sends her over the edge. They even give you an extra hand when the two you have can't find all her hard-to-reach passion points or when you'd rather call a rainout after only one inning. So use the toy advantage to keep her guessing and eagerly awaiting your next cool sex stunt.

THE PLAYTHING BREAKDOWN

■ Vibrators

From the ridiculously popular (and notoriously huge) Hitachi Magic Wand to the more familiar penis-shaped playthings, these devices vibrate at varying speeds to tickle the clitoris or anus—simulating what you can do with your tongue, hand, etc.

■ Genital and Anal Inserts

Dildos, G-spot ticklers, anal beads, and butt plugs all fall under the "inserts" category. They can be big or small, shaped like a penis or a thermos, soft and jelly-like, or hard and plastic, if you stick it in an orifice, it's an insert.

■ Restraints

Thrill heighteners because one person has all the power. Whether it's handcuffs, Velcro wristbands, bonds and fet-

SEX-TOY SUPPLIERS

Where to shop online, by catalog, or in-store.

■ Good Vibrations
www.goodvibes.com
(800) 289-8423 or
(415) 974-8990
Espousing the virtues of sexual health and pleasure for since 1977, this San Francisco emporium is the granddaddy of all adult stores. The shop's staffed with knowledgeable sales help, and the Web site sells toys for novices and sexperts alike, complete with reviews of staff and customer favorites.

■ Blowfish
www.blowfish.com
Definitely for more experimental couples, Blowfish sells the standard inserts, vibrators, and restraints, plus skin-contact electric gadgets, medical gloves for those with latex allergies, and other strange sundries.

■ Toys in Babeland
www.babeland.com
(800) 658-9119
Both the Seattle and New York City outposts mainly cater to women, but the slacker-esque staff is more than happy to assist hetero men and couples. Check out the in-store sex workshops and well-worn binder of porn titles.

■ Eve's Garden
www.evesgarden.com
(800) 848-3837
This female-friendly store and catalog carries toys, lingerie, even the "eroscillator," the first "scientifically engineered" vibrator that gets two thumbs up from none other than Dr. Ruth.

■ Adam & Eve
www.adameve.com
(800) 293-4654
This "sexy and secure" URL "for cheerfully consenting adults" ain't nothing like that other A&E. A comprehensive product list is organized alphabetically, and you can even join the e-mailing list to receive notices and special offers.

ters, or straps of the finest Corinthian leather, they're what you use when she says, "Tie me up, tie me down."

■ Clamps
From the simple garden variety clothespins to the more custom designed doodads, they're used to intensify sensation or pain on the nipples, genitals, and other body parts by blocking blood flow to the surrounding skin. Wussies can use clamps with an adjustable screw to change the tension level.

■ Costumes
Fantasy feeders. Who hasn't imagined his woman in a French maid's getup, cheerleader outfit, or McDonald's uniform? At some point she's probably had a costume in mind for you, too, like a slick 1920s gangster ensemble, or a firefighter's uniform.

■ Sex Games
Playthings that encourage experimentation such as Naughty Checkers (the pieces are shaped like penises and boobs) and Glow in the Dark Foreplay Dice are just two examples of wacky games that you can buy.

WHOSE IDEA WAS THIS?

Toys for the advanced, adventurous, and possibly psychotic.

■ Dungeon in a Box
It's the dungeon for the man on the go. The Tetruss is a portable, free-standing suspension system for folks who just don't have the space to maintain a fully equipped den of sin at home. (www.galensrealm.com).

■ Custom-Made Furniture
The next time she tries to drag you to IKEA, tell her that Sweden doesn't make Oral Sex Chairs, but Kinky Joe, a Brooklyn, New York, carpenter and self-proclaimed "pioneer of ergonomic erotica," does. His furniture for fucking (and other miscellaneous activities) blends almost seamlessly with the rest of your living room set. (www.kinkyjoe.com).

■ Electrode Sex Toys
Some erotic aids—including egg-shaped vaginal inserts, whips, cock rings, and butt plugs—are also available in electrical form. These goodies may come with voltage isolators, body contact pads, adapters, and other accessories. Whatever you do, don't place them above the waist—the electrical current could pass near or through your heart, stopping it in the process. Order these only from authorized dealers, which include The Noose in New York City (212-807-1789) and Blowfish, and keep away from water.

■ Cock and Ball Restraints
These are for encasing the penis, scrotum, or both in order to deprive your peter of all sensation and prevent orgasm. You can improvise with household bindings like string, rope or Saran Wrap, or you can buy torture sheaths of rubber, PVC, metal, or leather. After the restraint is removed, your dick is extremely sensitive and receptive to touch.

IF MAXIM MADE SEX TOYS

If the evil geniuses behind her love machines can rake in profits bringing faster-than-a-speeding-bullet orgasms to women everywhere, surely we can invent our own dynamite doohickeys.

Oral Sex Alarm Clock His/Hers Duo: These bedside appliances are remotely connected to a wireless Butterfly strap-on for her and a well-lubed silicone sheath for your manhood. Instead of a noisy alarm jarring you out of deep sleep, you'll both wake up getting slow, gentle head.

Sooper-Sexx Shakes and Softee Supplements: Sexx Shakes work quicker than Viagra, giving you that immediate erectile boost to make it through a long night of lovin'. If your sergeant is saluting at an embarrassingly bad time, pop a chewable Softee Supplement to instantly knock him down (regular and lactose-free available).

Remote Climax Control: For the TV junkie too lazy to slide over to her side of the sofa for a quickie, this remote control sex toy sees her slipping on special panties before you and she settle down for some boob-tube time. If she starts whining when *WWF Smackdown!* comes on, point the remote at her, punch in *69, and hit enter. The resulting orgasmic jolt will keep her grinning.

HER FIRST VIBRATOR: TIPS AND TRICKS FOR SEDUCING A SEX-TOY VIRGIN

You've decided to treat her to a sex toy. Good for you! But how to proceed? Unless you want to get smacked in the head with a half-unwrapped vibrator, it's probably not a good idea to just go out and get her one. Women are picky about shoes, for God's sake. Better to test the waters by doing the following:

ASSESS SEX TOYS FROM AFAR.

If you're passing a sex-toy store or come across a sex-toy catalog, ask offhandedly, almost academically, "Hmm, a sex toy. What do you think of that?" Sandor Gardos, Ph. D., a San Francisco–based clinical sexologist, suggests that this roundabout approach is especially helpful if your lady love is on the shy side. "Avoiding 'you' statements will give her a chance to air her opinions without feeling put on the spot," he explains. If she says she thinks sex toys are cool, that's good. If she thinks sex toys are all huge plastic penises and that sex shops are shady—debate her, even argue with her. Just keep it objective. No, "You're such a freak. What are you scared of?"

SHARE FANTASIES

A fantasy is the carte blanche of sexual communication: You can say what you want but don't need to follow through. "No one can disagree with a fantasy, because it's not meant to be a reality," says Gardos. After you've told her that you fantasize about her getting off with a sex toy, ask her if she's ever imagined something similar. If she says no, no harm done. If she says yes, that's a big green light. Proceed.

THINK TOY, NOT TOOL

A vibrator may cause your girlfriend to climax faster, more frequently, and in more positions than ever before, encouraging you in turn to bill this toy as the answer to all your problems. Don't be tempted. Why? Because this attitude turns your girlfriend's sexual apparatus into...well...a problem. "When suggesting a sex toy, don't say, 'You're not having an orgasm. Something must be wrong. Let's get a vibrator,'" says Carol Queen, Ed. D., a sex educator and author of *Real Live Nude Girl: Chronicles of Sex-Positive Culture*. Instead, treat sex toys like a romantic trip to Maui by saying "Wouldn't it be fun to try something new?" Women prefer adventures to repair jobs.

4. CHECK THE PRESSURE

"Since your upper lip has the equivalent number of nerve endings as a woman's vagina, testing it on your lip will give you a good idea of what a vibrator will feel like on her," says Juli Ashton, co-host of *Playboy TV Nightcalls*. Get her warmed up by starting on her shoulders or feet and work your way down or up.

5. FOCUS ON HER

Although toys demand a lot of attention, don't forget to check on the living, breathing woman on the receiving end of the goings-on. Look up at her from time to time and gauge her sexual response. It's not a race. Slow down and enjoy the scenery.

6. GET SOME PLAY

Follow those steps and she'll be a babe in toyland before you know it.

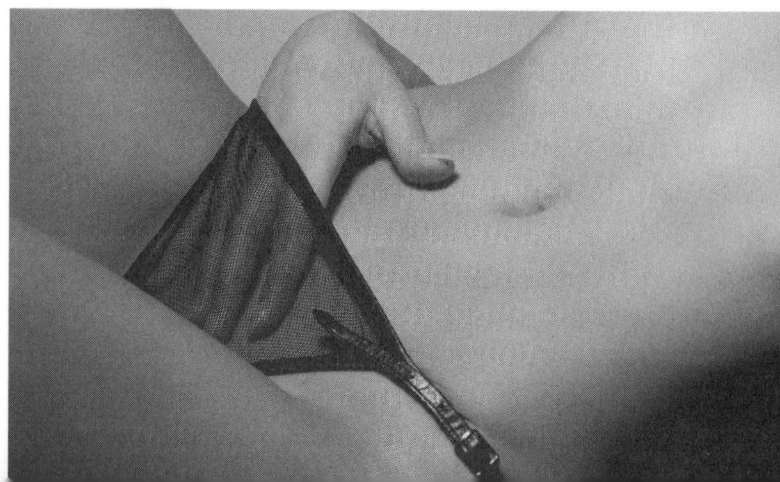

SAYS HER: SCREAM MACHINES

Got a hang-up about sex toys? They'll never replace you—they'll just make her want you more. One woman explains:

We thought you guys loved gadgets. You don't rake the yard; you Weedwack it. You'd never paint the house without some diesel-powered nozzle doohickey. And we womenfolk know how turfy you get with the TV remote. So what's with the hang-up over sex toys?

Relax, guys. We're not out to replace you. These battery-powered gizmos are fun every once in a while, but there will never be a machine that can open jars, get stuff off high shelves, and pay for dinner. Besides, we like being with you. So wine us. Dine us. Romance us. And for an occasional thrill, tickle our fancy with one of these toys. Don't think of them as a threat but as yet another electronic convenience. (Note: Listed prices are approximate.)

BESTSELLER #1

■ **The Hitachi Magic Wand, $45**

What it is: OK, let's acknowledge something right away. Jiminy Cricket, but it's big! The dimensions, however, are a function of this vibrator's efficient variable-speed motor, the feature that impresses us. C'mon, guys, you thought we'd love that Maglite flashlight because it was big and powerful. And you've heard this before, but it bears repeating: It's not the size of the instrument that matters but how you play it.

How it works: For external use only, puh-leeze. And exercise caution. Put the bulbous vibrating head somewhere in the neighborhood of her clitoris and let her talk you toward the bull's-eye.

Who it's for: An adventurous woman and a lover with a steady hand. "Often women's inability to reach orgasm has nothing to do with their bodies," says Patti Britton, Ph.D., a fellow of the American Academy of Clinical Sexologists based in Los Angeles, "but with their guilt about sex or their lack of understanding about their own sexual responses." The wand, Britton says, can "transcend their resistance—no matter what." If you can make room enough in bed for the three of you, more power to you—literally.

BESTSELLER #2

■ **Rabbit Pearl, $75**

What it is: Equipped with eyes, ears, and more pearls than your grandma's safe-deposit box, the Rabbit Pearl vibrator looks like no bunny—and no other sex toy—we've ever seen.

How it works: The Rabbit's Rube Goldberg combination of moving parts hits all the right spots. "It's one of the only vibrators designed to stimulate the vagina and the clitoris at the same time," says Claire Cavanah, co-owner of Toys in Babeland. The phallus rotates in two directions, and when it's inserted, a ring of pearls at the base of the shaft stimulates the vaginal opening. There's also a separate clitoral stimulator protruding from the toy. Turn it on and the ears (this is actually the only part of the toy that even vaguely resembles a rabbit) wiggle back and forth over her clitoris.

Who it's for: "The Rabbit isn't a starter toy," says Ellen Barnard, co-owner of A Woman's Touch, a Madison, Wisconsin, sex-toy store, who sometimes writes up a list of instructions for customers who buy it. And will all the Rabbit's wiggling and swiveling leave any room for a guy to jump in? Of course! Because if you're holding it when she comes, you get the credit and rack up a year's worth of good-sport points. Redeem them then and there for what I guarantee will be spirited lovemaking, or later for GET OUT OF BRUNCH FREE cards.

BESTSELLER #3

■ **Juli Ashton's Pink Pocket Rocket, $44**

What it is: Remember what I was saying about size? One of the most popular vibrators on the market is only a little bit bigger than your middle finger. Since its debut by Doc Johnson last year, three million of the four-inch Rockets have been sold. Last Christmas, bidding wars actually broke out. "We auctioned off the last Rocket in the store for $400," says Amy Murphy, a former marketing director for Fairvilla Megastore, a sex-toy store in Orlando, Florida.

How it works: Powered by a single AA battery, the Rocket fits neatly in her makeup bag for those romantic weekends away (hint, hint). And here's a neat trick: Put the Rocket inside an unlubricated condom that you tie off at the end and you've got a waterproof vibrator for late-night fun in the hotel pool.

Who it's for: The gal on the go and her equally active guy. It's the sex-toy equivalent of a roll of Mentos. You know the commercials where all those cute blond young people have spontaneous fun after popping a mint? The same principle applies here. It's the freshmaker!

BESTSELLER #4

■ The Butterfly, $25-$40

What it is: A couple-friendly—hell, a threesome-friendly—strap-on vibrator that will give everyone involved a bit of a buzz. "Unlike other vibrators," says Britton, "this one leaves your hands free to wander and stimulate each other wherever you want."

How it works: A woman wears the Butterfly like a jockstrap. Turn it on and it starts jiggling right where she wants it to. From then on the vibrator takes care of itself. "The Butterfly's big plus for me was when doing it doggy-style," says Michele, 29. "I like the position, but I usually don't get enough stimulation that way."

Who it's for: Cool couples. "Since sexual communication is opening up, people are breaking away from the idea that toys are a clandestine, one-person affair," says Cavanah. "We get a lot of dates in our store," she adds. "Definitely not first dates— probably fourth."

BESTSELLER #5

■ Lubricant, $6-$18

What it is: Don't take it personally if she's not as juicy as an overripe peach. It's probably not your fault. Bring a tube of lube along with the flowers, wine, and condoms. It shows you care.

How it works: Lube is a necessity when using sex toys, and a veritable stroke of genius when using condoms. The trick: Put a drop inside the condom as well as on the outside. "Just a drop will keep the tip moving around more, while the base of the condom stays put," says Barnard. "Some couples say lube works so well, it makes the condom disappear." Couples may not stop there. "We use it everywhere," says Michele. "It just makes whatever we do in bed feel sexy."

Who it's for: Everyone. "If you can take one thing onto a desert island, take lube," says Rebecca Suzanne, a former marketing manager at Good Vibrations, the original sex-toy store for women. Some of the bestsellers are Astroglide, a glycerin-based lubricant originally made to help NASA astronauts get in and out of their spacesuits and Liquid Silk, a water-based lube that's also a great moisturizer.

WHAT A GIRL WANTS

Women give their tips on using toys.

"The patterns and colors that I like for my clothes are also the ones I like for my sex toys. If your girlfriend's favorite color is purple, get her a purple dildo." —Aimee, 29

"My boyfriend had always fantasized about having sex with a cop, so I bought a skimpy police uniform for me and a prisoner's outfit for him. I had so much fun 'arresting' him and bossing him around."—Tammi, 33

"One guy worked a cute, medium-sized, life-like pink number like a pro, slowly entering me. And his eyes never left mine—eye contact is so sexy. And I appreciated the fact that he was ultraconfident and recognized sex toys as just another means of giving a woman pleasure."—Alexis, 24

"Don't bug her about wearing trashy-looking undies that she hates. Help her find something she likes better, or ask her to surprise you."—Rebecca, 30

"Don't use the vibrator to do something really kinky or unexpected. Just lube her up, put it gently on the clit, and let her guide you. And don't work harder than you have to—the vibrator will do the work."—Brianna, 29

"With a dildo or butt plug, size does matter, so find out her size and accommodate that. It's easy to get one that's either too big or too small. Some guys might not want to do themselves an injustice by getting a dildo bigger than their own tool."—Meg, 33

CLEAN OUT THE CUPBOARDS: THE POOR MAN'S SEX SHOP

Just because neither of you has the bucks to spend on anal beads and chains doesn't mean you can't invest a little time and imagination into spicing up your sex life. In fact, most of what you need to get creatively kinky is probably sitting in your fridge, closet, cabinet—just about anywhere in your house. Just get MacGyver about it.

Lots of common household crap can be turned into sex gizmos like those mentioned above. (If you've never seen *9 1/2 Weeks*, you just can't call yourself an American.) For a makeshift dildo, use a zucchini or cucumber, a candle (no wider than one or two inches across—you don't want to hurt Sweetie), or anything else that's about the same width and length as your own love rocket. Make sure to slip a lubricated condom on it so that she doesn't end up with a yeast infection or internal cuts. And even though she's never said one word to you about vibrators, at one point she's probably used the washing machine or the handheld massaging shower head or the bubble jets in the Jacuzzi to give herself a quick O before you had a chance to catch her in action.

Snoop around to see what other playthings you find, like a rolling pin (you can gently roll it up and down her body for a relaxing massage), a feather duster (to tickle her), or a spatula, ruler, or small paperback book (for spanking that naughty, naughty girl). Use an electric toothbrush to gently play with her nipples or ear lobes, but to avoid electrocution or anything equally bad, don't insert it anywhere.

If the thought of handcuffs and shackles creeps her out, why not reach for something on the softer side—like handkerchiefs, neckties, or tube socks—to tie her up with? "For inexperienced women, scarves have a romance to them that chains or leather ties do not," says Betty, 28. Whatever you use, you've gotta be careful—thinner restraints tend to tie a lot more tightly than handcuffs or chains, and you don't want to cut off her circulation. (The more daring might want to try extension cords or masking tape.)

Those too embarrassed to pop into a sex shop and pick up a game of Lovers Lotto can instead create their own "dirty deck" of cards, each with sexually explicit instructions, or love coupons, redeemable for sex acts, massages, full-body sponge baths, or breakfast in bed. "If you feel like buying sexual board games for the novelty of bringing in something new, go for it," says Ron, 32. "But many of these are either really sophomoric or really hard-core, and expensive. Playing strip poker or truth or dare can be far more innovative than anything in a store."

KINKS AND HIGH JINKS

Even in these enlightened, horny-as-all-get-out times, the mention of anal sex or bondage still elicits many an "Ewww! That's sick!" from people who are now thinking what a friggin' deviant you are. (And they're right, but no one needs to know that.) However, the good news is that formerly forbidden, "kinky" stuff is becoming—dare we say?—mainstream: Madonna in a vinyl catsuit, tied to a chair, in her "Human Nature" video, Midwestern tourists flocking to S/M theme restaurants; Britney Spears getting her bellybutton pierced.

Kink's as much about crossing psychological barriers to try out the taboo as it is about personal taste; doing it doggy-style might be kinky for her but ho-hum for you. Before you and she experiment with anal sex, porn, or fetishes, read on for the best conversation starters and how-to tips.

STARFISH TROOPER: HOW TO BE A BEDROOM ASS-TRONAUT

For most people the ass is for shipping and not receiving, leading them to think that anal intercourse is about as thrilling as a root canal. Porn hasn't helped sway the masses, either. "You'll see some actor wailing away on a slab of meat, and you think that anal sex has to be painful or hard-core," complains Anna, 31. Not so. If done right, the Devil's Onion Ring can be enjoyable for all parties involved.

■ How to Initiate Anal Sex

Whether either of you is a buggering novice or veteran, you still shouldn't sneak in her back door unless you're looking to sleep on the couch for the next month. Or as Beth, 30, so eloquently puts it, "If you go there and it's not the right time for her, it can fuck the whole night up." Like your little pookie-bear herself, her anus is delicate and unpredictable—you don't want to, or have to, hurt or aggravate either of them. Remember when you first hit on her, trying to win her over with your sensitivity and charm? That's how you must treat her bunghole—in a gentlemanly fashion—in order to get anywhere. And you've got to lay down the groundwork. This isn't the kind of evening activity you decide you want at four in the afternoon.

To find out whether she's ready for an anal adventure, consider her proclivities for other perversions, like bondage or sex in public. If she's daring anyway, talking her into rectal recreation will be a piece o' cake. The woman who's hesitant to even use a sex toy or admit to masturbating is the one who's gonna give you grief.

■ Sly as a Fox

Plant the anal-sex seed. "Just ask if you're really that curious, but preferably when you're snuggling after sex and she's somewhere on cloud nine," suggests Megan, 27. "As long as you're nice about it, she won't feel like you're nagging her." Which means a little polite persistence on your part could turn tonight's no into tomorrow's yes!-yes!-yes!

■ When the Truth Will Hurt You

She'll definitely wonder why you're so eager to experiment and ask you questions like "Where the hell did you get the idea I'd want to do that?" Even if she's defensive, don't you get all defensive. Just tell her the truth: You saw it in a movie, book, or magazine, your friends were talking about it, or you've never felt so close to anyone else to try something this intimate before. Do not mention any exes you've had the exquisite joy of butt-banging in the past. If she asks, and you get the sneaking suspicion she's trying to pick a fight with you, lie, lie, lie—tell her it was lousy or that none of your old girlfriends ever wanted to try it—or else change the subject.

An already open-minded or anally experienced woman will more than likely indulge you at least one time, possibly more; whether it's your first or 50th time, consistently reassure her that her comfort is your goal. With the most rectally reluctant woman, however, you've done the equivalent

WHAT IS RIMMIING

Rimming is working your way around her butt area—cheeks, crack, butt-hole, perineum, maybe even inserting the tongue into the anal opening. And it's called the same thing when she talks to the ass.

Since this kind of oral sex involves putting your mouth to a hole that spews bodily waste, the butt licker might want to request that the lickee wash the area thoroughly, though some people get turned on by anal aromas. Even if your butthole is clean as a whistle, if you rim without a barrier (like a latex condom or dental dam), you're at risk for contracting intestinal parasites that might be native to your partner's rectum but can cause you serious illness if swallowed. Oh, there's also the problem of getting or transmitting major STDs, such as herpes.

To test the waters shower or bath together, slowly kissing and licking your woman in her front and rear nether regions to see how receptive she is to rimming or being rimmed. (You could also let her try it on you, ya know.) "Guys should understand that having that area played with feels good, too," says A.J.

of climbing Mount Everest if you got her to agree to try it even once. If you're gentle and patient and she still hates it? Resign yourself to the fact that the only anal action you'll get is gonna be in VHS or DVD form.

■ Charter the Territory

To commune with the anus, you must first know the anus. Sounds pathetically Zen, but understanding how the asshole works is essential to enjoying it. Two sphincter muscles, one on top of the other, surround the inside of this opening. You control the external sphincter when you take a dump or pass gas, while the internal sphincter tightens and relaxes at will, clenching up (and causing excruciating pain) if anything tries to unexpectedly break and enter.

Before even trying to stick your saber or a sex toy up her butt, you two need to spend time exploring this undiscovered land. Way too many people hold tension in their anus, like those "anal-retentive" types who have "a stick up their ass." Not that she's like that, but you still have to help her decompress before the anal action begins.

Shower together, draw up a hot bath for yourselves, or give her a full-body or bum-only massage. Once she's settled in to bed, do whatever you usually do to get her all wet, hot, and bothered—you can't just flip her over and start poke, poke, poking away. Proctology jokes aside, slip on a latex glove to keep from hurting her with your raggedy-ass fingernails, and squirt plenty of lubricant on your fingers. (And for God's sake, stick with water-based lubes, not Vaseline, which will take a solvent enema to clean out. Poophole potions advertised as "anal lubes" are pricey and loaded with harsh numbing agents—the water-based ones like Astroglide will suffice.)

■ We Have Entry

Lightly stroke the outside of her anus to get her used to that feeling, but make sure she's deeply inhaling and exhaling, 'cause holding her breath will tense up her whole body, including the inner sphincter. After getting her anus loosened up a bit, try inserting the tip of your index finger (but get her permission first, buddy). Aim for the front of her body, where the first part of the outer rectum curves, and pay attention to when the sphincter relaxes or tightens. If she's loosened up, you can go deeper into the rectal cavity until she tells you to stop; if she's still rigid down below, keep your finger closer to the opening and gently massage the area. And, of course, remove said finger when she's had enough. You may now return to your regularly scheduled screwing.

■ Don't Be So Anal

Practice makes for near-perfect pleasure, so get her to touch herself there whenever she normally masturbates, until she graduates from fingers to butt plugs or dildos. When she's got the art of anal relaxation and self-pleasure down pat, you kids will be ready for the show.

She should be relaxed, happy, and looking forward to the evening's erotic

WHAT IS FISTING

Remember the fisting demonstration in *Chasing Amy* that made Jason Lee and Ben Affleck cringe? Fisting, hand-balling, or whatever you want to call it, is an advanced maneuver that requires the gentle hand of a diamond-cutter with the patience of a championship-starved Patrick Ewing. It's the insertion of a hand, one finger at a time, into the vagina or anus. Once the full "fist" has made its entrance, you can penetrate deeper to the end of the birth canal (you'll hit the opening of the cervix) or the anal cavity through the rectum to the colon, or gently rock or twist your fist.

Believe it or not, fisting was not created on a drunken dare: People who enjoy this say that it creates a deeper trust and bond with their partner, while others claim the joy of fist-fucking is similar to the sensation of taking a dump or of a woman giving birth. However, it is not considered a safe sex act—be sure to use latex gloves and heavy amounts of water-based lube—and serious injury can result if you attempt it.

agenda. "Get her drunk," advises Beth. "I don't drink a lot, but if I'm cocktailed it's easier to get me in the mood." That still doesn't give you the right to surprise her with an unexpected anal intrusion. "You have to earn anal sex," adds Raquel, 29. "Take baby steps, let her control the moving, let her give you signs that she's ready."

Revving her up for the backyard boogie requires extensive foreplay (toys not mandatory), if not oral and vaginal sex, beforehand. It's her anus we're talking about here, so her enjoyment is crucial if you ever have hopes of pulling this off or doing it again. Some neat freaks prefer to clear the lower rectum with an enema or New Age-y laxative teas, but the healthy bacteria that's supposed to be in (and stay in) the intestines might still be hanging around. For most anal activity, a bath or shower cleans the area just fine.

■ Protection Where the Sun Don't Shine

Always, always, always use a latex or polyurethane condom for STD prevention, but also when you and she are 100 percent disease-free. Because you're dipping your stick into what's essentially a sewer, you can contract intestinal parasites and develop urethritis if you party without a hat. For that very reason, you may want to get some vitamin P before proceeding to the anus—you can't switch back and forth between the two without discarding one rubber and slipping on a new one.

When it comes to choosing your anal contraceptives, the Reality Female Condom may be superior to the standard jimmies you use. The condom is a larger, looser sheath of polyurethane, which is softer and stronger and allows more sensation than latex. Each Reality has a plastic ring on each end, one of which can go into the anus minutes or even hours before sex; these help it stay in place better than male condoms do. And you can easily alternate between, oral, vaginal, and anal sex without removing it.

■ Easy Does It

Another reminder that her arsehole and love canal are not one and the same: Rectal tissue is drier and easier to tear than is the self-lubing vaginal mucous, so you cannot pump her from behind as fast and hard as you do up front. You might not even be able to stick your shaft all the way into her rectum. Spooning is probably the most comfortable positions for anal intercourse—she'll love the ease with which she can back into you as Mr. Happy slips in as well as the emotional symbolism. Doggy-style, woman-on-top, or even missionary-position might be a little more animalistic than what's she ready for this early in the game.

Neither of you should make this rectum reconnaissance solely about her orgasm—a cunnilingus-loving lass or a vaginal-favoring female probably won't climax from anal sex alone. (Maybe she'd like a vibrator on her clit, or a dildo in her pussy, or handcuffs on her wrists to enhance the experience.) But if she doesn't want to feel like she's being diddled by Edward Penis Hands, she might enjoy just the anal stimulation. In which case, it's really not bullshit when she says, "It's OK if I don't come."

TAKING YOUR (SEX) ACT ON THE ROAD

How bashful or bold your gal is in her daily life (Is she outspoken or terribly polite? Does she ever wear anything revealing?) will affect her openness to trying toys, being photographed, or doing anything different in the sack, especially when it comes to public sex. And even then, you can't predict what, exactly, will turn her on—she might be OK visiting a titty bar with you but nauseated just thinking about doing the deed with an audience in plain view. You've got plenty of options—*Maxim*'s going to help you figure out how to exercise as many of them as possible.

SEX IN THE GREAT OUTDOORS

Aaahh…there's nothing like getting outside for some nookie, especially if you've been cooped up with the flu or at the office working long hours. Though you're now removed from the privacy of your home, that doesn't automatically mean you'll be happily humping away with an audience…But just in case you are, good planning on your part will increase your chances of remaining undercover (in a matter of speaking).

START WITH THE GREAT INDOORS

To get a skittish woman geared up for, or at lease willing to attempt, public lovin', you and she should indulge in a little mutual exhibitionism at home. Take turns jacking and jilling off in front of each other, add more nudity to your life (like walking naked around the house—but not in front of the kids!), or encourage her to wear more revealing clothes when you and she go out. You can also make public sex into a game as Matt, 27, did in college: "My roommate and his girlfriend, and me and my girlfriend, had a 'competition' to see who could do it in the craziest places—the St. Louis Arch, the 50-yard line at the stadium." If you're woman is competitive, she'll be just as motivated and gutsy as you.

DRESS FOR SUCCESS

Because of the high risk of getting busted, keep it short 'n' sweet. (The janitor's closet at the local DMV is no place for an hour-long schtup, jackass.) On that note, leave the underwear at home and wear clothes that are easy to remove and put back on again: Anything held together with Velcro, snaps, or zips, good; button-fly jeans and wraparound halter tops, bad. She should wear a skirt or dress that falls above the knee for the quickest, easiest access to her juicy fruit, or a longer skirt if you want to better camouflage your covert operation. If safe sex was the bargaining chip for getting her to publicly boff you in the first place, pick up a box of Reality Female Condoms—she can insert one hours before you and she get down to business.

It helps if you're totally confident (or can fake being confident) about your ability to make this particular fantasy work, even if the cops show up or things don't go exactly as you'd planned. "If you have the slightest doubt, take me back to your bedroom!" groans Sasha, 27. "Don't look around every 20 seconds like a gopher peeking out of its hole—you're supposed to be focusing on me, not on getting caught. So long as we're not doing it in front of a daycare center, chances are people won't bother us."

USE YOUR HEAD

Unless you can tell the difference between poison sumac, poison oak, and poison ivy from 30 feet back or know the habits of black bears and coral snakes, city slickers might want to steer clear of having sex in the woods. (People with insect-bite allergies will probably want to stay indoors, too.) Those who want to feel at one with nature need to check for dirt, grass, sticks, and stones before settling down on a waterproof tarp or tent. And beware of extremely hot (over 85 degrees) or cold (below 40 degrees) temperatures—the last thing you need is to freeze your asses off or faint from heatstroke.

Since you're usually thinking about sex on the job, anyway, why not treat yourself to a little rumpus around the office? (Not during work hours, of course, unless you want to take your job and shove it.) But forget the office copier—you have no idea how much, or how little, weight a thin plate of glass can hold—and aim for the boss's desk or kitchen counter, instead. Love in an elevator requires a little more discretion than a cubicle screw. Cover up the closed-circuit security camera inside (yes, even in the freight elevator); it'll be either very noticeable or tucked behind one of the lift's ceiling panels. In newer buildings, don't pull the emergency stop—help will be on the way within five minutes of activating it, whereas with older models, it can take up to two hours to respond to a call, according to Bob Farley, executive director of the National Association of Elevator Safety Authorities.

PLANES, TRAINS, AND AUTOMOBILES

Plane, train, or automobile sex can be the most thrilling hanky-panky you'll experience—but it comes with its own rules and pitfalls. To become a mile-high club member, shoot for a longer, later flight like a red-eye or trans-atlantic trip and sit near the rear-most restroom. Let her go in first, and enter her from behind (but for chrissakes, put the toilet seat down and shut the door). If you're gonna fool around in the car while driving, limit the action to driver-side blowjobs and cunnilingus only—no screwing. (Do you wanna get yourselves killed?!?) Also, stick to daytime hours and long stretches of open highway as much as possible. Keep both hands on the wheel and both eyes open and on the road. Look out for animal crossings, speed bumps, or anything else that might cause you to make a sudden stop or slow down. Oh, and don't forget to set the cruise control.

Loud, pumping music, freely flowing booze, shoulder-to-shoulder crowds—there's nothing like a nightclub or bar to get the adrenaline and hormones going (or to give you the perfect cover-up for a little X-rated bump-n-grind action with your girl). But avoid slipping into the restroom without investigating the scene first—at dive bars they can be positively filthy, and at dance clubs they're not only dirty, they're usually guarded by a 280-pound bouncers named Dino.

SEX CLUBS AND STRIP JOINTS

Sex clubs do exist but are really hard to find in the United States. Once you do discover one, keep in mind, too, that at the, ahem, lower-end establishments, roughly nine out of 10 customers are guys—and roughly 10 out of 10 of them will be jerking off to the surrounding action at some point. "The one time I went to one I was disgusted," says Beth. "Feces everywhere, dirty rooms, all marketed at a day rate. It was like an interactive theater where actors are 'planted' as audience members, except it was prostitutes planted as regular people."

ALSO ON YOUR TO-DO LIST

Pick up some lube—and use it—before doing the job downstairs (Good Vibrations sells single-use variety packs of lube), or in a pinch use saliva.

Any liquid environment (the ocean,your bathtub,a swimming pool) makes it really difficult to put on a condom underwater, so roll one on beforehand. She's also gonna need lube—water washes away her natural moisture.

Even though you want to reassure each other that you're having a good time, try to keep the grunting and moaning to a minimum—you don't want to arouse suspicion or call attention to yourselves.

One more thing: "The best situations are the spontaneous ones," says Mark, 37. Several years ago, he masturbated his girlfriend off on the front steps of New York City's largest post office. "She just wiggled out of her undies, really discreetly, and shoved them in her bag. I found it incredibly erotic. If either person has talked about public sex as a fantasy, it can be exciting to get to finally act it out. But be careful—it can also be too scripted."

To find a business with a higher quality of patron and cleanliness, flip through dirty magazines or local papers, or surf the Web.

A safer, and legal, form of live entertainment for you and your lady is a strip club. But convincing her to join you—and that she is really the one that you want, and not the silicone-enhanced, spread-eagled blonde named Candee—is going to take a lot of sensitive coaxing. And maybe bribing her with a year's worth of daily oral sex.

In case you hadn't already figured it out, most women get pissed off about your gentleman's club visits with the guys because you're doing it on the sly. Yeah, it's understandable that you'd sneak out to a strip club if she's uptight about erotic experimenting, but if you've always been honest and open-minded about sex, you have no right to go behind her back on this. Just tell her already.

Even though you went to strip joints on a far more regular basis when you were single, now that you're seeing someone, you have to ask her, and yourself, how confident she is about herself and the relationship before setting foot in one again. "So long as she is just as turned on by the women dancing as you are and knows that it's not a competition, she may very well be part and parcel of the adventure," says Michelle.

GROUP SEX

According to the North American Swing Club Association, horny hordes of people—over 5 million, in fact—enjoy swinging in their homes or at resorts catering to their erotic preference. Swinging includes group sex (you, her, plus one or more other people) and partner-swapping. Plenty of singles are into swinging, though the scene is mainly couples who relish recreational nookie with someone other than their better half. Seasoned swingers say their relationships are so strong and honest that sharing sex doesn't hurt their primary partnerships—the fact that they've boffed many others has actually helped them learn a thing or two about how to please the Mister or the Missus at home.

You and your woman have to be equally enthusiastic about experimenting to really enjoy yourselves in a group sex scenario. "Are you interested in watching each other fool around with or bang other people? If not, you're opening a can of worms," says Robert, 30. "Be open and nonjudgmental and you'll find out more about the scene." If you're overprotective of her, or if she's the kind of chick who gets miffed if you're friendly to the waitress at Hooters, swinging is not for you. However, those ready for a little rumpus can go to NASCA International's web site, www.nasca.com, to find out about swingers activities near you.

THREE'S COMPANY

So an all-out orgy with a cast of several is scaring your wee-wee into hiding (and just plain freaks her out), but you've always been curious about a ménage à trois. Most women have at least thought about gettin' it on with another female, so tricking her into... er, persuading her to give a trio a chance isn't as tough as you think. But you're pretty much asking the hetero woman in your life to engage in bisexuality. Even if it's been a fantasy of hers, making that dream come true takes finesse. As A.J., 24, an orgy veteran, so astutely points out, "You can't just say 'I want to have a threesome.' If she has a problem with toys, even, she's not gonna go for the idea of having sex with another person."

When you're reading a magazine or watching a movie or T.V. show with really hot chicks in it, casually mention how sexy you think the women are to see whether she'll respond in kind. (Warning: Don't comment on real women that either of you might see at the beach or the grocery store. There's way too much potential for a jealousy-fueled spat.) Or start talking about closing the deal with an audience—like when you're in the throes of passion, whispering, "Hey, wouldn't it be cool if someone were watching us?" If she responds with a yes, keep going with the whole idea of having another person observing...and eventually, participating in the action. If she's not so sure about it, sell the ménage experience as a way to expand your sexual repertoire. "Whether she can handle talking dirty about it or she's close-minded, she'll tell you right away," says A.J.

Watch lesbian or threesome porn films to get an idea of her interest level (or lack thereof) and to get some pointers on how you'd physically pull it off. Also, ask your girlfriend about whether she'd "interact" with the other woman or just with you; her biggest problem with a threesome might be that she just doesn't want to engage in lesbian sex play.

Now that her interest is piqued, you have to pick a woman to join you two. Tread lightly if she suggests one of her closest friends—it'll come back to haunt you if your gal suddenly thinks you're going to dump her to be with Sarah, her old college roommate. (Stay away from any of your close female pals, as well, especially the ones who have a not-so-secret crush on you. Do you want to deal with a potential stalker? Didn't think so.) But definitely don't go pick up a random female at a bar or club. (This is self-explanatory.) A sexually adventurous acquaintance would probably work best.

Once you've settled on a time and place for the ménage à trois to happen, plan a night out for the three of you, preferably with a group of friends (surrounding yourselves with familiar people will calm your nerves) and lots of booze (to loosen your inhibitions). How you decide to carry out the threesome is your choice, but remember this: Even though you're messing around with two women, your number-one priority is making sure your girlfriend is having a good time. Keep the action more intense with her than with the other woman—verbally reassure her that she's gorgeous/sexy/giving you the best blow job ever, and put 200 percent effort into getting her off. You can't totally ignore the third party, either, but don't come on to her the way you'd approach your girl: Let her attack you first, and for the love of God, avoid penetration with her.

Because it can be really awkward for Number 3 after the sex games end, let her know what a great time you and your girlfriend had, and ask her if she'd like to spend the night or if she'd feel too weird staying over. (If she wants to stick around and you and your woman want privacy, you can always tell her, "We have to get up really early tomorrow morning to go to church with my grandparents." That should get the other girl outta there, pronto.)

You've tried every tactic for coaxing your girlfriend into a threesome and she's still revolted? Respect her wishes if she's really scared because neither of you will enjoy yourselves if you have to browbeat her into trying it.

SPEEDY CINEMA

The biggest problems with porn is not whether she'll be into it (most women like porn or at least some form of celluloid sex), but how she'll react if you try to bring her into your dirty little world. In porn films of the past, all that mattered was sex—but porn was and still is also all about fantasies that are probably never gonna come true anyway (drill this into her head). More female and feminist directors are gearing their productions toward a female audience—upward of 40 percent of all porn is bought or rented by women or couples—which means there's more porn than ever for the two of you to choose from. You're just one step away from making it a better-than-blockbuster night.

HOW TO SELECT A PORN FILM

Let's get one thing straight: "Most pornos are stupid and made for guys," says Mark, 37. The sooner you realize this, the sooner you'll be able to actually find a film both you and she will dig. Or you could always spend Saturday night with the *Super Alien Anal Intrusion Adventure* series instead of in bed with her.

Check out online reviews for film-selecting guidance, and ask her what sounds good. BlueDoor.com, Blowfish, and Good Vibrations offer a wide range of porn in categories for all tastes, including couples, softcore, real and raw hardcore, and S&M, and smart descriptions of each video. Reviews on these sites and on Adult Video News (www.avn.com) will tell you exactly how intense the content is. "You might also want to rent three or four films and preview them for your girlfriend, but if she's so leery of porn that you have to screen it for offensive stuff, you probably shouldn't be watching it together," says Lena, 27.

"There's porn, and there's denominations leading up to it," says Elaine, 28. "Like most women, I like erotic, artistic movies like *Belle De Jour*, but when it comes to porn itself, I'd have to go with *Behind the Green Door* (Mitchell Brothers Film Group). It's a genre classic, like *The Rocky Horror Picture Show*." In case you didn't know, this sexy, surreal movie launched the career of the one and only Marilyn Chambers. A handful of top porn directors have become a huge hit with women and couples because of their movies' interesting, engaging story lines, attractive and realistic-looking actors, and beautifully shot sequences: Michael Zen, Michael Ninn, Andrew Blake, Candida Royalle, and Paul Thomas. (When in doubt, pick up a flick by one of these talented filmmakers.) A legitimate film—maybe a romance of historical proportions like *Henry & June* or an erotic romp like *Wild Orchid*—from the video store, or a softcore film on cable or pay-per-view TV, is also a good way to get her heated up to the idea of porn.

"You can also choose a cheesy film from the '70s with a bad funk soundtrack, like *Deep Throat* or *Debbie Does Dallas*," says Mark. "Starting with one of these can be an easy way to help her nervousness, because they're genuinely funny and campy."

Looking for female-on-female action? Stick to porn produced by and for lesbians. "If she's bisexual or has fooled around with other

CALIFORNIA CREAMIN'

Next time you get a video for the kids, you may want to double-check that title. No-budget production values? Of course. Tasteless? We hope. Utterly devoid of artistic merit? We think not. Note the clever plot revisions in these skillful XXX-rated interpretations of Hollywood blockbusters—some of which actually improve on the originals.

■ ***Edward Scissorhands*** (Fox Home Entertainment)
Hero wins suburban housewives over by skillfully clipping their bushes with his freakish scissor-fingers.

Edward Penishands (Video Team, Inc.)
Hero wins suburban housewives over by skillfully clipping their bushes with his freakish penis-fingers.

■ ***A Clockwork Orange*** (Warner Home Video)
Gang of boys with appetite for "ultraviolence" wreaks havoc on futuristic London.

Clockwork Orgy (Pleasure Productions)
Gang of girls with really, really bad cockney accents and appetite for "ultrasex" wreaks havoc on futuristic London.

■ ***Top Gun*** (Paramount Home Video)
During flight maneuvers, navy pilot Tom Cruise urges fellow flyboy to "ride his tail."

Top Buns (Essex)
During sexual maneuvers, assorted porn starlets urge studly co-stars to ride their tails.

■ ***Ben-Hur*** (Warner Home Video)
Ben-Hur, a slave in Rome, spreads his name far and wide in thrilling chariot race, circa 0 A.D.

Dun-Hur (Sin City)
Dun-Hur, a babe in Rome, spreads her legs far and wide in decadent pagan feast, circa 69 A.D.

■ ***Saving Private Ryan*** (DreamWorks Home Entertainment)
Squad of WWII soldiers comes to discover that their mission is a man.

Shaving Ryan's Privates (All Worlds Video)
Squad of gay porn stars come, then discover that their mission is a man.

women, the 'lesbian' scenes in male-directed films are going to look so fake and plastic it'll be a yawn," says Rio, 24. But if she's insecure or nervous about lesbian-esque films, remind her that one of the best ways to learn how to please your own honey-bunny right is to watch other female bodies in motion.

To find out how she feels about porn, just ask her. She might have a mind and a preference that are as filthy as your own, or she might want a soft core pick, instead, where the sex that is tasteful rather than ridiculously hardcore, and male performers are actually good-looking. "When it comes time to picking the movie, if she's thinking 'love' and you're thinking 'sex,' she'll be scared or think you don't care about her," says Gwen, 27. Whatever you do, don't keep it a secret from her, either, or else she'll think you're addicted (and wonder what else you're hiding). "Doing it together is huge. There's nothing wrong with looking and fantasizing, but I want to know if my man is looking at porn."

HOW TO MAKE YOUR OWN PORN FILM

Do-it-yourself erotica can be every bit as enticing as the stuff you rent from the back of the video store and, compared to same, have the same production quality. Just focus on how much fun it is to play porno flick director and you're guaranteed a good time.

■ Plan Ahead

Unless she's naturally sexually aggressive (go ahead and pat your back for us), it's going to probably take some serious bribing to get her to let you film your bedroom tangling, as she probably figures you're going to post it on porno4pervs.com (admit it, we know it crossed your mind, you dog). Reassure her that the tape stays with her, in a lock box, buried under the house. Better yet, bring the intimidation down a notch and start with simple Polaroids. We suggest the instant kind, as we figure you don't want some pimply faced teenager at the 1-Hour Foto Shack seeing 'em (and then have *him* posting them on the Web).

For those filming the festivities, don't worry about getting the high-end video cameras that'd make George Lucas jealous. If it's only for you, any old VHS camera will do. If you're worried about quality, there are plenty of digital cameras that give plenty of bang for the buck (pun intended).

■ A Seedy Spielberg

You can't forget good lighting and sound, either, unless you want a tape full of nothing but blurred shadows and barely audible grunting. "There's no bigger bummer than when you watch the tape and can't see anything," says Mark. "A good microphone helps, too, though you do have to be worried about giggling and breathing and talking that you might not want to hear."

When it comes time to figuring out the action, Beth recommends just being yourself—but taking it to the *n*th degree. "The fact that it's an exaggeration of what you are is what you'll like about it," she says. "So if you have a specific talent, like going downtown, make that the focus of the video. If you have an incredible body, strip for the camera."

And if you don't...just keep in mind, this is amateur with a capital A, as well as the fact that there may be a reason you aren't currently starring in bigger-budget pornos. "You tend to think of it in fantasy images, and then you see reality," says Sean, 31. "It's really an ego deflater. You don't think of your hairy ass or love handles—you think those everyday things you see in the mirror are going to be gone because you're having a good time on film."

"The most fun of the video is making it," agrees Mark. "The ones I've made I've only watched once, anyway."

THE BEDROOM'S BUT A STAGE: FUN WITH ROLE-PLAYING

As the sexologists like to say, our biggest sex organ is our brain—and a wild imagination can be the best and cheapest sex toy you could ever want. But there's a time to guard a sex fantasy for your own erotic use, and a time to bring it to life. Relax: It ain't Shakespeare, just a little play-acting to keep things interesting and spontaneous. Here's how to make it happen.

Whether you use fantasy to get aroused or to tide you over until your next night of mattress mambo, "fantasies are crucial to keeping passion in a relationship," says Taryn. "Without that kind of playfulness, things can get stale really quickly." A daydream (or wet dream) exists in a totally pretend world, allowing you to "experiment" without worrying about crap like who's gonna tie who up or how the hell you'd have sex on a roller coaster without getting killed. "I think mental fantasies—the anticipation—is the best foreplay," says Tracey, 31. "Sometimes the idea of getting something you're craving is better than the real thing."

Communicate, communicate, and communicate some more so that everybody involved gets something they want and doesn't get anything too freaky. There's always the direct, just-ask-her-already approach to discussing fantasy, but when you're talking about crazy, totally make-believe ideas that'll never be brought to life, you might want to get a little more creative, bub. "Women are naturally more communicative, so why not buy her a journal and have her right out all her secret desires?" says Beth, 30. "She'll write off the cuff, without having to look you in the eye or worry about what you're thinking. You'll get total honesty from her. You should write in it, too. Building up trust and her interest is sexy." You can also read books of erotica, where the fantasies are spelled out in vivid, explicit detail, to each other. If you can learn to read someone else's sexy

MOST POPULAR HIS-AND-HERS FANTASIES

As you probably guessed (and perhaps found out, much to your chagrin), what a female fantasizes about is different from what you spend your days dreaming of. While you're thinking about a three-way between you, your eighth grade English teacher, and Brenda from accounting, women tend to focus (surprise, surprise) on love and romance. Here are men's and women's 10 most common fantasies, according to Tracey Cox, author of *Hot Sex*.

Men's Favorites

1. Sex with your sweetie (well, that's what you told Cox anyway)
2. Sex with another woman
3. Receiving oral sex from a super enthusiastic gal (next, we'll tell you something you don't know)
4. Sex with two or more women
5. Watching other people do it
6. Watching her masturbate
7. Being penetrated
8. Bondage
9. Overpowering her, or letting her overpower you
10. Sex with another man—er, if someone reported it, it must be true

Women's Favorites

1. Sex with you (unlike you, we believe women when they say this)
2. Sex with another man.
3. Sex with another woman (yes, all your hopes and fantasies may indeed come true)
4. Miscellaneous out-of-the-ordinary sex—from bondage to public sex, she's indulging her wild, exhibitionist side by escaping from her shy shell and performing for a horny, adoring audience.
5. Receiving unconditional oral sex.
6. Romantic fantasies—You know the drill: candlelight dinner and moonlit walk on the beach, a handsome gentleman whisking her onto his horse and galloping into the sunset—in other words, fairy tales and Harlequin novels combined, times 10
7. Sex against your will—yeah, right—like you'd ever say no to sex.
8. Being the object of men's desire
9. Working as a prostitute or stripper
10. Sex with a stranger.

words, you'll get comfortable with creating some of your own. (Check out Amazon.com or erotica Web site Nerve.com for recommendations.)

Oh, sit down. Not all your sexual wishes can come true. In the real world people fart and sneeze, cars break down on the way to the country house, and moonlit picnics on the beach get rained out. Having unrealistic expectations about how a fantasy should play out is setting yourself up for astronomical disappointment. "If you want to act out a fantasy, don't get incredibly specific," says Sean. "That perfect fantasy's not gonna happen. Pick one that can be molded as you go along." There's a delicate balance between spontaneous sex and scripted staleness.

Jen, 26, a photographer, sees the carrying out of a fantasy the way she'd look at a photo shoot: "You have to clearly get across what you're envisioning, while also making her comfortable and interested in what your 'vision' is."

When one partner wants to turn a dream into reality, trust, understanding, and patience are of the utmost importance if you want the show to be a success—and have a repeat performance. "When my boyfriend broached the subject of a particular desire two years ago, we didn't realize the fantasy for a while," recalls Taryn. "We just fed off the idea and were content with it. But when we were ready, it turned out to be something that we both immensely enjoyed because we were open, honest and unrestrained."

PHONE SEX: LET YOUR FINGERS DO THE WALKING...AND HER FINGERS DO THE FONDLING

When you can't just reach out and touch that special someone 'cause she's visiting family in Cleveland, or she's stuck in traffic or at the doctor's office, phone sex can hold her off until she's back in your bed again. Getting her off long-distance style's kinda like *Whose Line Is It Anyway*? (minus the fat guy in glasses and studio audience): You gotta play off what she's saying to you (and doing to herself) and think fast on your feet to keep her entertained. Here's a 10 step plan to dialing.

1) You and she should plan the best time to call if you know the conversation's going to last more than just a few minutes. She'll probably be annoyed if you surprise her when she's in a meeting with her boss, but more than happy to talk if she's home alone. As long as you don't call when *Ally McBeal* is on.

2) Sean, 31, suggests requesting that she wear a certain item of clothing: her black leather high heels, thigh- high stockings...or no panties at all. "If she asks why, just tell her, 'I'll explain later.' She'll be dying to know what you're up to."

3) At your respective houses, you should each set the stage for some filthy phone time: Turn the TV off, put on some sexy background music, light some candles, dress (or undress) for the occasion...

4) and get comfortable. Figure out how you'll hold the phone and masturbate at the same time. Any sex toys, lube, or towels (for cleaning up your juicy mess) should be within arm's reach.

5) Even a routine chat can morph into phone sex. "'What are you wearing?' doesn't work because it sounds bad," says Sean. "You don't want to sound cheesy like Chester the Molester. A conversation like, 'Did you think about me today? No? What did you think about?' does work."

6) Follow her lead: Does she want to share her deepest, darkest fantasies with you? Are the fantasies totally unrealistic or of the "I've-always-wanted-to-try-this" variety? Is she giving you a stroke-by-stroke account of how she's playing with herself? Give her your own play-by-play report. Is she too shy to blurt out what she wants? Ask her questions about what she likes or what she'd be interested in trying, or take turns making up parts of a sexy story.

7) Be explicit about what you want to do, or will do, to her, and when: "I'm

MAXIM FANTASIES

Forget Princess Leia, we give you the most popular fantasies round the *Maxim* offices

The Lucky Burglar
He was looking to get off scot-free, she was just looking to get off.

Auto Mechanic and Customer
"Hey lady, you wanna see a real grease monkey?"

Priest and Parishioner
"Forgive me, Father, for I'm about to sin"

Warden's Wife and the Escaped Prisoner
He was looking for revenge…and so was she!

Commanding Officer and Enlisted Soldier
She barked out orders to the lowly private, making him drop for 20…minutes…in between her thighs.

Way off the Beating Path
Now we get to the real hard-core shit. From fetishes to serious S&M, the tawdry details on deviant behavior.

going to tie you up/tickle you with a feather/ give you a sponge bath when I see you next week, tomorrow morning, at the beach house." Are the creative juices just not flowing? "Tell her, 'It was so cool when you did [sex act] to me the last time we were together,'" advises Sean.

8) If she's not using four-letter words, try descriptive language to paint the best pornographic picture possible—your words don't have to be filthy to turn her on.

9) Because you're not looking each other in the eye, just about anything you say goes. Take advantage of the telephone's "anonymity" to pretend to be someone else or to find out each other's erotic likes or dislikes.

10) Whether one or both of you are phone-sex virgins, if playing dirty telephone is a new activity, keep the first few calls fairly brief. You can even just dial up and say something like, "I can't wait to see you so that I can [fill in the blank with a descriptivebut not super-dirty act, like undressing her and giving her a massage]." The idea is to get her wondering what else you've planned for the night.

FETISH FANTASY

Sure, the sight of a naked woman in high heels might get your hornier than a three-peckered billy goat, but don't dial Dr. Ruth to find out if you're a fetishist who should start frequenting leather bars. Simply consider the fact that there's a big difference between being turned on by something and being a legitimate fetishist. As Michelle Surchuk, a New York City-based fetish photographer says, "You're either a fetishist or you're not."

■ **First Fetish Feelings** Most fetish worshippers "discover" their particular sex objects before they're even adults, since a lot of fetish favorites—like aprons, shoes, diapers, or rubber—remind them of being nurtured. A baby boy's first memories of his mama are often her shoes, since he's crawling around them; fur clothes are associated with pubic hair; and rubber sheets and diapers let him know that only very bad, bad boys pee when they're not supposed to. And, as we all know, bad, bad boys must be punished.

At the highest extreme, a fetish replaces a person as the focus of erotic desire, so rather than, say, getting off on seeing your girlfriend in a leather bra and panties, she needs to wear them in order for you to enjoy sex. Fetishes can be partial (as in body parts or characteristics such as obesity or skin color) or inanimate (miscellaneous objects, clothing items, fabrics, and materials fall into this category). And, no, despite the fact that you can't stop thinking about it, and the very thought gets you physically aroused, you don't have a naked woman fetish.

■ **Getting Her Involved** Before talking her into doing anything you'd really like to try, you have to reassure her the fetish experiment is not going to replace her or anything else you do in the bedroom. (If it does, buddy, you might want to go to a relationship counselor—we at *Maxim* can only do so much.) Here are a few of the more common fetishes and how to get your girlfriend to indulge you:

■ **Hair** The next time you two bathe or shower together, give her a slow, soothing scalp massage or shampoo. If she has long, straight hair, gently brush it with long, slow strokes. Back in bed, she can tickle your chest or legs by "stroking" your body with her hair.

■ **Feet or Shoes** Treat her to a pedicure so that her peds are in beautiful shape for slipping into a sexy pair of sandals, and squeaky-clean for kissing, licking, and sucking; you can paint her toenails yourself, as well. If you're going to insist she parade around in trashy stilettos, at least massage her feet after she takes them off, or have her wear them only in the house or bedroom instead of when she goes out. (High heels hurt!) She can also use her footsies to play with just about any part of your body.

■ **Corsets** Besides giving her an exaggerated hour-glass shape, the squeezing of her waist forces her to breathe from her chest, not from her diaphragm (the muscle below the lungs)—making her lightheaded and aroused more easily. Lingerie boutiques and catalogs, as well fetish shops, sell corsets that can be laced at different levels of tightness.

■ **Latex** A sheer latex dress or top is one of the sexiest things she can wear—you can see through it, and condoms are made out this stuff! "At first I was hesitant to put it on a latex dress—I'd only worn leather fetish gear," says Surchuk. "But I covered myself in baby powder before putting it on for a party. I walked around and felt like a goddess." If she feels uncomfortable or slutty wearing latex clothes, you can take turns "painting" each other with Liquid Latex (available at www.18tex.com), or using latex medical gloves to fondle and massage each other. (Lube up first, and make sure neither of you has a latex allergy.)

■ **Leather and rubber** Black. Shiny. The perfect outfit for a *Matrix*-inspired sex scene. Turn the fan or A/C on—this stuff is hot (literally). You don't want her getting overheated and faint.

NOW THAT'S CREEPY

When foot worship just won't satisfy your sexual-obsession needs...

Acrotomophilia and apotemnophilia Fancy-shmancy words for, respectively, getting off on real (or imagined) sex with an amputee, and fantasizing about one day having a body part removed or cut off. Has John Wayne remembered to thank Lorena for his porn career?

Spectrophilia Getting turned on by spirits, ghosts, angels, or gods. Safest sex ever—you can't get a poltergeist pregnant! Just don't piss it off, or you'll never be able to prove that an apparition chopped off your pee-pee (see above).

Dysmorphophile Someone turned on by a face that only a mother baboon could love, plus other deformities, like chicken-pox scars, club feet, and hunchbacks. Not you, you say? Have you seen your ex?

Dendrophilia Intense sexual arousal caused by having sex with trees rather than with humans. Brings a whole new meaning to the word "woodpecker."

Emetophilia A fetish for throwing up and being thrown up on; also known as a Roman Shower (if anyone knew how to have a good time, it was the Romans).

Iatronudia Think reverse hypochondria: Perfectly healthy people who pretend to be sick so that they can undress in front of a doctor. Still kicking yourself for dropping out of pre-med your freshman year?

Gerontophilia Otherwise known as Cocoon syndrome, or sexual attraction to someone decades older than you. At least we now know that Catherine Zeta-Jones's mating habits are a psychological "condition."

Menophilia A fixation on menstruating women, and...maxi pads. Do you have any idea the kind of brownie points you'll get for this? (Just don't mention how much water she's retaining.)

Pony play Giddyup! If having sex with an animal is too weird for you, at least you can screw someone pretending to be lower on the food chain.

Ophidicism Using lizards, snakes, and other reptiles for sex. If Godzilla and the 50-Foot Woman had a kid, who would it look like?

Avisodomy Sex with a bird (you can't make these up, folks) Would Elmo and Big Bird lose their jobs for getting caught doin' it on Oscar the Grouch's trash can?

Agalmatophilia A doll, statue, or mannequin fetish At least Barbie's not gonna dump you for that Swedish model/video store clerk.

THANK YOU MISTRESS! MAY I HAVE ANOTHER? AN INTRODUCTION TO BDSM

Contrary to what 700 Club–watchin', Michael W. Smith–listenin', missionary-sex-only-havin' people think, the great big world of BDSM is not the same as fetish worship or sexual torture. While fetish-scene folks might also be into dominance and submission scenarios, neither BDSM nor fetish allows physical or emotional violence against another person.

"SORRY, I'M TIED UP."

BDSM involves artful, and consensual, power plays between a "top," or dominant, and a "bottom," or submissive, from light, playful spanking to flogging and whipping; loosely gagging to tightly shackling your partner; and piercings, branding, tattoos, and self-scarring. There's also coprophagy (eating shit—literally) and coprophilia (just playing with it), water sports (using urine, semen, or enemas during sex), and blood sports, all of which are unsafe (the risk of STD transmission is high).

Tops and bottoms play with the senses in other ways, too, like using gas masks, blindfolds, or mummification for sensory deprivation; or enhancing the senses by, say, numbing a partner's nipples with ice before heating them back up with candle wax, for instance (hey, we told you this was going to be fun, didn't we?). Whatever the fun and games may be, the details of each game—down to code words to tell the Mistress when you've had enough—are hammered out beforehand so that each party knows how far they can go. Even in a master-and-slave scene, the "punishments" aren't cruel—they just create the illusion of a scary situation, like the fear, euphoria, and turn-on from riding a really fast, tall roller coaster.

FIRST, THE GROUND RULES

If you're domming, you are the cruise director, in control of the scene but also responsible for the bottom's safety and enjoyment—in other words, you call the shots but are still there to serve and protect. If you're the bottom, thank your lucky stars, 'cause you don't have to do anything but get aroused and lose control.

Bottoms can go to a professional top, or dominatrix, for BDSM play; but absolutely no sex is involved. Still, the dom's first priority is engaging and arousing the client—the bottom can only "surrender", or submit, if the top makes it clear who's running the show. "A true mistress is going to pay homage to her bottom," says Magenta, a former mistress and "dom" trainer. "If she doesn't, she's not for real."

"A TRUE MISTRESS IS GOING TO PAY HOMAGE TO HER BOTTOM."

As with swingers' clubs, you have to research the BDSM scene in your city before just showing up at a party, since participants tend to find spectators annoying. (Start schooling yourself in BDSM's finer points at www.altsex.org/bdsm and the Society for Human Sexuality's link, www.sexuality.org/bdsm.html and www.tes.org, the home page of the Eulenspiegel Society.) Also, if you're looking for live sex acts, you won't see any, since safe-sex laws across the country prohibit penile penetration and body-fluid exchange. "You can think you'll have an idea of what to expect, but then you'll see older people, yuppie-frat boys, just about anybody walking around," says Magenta. Maybe even *700 Club*–watchin', *Michael W. Smith*-listenin' folks.

Sex-Machine Maintenance

You've now made it to a higher level of sexual intelligence. Well, almost. You possess the moves and toys necessary to take your lady to the edge of ecstasy and perhaps even beyond. But if you don't keep your equipment in tip-top shape, prepare for a booty breakdown. Think of all the stuff that can screw up your screwing: disease, babies, blue balls, or the dreaded limp biscuit. That's why this chapter will answer all your itching (literally) questions about sexual health. We fire away on everything from buying the best condoms to avoiding nasty diseases that'll wound your willy and ground your swimmers. Best of all, we'll prove that a little nookie every day can help keep the doctor away.

TROUBLESHOOTING THE TROUBLESHOOTER

Even the most well-hung, longest-lasting, macho-manliest would-be porn star experiences the occasional penis pitfall—such as premature ejaculation or whiskey dick—or tosses and turns at night imagining all the cock complications he could face (or may have contracted, depending on who's lying next to him in bed). Here we explain the causes of an assortment of sex organ snarls and ways to ward them off.

PREMATURE EJACULATION

The night of his best friend's Halloween party, Jack was struggling to decide on a get-up when he suddenly had a bright idea, got into costume, and headed for the shindig. When his buddy answered the door, he found Jack standing there with no shirt, no shoes, and no socks on. "What the hell are you supposed to be?" asked the confused host. "A premature ejaculation," answered Jack. "I just came in my pants!"

Hey, it's all fun and games until you really do spurt too soon, at which point your woman rolls over in disgust, gives you the perfunctory, "It's OK!" then falls asleep, and notifies every last one of her friends about your "problem." If you're lucky, that scenario will only be a bad dream.

Because you're up against some sensitive, unpredictable variables—you haven't gotten any in a while, her take-me-now horniness after you've downed eight beers—your manhood's response under pressure isn't easy to predict. But according to the experts, you shouldn't be so, er, hard on yourself. "Ejaculation that occurs before it's desired is really the best way to explain it," says Ira Sharlip, M.D., assistant clinical professor of urology at the University of California at San Francisco and president of the Society for the Study of Impotence. "What's 'premature' for some men isn't the case for others." He also points out that because this member mishap involves the erotic bliss of more than one party, diagnosing and treating it can be tough. "If a guy's partner has a problem achieving orgasm, that could create a situation where his ejaculation is premature for her but it's not always medically abnormal."

CAUSES OF PREMATURE EJACULATION

There is no one universal reason for the occasional quick release. Three of the more common sources include:

■ Maybe you're born with it. According to studies, for some guys in their 20s and 30s, it doesn't matter how much they're getting laid. They are, in layman's terms, horny as hell, and that's going to make them preemies.

■ Been a long time, been a long time? You might also notice that when you've gone for an extended period of time without hittin' it, the sudden onslaught of stimulation can make you come more quickly. Duh, right.

■ In your head? Or it could just be in your head (and we ain't just talkin' about the one between your legs). "Some men are very good at controlling themselves; when they feel they're reaching ejaculation, they back off and hold off," notes Sharlip. It has also been his observation that "other men don't have that ability, or the confidence that they'll be able to maintain their erection, so they come right away to save themselves the embarrassment." Over time that kind of sexual performance anxiety can cause chronic equipment failure.

THE QUICKER PICKER

Jed C. Kaminetsky, M.D., a sexual dysfunction expert and assistant professor of urology at New York University School of Medicine, recommends four tactics for tackling premature ejaculation.

1. Unlearn how to come. Increasing your latency period means retraining yourself to know when you're about to bust a nut and letting that feeling subside. "Most men who ejaculate prematurely were as kids, or are as adults, frequent masturbators," explains Kaminetsky. Such spirited salami-spankers don't want to get caught, so they finish off immediately, if not sooner, which doesn't improve stamina. Aside from imagining sex with Barbra Streisand, one way to keep from coming is to use Masters and Johnson's squeeze technique or the stop-start technique.

2. Assume a different position. When you're thrusting in and out, the motion and sensation are similar to the feel of your hand sliding up and down your saber during a self-pleasuring session. Your unit doesn't sense much of a difference, so you end up spewing semen sooner than you wanted. The solution? Stop pumping and start rocking. "Penetrate deeply and rub your pelvic bone against her genitals," suggests Kaminetsky, "which gives her more clitoral stimulation and is less intensely stimulating for you. She'll be happy, and you'll last longer." Or try lying face-up—or better yet, sit up—while she straddles you and "rocks" herself back and forth; screwing in an upright, seated position helps maintain the blood supply to the penis, resulting in longer-lasting boners.

3. Check out your medicinal options. That little blue defender of potency, Viagra, not only gets your love muscle ready for action, but it also seems to help speed up the refractory period and allows a man to maintain a hard-on after ejaculation. But if Viagra puts into your mind the frightful image of your future as a flaccid grandpa, you might want to try a class of antidepressants called selective serotonin-reuptake inhibitors (SSRIs) such as Zoloft or Prozac. "Men treated with these medications for depression sometimes complain of delayed ejaculation," observes Sharlip. (Uh, what's to complain about?) However, you've got to pop these pills daily, as recommended by your doctor, or else two to four hours prior to gettin' it on, "though predicting when you'll actually have sex can be a problem," he adds. The SSRI dosage is low enough to not cause any side effects, but you do have to worry about the antidepressant's interaction with alcohol or other drugs. That said, this regimen might be just what the doctor would already have ordered. Says Kaminetsky, "If someone has a big enough problem with premature ejaculation, he's usually a little depressed, anyway."

4. If all else fails...As a course of last resort, you should try to physically decrease the sensitivity of your unit. Use common sense and be sure to avoid any activities that might cause you pain or injury. Although Kaminetsky is not advocating recreational drug use, he does concede that "most drugs will delay orgasm." Same goes for having sex when you're three sheets to the wind. Since the messages from your genitals to your brain's pleasure center are tra-aa-veling...more...slowly on account of all that booze you've drunk, you'll have difficulty ejaculating at all (assuming you can achieve and maintain a stiffy in the first place). Just hope your sperm is also too toasted to find their way around anywhere.

THE STOP-START TECHNIQUE

Your aim: to fight millions of years of evolution. Our ancestors learned quickly that the best way to get eaten by animals bigger and hungrier than them was to get sidetracked. They needed to get in and get out before trouble came to get them. Those prehistoric instincts extended to sex, which explains most men's orgasms. But sometimes you promise your girl you'll go "all night long," and she assumes that means longer than a Jay Leno monologue.

The goal of this exercise is to learn to keep yourself below the point of no return for as long as possible. You must practice the six steps. It's not as bad as it sounds—after all, you get to wank off. The first three steps you'll do solo. though they aren't part of the stop-start technique, we kind of like'em anyway. For the final three you'll need the cooperation of a partner other than Rosy Palm and her Five Sisters.

Step One: Pet Your Friend

Masturbate with a dry hand, but avoid thinking about that new girl in accounting. You're trying not to get off here. Just focus on the sensation in your penis. Let

THE SQUEEZE TECHNIQUE

This favorite of sex gurus Masters and Johnson (yes, we're sure they've heard all the jokes), the "squeeze" technique is designed to help you slowly lose a bit of your erection, and it can be applied every time you get too close to ejaculation. Your partner performs the squeeze by gripping your penis firmly and pressing with her thumb on the frenulum. This is the place on the underside of the penis where the head joins the shaft (you did read Chapter One, didn't you?). At the same time, she presses on the opposite side of the penis with her forefinger, with her other fingers curled round the shaft. It's key that she press fairly hard on the penis (hope you haven't had an argument recently) and doesn't move her hand while doing so. Too light a touch can cause you to ejaculate straight away. To perfect this maneuver, some prepping is required:

Step One: Just like with the stop-start technique, have her give you a hand job without any lube. Anytime you feel the soldiers ready to charge, signal to her to stop and squeeze your penis, for a few seconds. As with the stop-start technique, aim to last for three consecutive 15 to 20 minute sessions before moving on to Step Two.

Step Two: Get your partner to masturbate you slowly and gently as before, but this time ask her to lube up first, then do as directed in Step One.

Step Three: Time for the main event—i.e., actual intercourse, with no thrusting. Instead, lie on your back and ask your partner to sit on top of you, with your penis inside her, and neither of you moving (fun, eh?). As soon as you feel the urge to come, your partner should rise off you (this movement is dangerous, as it applies stimulation) and immediately hold your penis in the squeeze grip. Repeat the exercise a couple of times before you allow yourself to ejaculate.

Step Four: When you think you've got a handle on your feelings, you can go ahead and move gently while she sits still. When you feel the urge to purge, she should move off you and squeeze as before, until you can last 15 minutes without ejaculating.

Step Five: You're now ready to try other positions, but remember: When you're on top you'll have less control. As with the stop-start technique, you should focus all the attention on yourself, taking care of her either before or after (and now, thanks to your newfound longevity, maybe during!).

the pleasure build up but stop immediately when you feel you're about to cross the line that'll unleash the hounds. Relax for a bit, still keeping your mind free of fantasies, until the dreaded 'danger of ejaculation' has passed, then begin again. Keep repeating this for 15 minutes without orgasm, if you can. You may not be able to succeed at first, but try, try again; eventually, you find that you have to stop less often. When you've completed three 15-minute sessions on three consecutive occasions (not necessarily one immediately after the other, unless you don't mind major chafing), proceed to step two.

Step Two: **Lube Job**

Instead of dry heaving, now get a bit of lubricant (we suggest shying away from non-phallus-friendly substances like Crisco, Windex, or Dippity Doo—E.R. doctors tell us it happens). Lubrication will heighten the sensation and make it feel more like real sex, making delay more difficult. Use the same techniques in Step One until you've done three more consecutive sessions as above.

Step Three: **Different Strokes**

Congrats, you're well on your way to being a marathon man in the bedroom. For this step do just as you did in Step One, but instead of stopping the party when you feel the dam about to break, change the rhythm or alter your strokes in such a way that the pressure to ejaculate fades. Now experiment to see which strokes excite you most and which allow you the most control. As with the others, work on this step until you have completed three consecutive sessions just like before.

Step Four: Couple Up

As much as you may have enjoyed these sessions with the one you love, it's time to get another party involved, preferably your girlfriend and/or wife. Start by telling her heard that practicing this will help you go longer—so she doesn't think you're a freak. Then ask her to do Step One for you (not on her, on you), masturbating you with a dry hand. Be sure to tell your partner to stop when you get close before the 15 minutes is up. So she doesn't feel like there's nothing in it for her, after the session don't forget to take care of her.

Step Five: Get a Hand

Repeat Step Four (again, not all of this on the same day), but have her use lubricant while she masturbates you. Again, once you have mastered three consecutive 15-minute sessions, you are ready to try the stop-start technique with actual two-person intercourse.

Step Six: Show Time!

Don't just dive right in and start pounding away doggy-style, Rover. The best position for delaying ejaculation is with the woman on top. Once you're inside her, ask her to move gently. Put your hands on her hips so that you can let her know with your hands when you want her to stop and when you're ready for her to resume. Again, aim to last for 15 minutes, but if you can't, don't worry; you can start again once you recover your erection, and the second time you'll probably have more control. While it's OK to be selfish and concentrate entirely on yourself at first, take care of her needs...afterward (or if she can't wait, before).

SEXUALLY TRANSMITTED DISEASES: THE GIFTS THAT KEEP ON GIVING

No matter how well you think you know women, the dilemmas of dating—Pleated pants or flat-front? Roses or daisies? Nipple clamps or dildo?—have nothing on the nasty ding-dong discomfort that can result from slayin' some sick snatch. Even if your peter doesn't feel any different, it could be pickled. The hell of many STDs is that they sometimes show no symptoms until they are in their advanced stages. So you need to know how to keep from contracting some nasty and what to look for if you've had the bad luck of getting one. While some of these penile presents can be "returned" (antibiotics and other prescription drugs will easily wipe out a pesky infection), others, like diamonds, really will last forever.

DISEASE: Gonorrhea, a.k.a. 'the Clap'

What it is: A nasty bacterium that can be spread vaginally, anally, and even orally.

Odds of getting it: More than 600,000 new infections occur a year.

How you know you've got it: Within a week or two of exposure, you'll have pus-like liquid oozing out of your pole (though 10 percent of who have it never show any symptoms), along with painful peeing. If you got it orally, you're going to have the mother of all sore throats.

Be afraid, be very afraid: Left untreated it can cause scarring of your urethra, which keeps you from fully emptying your bladder and inflamation of the prostate.

How you gonna treat it: The good news is, simple oral antibiotics will take care of it.

DISEASE: Chlamydia

What it is: The most common STD in the nation is caused by a bacterium.

Odds of getting it: Every year three to four million men and women are infected in the U.S.

How You Know You've Got It: This sneaky little bugger only causes symptoms in 60 percent of men infected, but if you do have symptoms, they'll include a goopy discharge from your penis, burning when you pee, and tender testicles. If you're sexually active—even if you use rubbers—play it safe and get tested regularly.

Be Afraid, Be Very Afraid: If it spreads, it can lead to Reiter's syndrome, which involves eye infections, arthritis, and urethritis.

How You Gonna Treat It: A round of antibiotics will send this bad boy packin'.

DISEASE: Hepatitis B Virus (HBV)

What It Is: A virus that lays waste to your liver.

Odds of Getting It: There are up to 77,000 new cases reported a year, with 750,000 Americans being chronically infected with sexually acquired HBV, which means, they've got it, but it's in remission.

How You Know You've Got It: Let's see; there's the typical hepatitis symptoms—brown urine and yellow eyes (jaundice), fatigue, vomiting, and fever. But during the time the virus is at its most contagious it may not bring on any symptoms. (Sneaky, huh?)

Be Afraid, Be Very Afraid: A chronic infection can cause permanent liver damage, including cirrhosis of the liver and even liver cancer.

How You Gonna Treat It: Sorry, man, no can do—almost 95 percent of HBV-infected adults completely recover in four to eight weeks, while the remaining infected folks stay contagious for the rest of their lives. If you haven't contracted it, a series of vaccinations will protect you permanently.

DISEASE: Herpes

What It Is: More than just cold sores and fever blisters, herpes simplex virus-1, like HSV-2, can spread via kissing or vaginal, oral, or anal sex, *or skin to skin contact*.

Odds of Getting It: Herpes finds a new home in 1 million people every year.

How You Know You've Got It: When you see fluid-filled blisters breaking out en masse on your crotch, its safe to assume you've got it, though you can get an outbreak on your penis, anus, and mouth as well.

Be Afraid, Be Very Afraid: Once you've got it, you've got it for life, and even if she doesn't show any blisters (it's in remission), she can still give it to you. Oh, yeah, condoms offer only mediocre protection.

How You Gonna Treat It: There might be no cure, but there are daily antivirals you can take that'll help prevent nasty outbreaks.

DISEASE: Human Papilloma Virus (HPV) a.k.a. Genital Warts

What It Is: A viral disease that makes your crotch look like cauliflower, transmitted by vaginal, oral, anal, or unprotected genital rubbing.

Odds of Getting It: Roughly 5.5 million folks get at least one of over 60(!) types of HPV each year; as many as 75 percent of American adults have been infected with some variation of the virus.

How You Know You've Got It: The soft, itchy cauliflower-looking warts will possibly appear on the genitals, urethra, anus, or even throat within three weeks, though, as with all STDs there may be no symptoms.

Be Afraid, Be Very Afraid: In surveys of college women, nearly half tested positive, though only 2 percent had any visible symptoms.

How You Gonna Treat It: Surgery, from lasers to liquid nitrogen to acid, will erase warts, but not the virus (you're stuck with HPV for life, even if you never have another out break.

DISEASE: Pubic Lice a.k.a. Crabs

What It Is: Tiny little blood suckers that burrow into your crotch after you've had sex with the infected. But you can also get them from toilet seats.

Odds of Getting It: Millions self-diagnose and treat themselves for crabs.

How You Know You've Got It: If you've had any kind of unprotected sex or the bad luck of sitting on filthy bedding, clothes, furniture, or toilet seats, be on the lookout for intense itching in the genital area and lice or egg sacks nestled in your short 'n' curlies. Pale gray "crabs" are newer to the neighborhood, while darker lice are swollen from blood sucking.

Be Afraid, Be Very Afraid: They also thrive in eyebrows, possibly causing, among other things, eye infections, so watch where you stick your face.

How You Gonna Treat It: For once in your damned life, wash your sheets in hot water and vacuum your carpet. And while you're at it, grab some RID at the drugstore.

DISEASE: Trichomoniasis, or Trich

What It Is: A whip-tailed parasite that, like most men, prefers bush to dick.
Odds of Getting It: As many as five million Americans contract trich every year.
How You Know You've Got It: Men rarely develop symptoms, but those who do have swelling in the groin area or painful urination from three to 28 days after vaginal intercourse with an infected partner.
Be Afraid, Be Very Afraid: More than half of all women with gonorrhea also have trichomoniasis.
How You Gonna Treat It: Drugs called 5-metronidazoles will do the trick (no pun intended).

DISEASE: Human Immunodeficiency Virus (HIV)

What It Is: Conspiracy theories aside, it is the virus that causes AIDS.
Odds of Getting It: HIV is the number five killer of American men ages 25 to 44, many of whom are infected in their reckless teens or 20s. About 40,000 people contract the virus yearly. roughly one in every 250 Americans is infected.
How You Know You've Got It: You probably won't, though within the first couple of weeks, you may get flulike symptoms that eventually go away. Once it goes on to full-blown AIDS, other symptoms include mysterious weight loss, lack of appetite, and diarrhea; regular fatigue, night sweats, fever, and dry cough; mental disorders; purplish, knoblike skin growths; and thrush, a thick, whitish coating of yeast that makes the tongue or mouth feel "hairy."
Be Afraid, Be Very Afraid: Is death scary enough for you?
How You Gonna Treat It: No vaccine, no cure. Plus, HIV camps out in your immune system for the long haul. Protease inhibitor cocktails can suppress the virus for a while, but AIDS and AIDS-related illnesses, like cancers and pneumonia, have a tendency to team up with new harder to combat strains to kill you.

DISEASE: Syphilis

What It Is: This potentially fatal—if left untreated—bacterium can be spread from not only anal, vaginal, and oral sex, but even by kissing.
Odds of Getting It: Each year about 70,000 people contract syphilis.
How You Know You've Got It: First you get the weeping chancre sores on your penis, anus, fingers, and mouth. Then there's the skin rash, with lesions on your hands and feet that quickly follow, and flu-like symptoms.
Be Afraid, Be Very Afraid: If it's left untreated, for the next two years you can enjoy hair and weight loss, nerve and major organ damage, and likely death. And in tertiary syphilis, the final and fatal stage, your flesh looks like it's decaying—which it is.
How You Gonna Treat It: Antibiotics will eliminate syphilis early on, but damage in its later stages is irreversible.

HAS SHE GOT IT?

It takes a little detective work to know if your partner might inflict Dick Jr. with some gnarly plague. "Infection in females is often up in the cervix, where there aren't enough nerve cells to reliably indicate a problem," says Paul Norris, M.D., a fellow of the American College of Obstetricians and Gynecologists and assistant professor of ob/gyn at the University of Miami School of Medicine. Some symptoms:

Disease: Chlamydia
Signs: Vaginal bleeding, painful intercourse for her, or "spotting" (light bleeding) after intercourse.

Disease: Gonorrhea
Signs: Check her panties for a yellowish or yellow-green discharge.

Disease: Trichomoniasis
Signs: Pungent and sometimes bloody discharge and vaginal itching.

Disease: Herpes
Signs: Pus-filled sores

Disease: Syphilis
Signs: Oozing chancres pretty much around any sexy orifice.

Disease: Pubic lice
Signs: Duh, there are little crablike things scurrying about on her pubes.

Disease: Genital warts
Signs: Her crotch looks like a cauliflower patch.

Disease: HIV
Signs: It's almost impossible to tell, but if you must have a symptom, the most easily noticed signs are purplish "knobs" on the skin or a constantly red, "sunburned" face (a side effect of taking antiviral medication).

PREGNANCY: THE NINE-MONTH SENTENCE

Congrats if you've made it this far without being benched for any of the previously mentioned penile predicaments. Now comes the next test: menstrual-cycle roulette. Whether you're ready for fatherhood or just "practicing" your baby-making maneuvers, here's what you need to know about the whole conception process.

PREGNANCY MYTHS DEBUNKED

■ **A woman can get pregnant all month long.**

Not true. The days a couple should worry about a pregnancy are around the time the female ovulates—typically, though not always, 14 days before she expects to start her next period. But since there are a few variables, the danger zone is about four days. Even if her menstrual cycle runs the exact same number of days every month, an egg cell can survive up to 24 hours after ovulation, while a sperm cell is good for up to 72 hours in her tuna tunnel. "Theoretically, a couple can have sex one day before she ovulates, and there could be some semen hanging around at the time her ovary releases an egg," explains Dr. Norris.

■ **Some women conceive only during periods.**

Not likely. A woman menstruates after her ovary's already released an egg. When she's riding the crimson tide, the uterine lining is shed, which wouldn't give a fertilized egg a chance to implant itself in the womb to develop into a baby. Since her body will need at least five days after she starts her period before she can ovulate again, the first five days of her cycle are safe from pregnancy. But as generations of couples who got pregnant using the so-called "rhythm" method can attest, sometimes following your body's patterns is not always the best contraception. Bleeding might occur for reasons aside from her period, so just remember that watching for spotting is not a guaranteed system.

■ **Douching, showering, or standing up will prevent pregnancy.**

Fuhgeddaboutit. None of these techniques kill sperm cells. Sperm-saturated semen has already shot up into the cervix—hell, maybe even into the Fallopian tubes—as a result of ejaculation and uterine contractions. Nothing short of the morning-after pill is going to help you here.

■ **If the drugstore pregnancy test comes up negative, you're home free.**

Clinic tests at the ob/gyn's office can establish a pregnancy within six to 10 days of fertilization, while most home pregnancy tests are less sensitive and require her to wait two weeks or until she misses a period in order to check her pregnancy status. (Then there's the impatient girlfriend who takes the test too early, comes up with a negative, and thinks she's in the clear.) "If there's any doubt in the woman's mind—and even the doctor's afraid it's too early in the pregnancy for a reliable urinalysis result—the gold standard is a blood pregnancy test," says Adelaide G. Nardone, M.D., medical advisor to the Vagisil Women's Health Center and a gynecologist in Mount Kisco, N.Y.

THE PILL IS SUREFIRE

Nothing's 100 percent certain. Short of a hysterectomy (where a surgeon removes the uterus), all birth control has a failure rate:

1 percent for Depo-Provera injections, Norplant implants, and IUDs

5 percent for the pill.

14 percent for condoms.

20 percent for a diaphragm or cervical cap.

26 percent for spermicide alone.

Why? She might get pregnant because of such screw-ups as not using the birth control correctly every time you do the mattress mambo. And some medications, including antibiotics, can seriously decrease the power of the pill and other hormonal contraceptives. There's even a one in 300 chance that a female who's had her tubes tied will get prego.

HOW TO GET PREGNANT WHEN YOU WANT TO

Ready to fulfill your Darwinian destiny? Here's what you need to know so that it can go off without a hitch.

Be Patient

1. Stop using barrier birth control as well as any hormonal contraceptives (duh). During the time between going off contraception and when the sperm actually fertilizes the egg, a woman's menstrual cycle can be erratic, and different forms of birth control will delay conception in different increments of time. Check with your M.D. about how long it may take before you and your partner can get pregnant.

Track Her Ovulation Cycle

2. Next, the little lady needs to track her periods so that you'll have some idea of when she'll be ovulating. That's the day she lays the golden egg that you want to fertilize. Time to work your mojo.

Here's how:

Mark the first day of menstrual bleeding as Day One of her cycle, then count all the days that follow until she gets her next period. The day before the new bleeding begins is the end of her cycle, so if she finishes a period and starts her next one 31 days after Day One, her cycle is 30 days long. To figure out when she's most likely to release an egg, count backward by 14 days. (With a 30-day cycle, ovulation should take place on or around Day 16: 30-14=16.) This way, you know when she's going to be cranky, too.

Change Your Underwear

3. While she's decorating her calendar with red X's, you might want to reevaluate your choice of underwear. Doctors have joined the boxers-versus-briefs debate, though not because they think you'd look just so much cuter in bikini briefs. Generally speaking heat hurts your swimmers,so if you're trying to conceive, steer clear of hot tubs(damn!) and bicycling(tight pants + crotch hump = reduced sperm volume). But remember there are other docs who believe that your drawers don't make a bit of difference.

No More Self-Love

4. Sorry, fella, but you'll have to take a break from polishing your bishop: Ejaculating more than once a day can lower sperm count, says Arnold Belker,

CLEVER CONDOM CATCH PHRASES

If rubbers had corporate sponsors, ad campaigns just might take on a whole new meaning…

Nike: **Boing.**

McDonald's: **We love to see you smile.**

New York Lotto: **You in?**

Microsoft: **Where do you want to go today?**

Nissan: **Enjoy the ride.**

California Lotto: **Who's next?**

Avis: **Trying harder than ever.**

Snickers: **Not goin' anywhere for a while?**

KFC: **How good is that?**

Capital One credit card: **What's in your wallet?**

Payless ShoeSource: **Doesn't it feel good?**

Buy.com: **Get in. Get out.**

Volkswagen Jetta: **Spread the joy.**

Ford: **The best never rest.**

Mazda: **Get in. Be moved.**

Visa: **It's Everywhere You Want to Be.**

FedEx: **Be absolutely sure.**

M.D., a urologist and male infertlity specialist in Louisville, Kentucky. "Generally we advise couples to have sex at 48-hour intervals, starting about four days before anticipated ovulation," he explains, so that a released egg has a greater chance of being fertilized. Also, it doesn't matter what kind of bedroom aerobics you use in trying to conceive, since sperm can swim in every direction possible, but it wouldn't hurt for the woman to remain lying down after sex.

Relax—Just Do It!

5. Make sure you chill out. If you face job-related or personal-life pressure, that tension can take its toll on your baby-making ability. Consider decreasing your number of work days a few months before trying to get pregnant, advises Belker. Give the excessive boozing and drugging a rest, as well: Marijuana, tobacco, and cocaine are all known to hinder sperm production. And while many a pregnancy has occurred after—oops!—drinking too many when out on the town, keeping your alcohol consumption at a moderate level is important.

The good news: Within a year of frequent, regular, unprotected intercourse, 85 percent of couples hit the jackpot. If you're among the 15 percent who've not yet conceived, it's time to head to the fertility specialist's office; Norris notes that of the couples who aren't yet pregnant, about half the fertility problems are in the male.

DON'T IT MAKE MY BALL SACK BLUE?

At the precise moment you and your girlfriend are about to lay some pipe, your bedroom door flies open, and your roommate's standing there videotaping your rendezvous for his Web site, www.other peopless exlives.com. You're now forced to postpone screwing in order to kick his ass, during which time your crotch starts throbbing in pain—yep, you've got "blue balls," or at least you think you do, because there's really no such thing. Although being left in lust limbo can cause some serious discomfort.

From French kissing to fondling to fantasizing about that fox in accounts payable, any sexual stimulation leads to a surge of blood to your genitals. (If you shined a flashlight on your crotch, you'd see that your scrotum might very well be a different color, albeit more purplish than actual blue.) "The testicles themselves don't do much in response to sexual excitement," explains Jed. C. Kaminetsky, M.D., a sexual dysfunction expert and assistant professor of urology at New York University School of Medicine. Most ejaculate comes from the prostate and seminal vesicles, so when a man doesn't bust a nut for a long time, the prostate becomes engorged with love juice, local blood vessels get congested, and your sack swells with pain. Ejaculation relieves this blood and fluid buildup, so when your erection goes away, the scrotal suffering also subsides.

If there's no chance of you ejaculating—she's "not ready" or that annoying roommate is watching—then quitting sex play completely will help you get over the discomfort. However, "This is not as immediate or effective a means as having an orgasm," explains Ira Sharlip, M.D., assistant clinical professor of urology at the University of California at San Francisco and president-elect of the Society for the Study of Impotence. (Thanks for the reminder, Doc.) For repeated instances of blue balls, forget the cold shower—that'll temporarily "shrink" Big Jim and the twins rather than tame them. Sharlip and Kaminetsky both suggest immediate ejaculation—masturbate or fantasize as needed—before you get to the point of achiness, since the best cure is coming. If your girlfriend's not feeling as frisky as you are, don't try convincing her you need sexual healing or your testes will explode or suffer some other ugly, permanent fate; blue balls constitutes absolutely no health risks.

SCARY STORY: POP! GOES THE ONE-EYED WEASEL

The prospect of shattering a shin or kneecap is scary enough, but the thought of your penis bending and breaking is enough to make you bawl like a newborn baby. When you're faced with a penile fracture, however, at least you won't have to spend six weeks hobbling around on crutches, your mini-me wrapped in a plaster cast.

THE BREAKS

Since your penis has no actual bone, the "fracture" is really a laceration in the corpora cavernosa, two chambers of fibrous tissue, blood vessels, and smooth muscles that run from the base to the tip of the organ. This mercifully rare cock crisis most often occurs when a man with a strong, eager prick rolls onto his stomach in mid-slumber, tries to push the big boy down to hide an untimely erection, or slides out of his partner's vagina and bumps his ramrod against her thigh or pelvic bone before he has a chance to stop it from happening. The penis will fold in on itself and make a horrible popping sound, and one or both of the corpora cavernosa will rupture, bringing on swelling, internal bleeding, bruising, excruciating pain, and, occasionally, urethra injury and bloody urine.

THE RX

If your boner breaks, go to the emergency room, stat, for a diagnosis. A surgeon may have to sew up the torn tissues so that blood stops leaking from the erectile chamber. Stitching may cause complications such as blood-clot accumulation, hematoma, or infection, so you might have to stay at the hospital for overnight observation. This is your penis we're talking about.

If you go to the doctor several days after the fracture occurs, he may not operate. But whether you choose to wait it out or get a professional to fix the problem, you could develop scar tissue at the spot where your scepter "snapped." When you get a hard-on, the scar tissue doesn't expand in quite the same way as the rest of the penis; the result is probably Peyronie's disease, a penile curvature which can produce a lump or bump at the area of the fracture, painful erections, or a bent boner. "I recommend vitamin E, which decreases the occurrence of Peyronie's disease, and anti-inflammatory medicine," says Kaminetsky.

According to Sharlip, a man's fertility, as well as his ability to prolong or maintain an erection, would not be negatively affected by a penis fracture. And don't worry too much about cracking your chubby: "Most people who have sex aren't fracturing their penises, so don't go into an encounter being worried about it," advises Kaminetsky. "This usually occurs when you're drunk, anyway, so don't drink so much." Or if you do knock back too many Buds, save the sex for when you're sober.

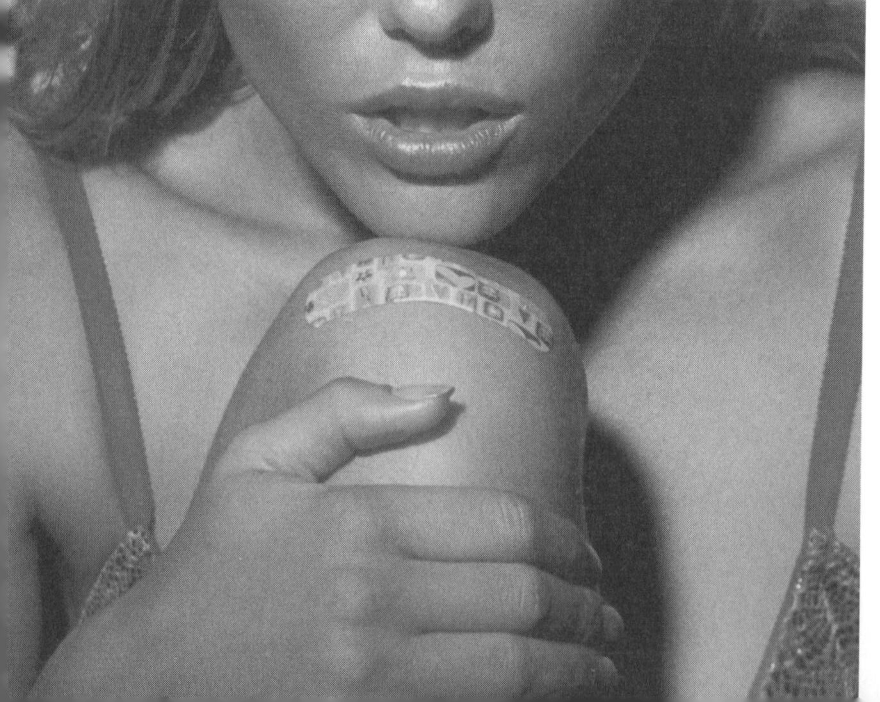

ERECTILE DYSFUNCTION: ARE YOU UP FOR THE JOB?

You finally brought home that babe you spent all night hitting on. And while you were a bit embarrassed when she sneaked a peak at your Happy Meal toys collection, it was nothing compared to being utterly demoralized when your little soldier failed to salute. But before you go and commit hara-kiri, or worse, go see a urologist, you'd best learn the ins and outs of getting it up.

■ Impotence Is a Dirty Word

To most men, "impotence" sounds an awful lot like "incompetence," not just between the sheets, but pretty much between all your waking hours. Now ego-friendly docs prefer the more benign (but equally disheartening) "erectile dysfunction" to describe it when you have "ascension deficit disorder."

"Specifically, these are erections that are consistently insufficient for satisfactory sexual function over a period of time," emphasizes Sharlip, not the occasional softies brought on by a couple of six-packs. "However," he adds, "this varies from one individual to the next." One man might not mind having a brief boner, but if his partner is unhappy about his performance with Flácido Domingo, it'd qualify as E.D. On the other hand, another guy might not be happy unless he's got an erection that lasts a minimum of 20 minutes.

■ Troubleshooting the Troublemaker

The best way to rule out a scary physical cause is to undergo what big-brained docs like to call "a nocturnal penile tumescence study," which is a fancy way of asking if you get hard-ons in your sleep. "If he has normal erections at night, that tells us the erectile 'mechanism' is working and that any dysfunction is most likely due to a psychological problem," explains Kaminetsky. No nighttime erections doesn't mean for certain that there's a physical problem, but it raises a level of concern.

■ Special E.D.?

Just because you're taking the gold at the Lake Flaccid Olympics, that doesn't mean you have clinical E.D. As Kaminetsky and Sharlip point out, actual clinical E.D. is often a symptom of a greater ailment. If you're in your 20s or 30s, your inability to get or maintain a proper erection could be a result of just about anything from depression to anxiety to relationship problems, or any psychological stress. Believe it or not, even excessive bicycle riding can damage nerves in your nether region. Obesity, smoking, and heavy drinking don't help matters either. And just in case you were wondering, yes, a good, hard kick to the groin can cause pelvic trauma, but because your nuts and bolt are pretty resilient, erectile dysfunction is a very unlikely result.

■ Curing What Ails You

If your floppy bone is a product of emotional factors, it's time for some communication, either between you and your honey or you, your honey, and a therapist. "An occasional erectile problem doesn't need to be medically treated, since it's probably psychological," assures Sharlip. But if the urologist figures that a hormonal imbalance or vascular difficulty is the real culprit, he'll prescribe a more serious treatment, like hormone supplements or surgery.

The *Null Monty* is often a result of high blood pressure, high cholesterol, smoking, or drinking, so your chances of suffering from this form of member misery will drastically decrease if you clean up your act. And make sure you and the little missus share romantic maintenance duties. "It is so important to have a good relationship," argues Kaminetsky. "Because, without a doubt, if you have relationship problems, it can lead to sexual problems."

On the scarier side, other troublemakers include diseases such as multiple sclerosis, HIV, arteriosclerosis (hardening of the arteries), high blood pressure, and hormonal imbalances. "The thyroid can sometimes elevate prolactin, a hormone secreted by the brain that usually causes testosterone levels to be low," notes Sharlip.

HORRIFYING REAL LIFE PENIS FRACTURE ACCOUNT

Richard Bray (not his real name) tetlls the tale of how he broke his penis during a wild ride (and you thought you were having a bad day):

OK, here's how it happened. My wife and I were alone, the kids asleep; we had stuffed our faces and downed a bottle of good wine. We'd just settled down for a long winter's romp. We were getting it on in the living room enjoying what you might call vigorous sex.

And then it happened. You know how during sex, sometimes you'll pop out and have to reinsert tab A in slot B? Well, this time disaster struck. I couldn't halt my energetic downstroke in time, and the angle was such that when I missed the landing pad, my penis nailed my wife's pubic bone dead on and folded back on itself like a jackknife, with all the pain the world could muster.

My stabbed wife was miserable herself, but I was far too busy shrieking like a little girl and curling up into a fetal position to offer sympathy. The agony was unbelievable.

As soon as I could force my eyes open, I cautiously surveyed the damage. Ugly bruises and swelling had already started to appear along my penis' broken length, but the worst was yet to come.

Over the next four weeks, my wife couldn't even glance toward me when there was a possibility of seeing the awful injury. A deep, purple, my blood-filled penis swelled beyond porn-star proportions and hung distended and stiff. My scrotum, bulging with blood, was almost round. The skin was drawn dry and tight over my monstrous genitalia.

No, I did not seek medical attention, though a surgeon later assured me that victims of this sort of accident normally rush themselves to the emergency room. I guess I felt something between embarrassment and the instinct of a hurt animal to hide and heal. I'd have licked my wounds if I could.

THE FIVE SCARIEST DISEASES A GUY CAN GET

Stop whining about how that groinful of hot, scalding coffee will leave you infertile and impotent forever (it won't), and just be thankful you aren't afflicted with any of these sexual maladies.

Elephantiasis of the Scrotum **The good news is your nuts get bigger. The bad news is they may never stop getting bigger. In an extreme case of elephantiasis, the scrotum can weigh over 100 pounds and the victim can sit astride it like a Hoppity Hop.**

Penile Cancer **Penile cancer occurs in four stages that, horribly enough, resemble the moves of an affectionate mate. It starts at the tip, works down the shaft, goes south to the rest of your crotch, and eventually consumes your entire body. The most frightening treatment—penectomy (yep, that's the removal of your penis)—is also, unfortunately, the most effective. Ugh!**

Peyronie's Disease **Also known as penis plastica, Peyronie's disease is distinguished by a painful crick in the crank. Right-angle bends can occur, and other configurations have been reported, including corkscrew (corkscrew?). In any case, it hurts.**

Gynecomastia **Where don't you want to see tits? In the mirror. An imbalance of estrogen and testosterone, common during puberty and advanced age, causes some men to develop firm breast tissue. This can range from tiny boobies to enormous Manchesters.**

Male Breast Cancer **Now that you have breasts, you need to take care of them. Men can get breast cancer, too. What's worse, male breast cancer intends to be far more aggressive than the female variety. Risk increases with age and with other conditions such as obesity, and liver disease.**

But the gods had more in store for me. A week or so after the Incident, I developed a freakishly huge Elephant Man erection that would not go away, even under ice water. I decided that the only way to make it disappear was to have an orgasm, and during those lonely days, I somehow managed to achieve release several times without blacking out from the pain.

The bruising slowly receded, and after about a month, with my wife's blessing, I tried getting back on the bicycle. The first time was pretty bad: My wounded soldier kept collapsing with posttraumatic stress disorder. But eventually, with a little patience and a lot of good humor, a very restrained act of sexual intercourse took place, and in a few weeks things were normal. Well, almost. My erections would sometimes simply vanish at inappropriate times. And nothing bolsters your ego quite like that.

There were other signs of permanent damage. The accident had left a ridge of lumpy tissue under the skin of my penis. When erect my member had a little bulge, like a snake after a light lunch. Worried about whether this would get worse, I finally consulted Vinton Crawford, M. D., a urologist in Anniston, Alabama.

"It's a fracture of Buck's fascia," he said. "That's the covering tissue of the corpora cavernosa, which are the two cylindrical erectile bodies in your penis. Think of them as blood-filled sponges during erection."

In layman's terms, my mishap had torn the "second skin" inside the penis, which holds the blood-swollen tissue of an erection; and the lump under the skin was the scar that closed the tear. Dr. Crawford told me that because there was not more significant deformation, there was no need for surgery.

"If a doctor sees the injury just when it's happened, during the first day or two, often you can correct it surgically," he said. "It is a fairly minor procedure." Now I felt like a real dick.

When Dr. Crawford learned that the difficulties I experienced in maintaining an erection were occasional and always brought on by memories of that dreadful night, he told me not to worry.

Even in a urology practice, Dr. Crawford said, he only sees such injuries a couple of times a year. "We get really interesting stories about how it happened, as you might expect," he said. "Most men are a bit embarrassed about it, so I'm not sure I get the true story; but that's all right."

Today, several years after I broke my penis, the physical scarring has almost disappeared, but I know that sex will never be the same wild ride. In positions where I don't control the action, or when the injury comes to mind, my erection can rapidly fade. My advice to you is tight coverage. Don't pull out too far, especially if it feels like you're almost slipping. Stick to your lover like Gary Payton on a point guard.

And whatever you do, keep one eye on the ball handler.

DOES IT REALLY MATTER WHAT KIND OF CONDOM YOU USE?

Does it matter what underwear you wear? Will Underoos help you do the deed? When it's time to get down and dirty, wearing the wrong condom can be even more disastrous than dressing up like a six-year old Superman.

When choosing a condom, the only important consideration is fit. According to experts, 80 percent of men will be fine in most condoms. If you're a Slim Jim and you use an oversized condom, not only will you look ridiculous but the condom can slip off, increasing the risk of both pregnancy and pustular things on your wanger. On the other fist, if you're a fat man in a little coat, packing yourself into a small sheath is uncomfortable and could decrease sensation or even burst the bag.

Still not sure how you stand? Take the cardboard cylinder from a toilet paper

TROJAN HORSEPLAY

While you're out humping everything in sight, the Food and Drug Administration makes sure your condoms meet rigid standards. Jizz jackets sold in the U.S. must pass several basic tests. Here's what some major condom manufacturers do to make sure their prophylactics go the extra inch.

■ **Durex final test:** Condoms are filled with 300 milliliters of water and suspended for three minutes, then inspected for "minute fluid leakage." Hey, it happens to the best of us.
Home version: Drop water filled condom off balcony. If unbroken, check for leaks; if broken, take pounding from soaking-wet gentleman to your left.

■ **Lifestyles final test:** Several samples from each batch of approximately 1,000 condoms are inflated with 16 liters of air each. If more than four break under the pressure, the entire lot is destroyed.
Home version: Inflate condom to maximum size (using someone else's lips if possible) and tie off. Have a circus clown twist condom into giraffe or poodle. Watch for breakage. Discard.

■ **Trojan final test:** Condom is placed in water and zapped with high-voltage current. The condom is then examined for flaws as the lab testers reflect on the innumerable real-life situations that call for a perfectly insulated penis.
Home version: While wearing rubber shoes, unroll condom and wrap around cake pan. Touch pan to bug zapper or lighting fixture. Inspect condom for holes; swear off cake forever.

roll and slip it over your erect penis (whoa, cowboy, try not to enjoy yourself too much). Don't panic—unless you're a porn star, you should have room to spare. If it fits comfortably, wear regular condoms. If you could squeeze a second penis inside (what you do on your own time is your business), try snug brands like Beyond and Exotica. If you have to struggle to get in, bandage the paper cuts and reach for larger condoms such as Magnum and Bareback—and pray that nobody saw you abusing the Charmin.

While searching for size, take stock of the latest in jimmy hat technology.

Condoms have come a long way since your first one shriveled up and died in your wallet. If your gal has trouble getting her juices flowing (or you just suck at foreplay), try a prelubricated condom; many of these also have spermicide for extra insurance. Avanti by Durex and Supra by Trojan are made of polyurethane, which conducts heat and is twice as thin and strong as regular latex. Pleasure Plus and inSpiral have loose-fitting pouches at the tip that increase the friction. These types are all light-years ahead of those old French-tickler, ribbed, and textured rubbers, which really do no more than make you look like some randy kitchen appliance.

APHRODISIAC ATTACK

Still praying for a magic potion to get women turned on and tuned into you? We'll give you the next best thing: foods, scents, even a cream scientifically proven to get her hotter than a redneck at a family reunion. Plus a couple of rumored ones that don't work.

■ **Raw oysters**
Why they work: The favorite of the ancients because of its uncanny resemblance to a labia, this shellfish is actually rich in zinc, which get helps the sex drive hormones raging. We suggest, however, for maximum effect, to avoid mentioning the labia-oyster connection on a first date.

■ **Bananas**
Why they work: It's not because the fruit looks like a penis. Bananas are rich in potassium, a mineral needed for nerve and muscle function.

■ **Asparagus**
Why it works: Sure, it makes your urine smell funny, but a spear of asparagus may increase her interest in your love spear. Asparagus is rich in vitamin E, another sex hormone stimulant.

■ **Damiana (wild yam)**
Why it works: It's scientific name is actually *Turnera aphrodisiaca*, and it's usually taken as a tea. It reportedly increases sensitivity in the genital area,

but no one's quite sure whether it serves another rumored purpose: inducing erotic dreams when chugged before bedtime.

■ **Chili peppers**
Why they work: Spicy foods get the endorphins pumping and her heart racing, and will leave her sweaty and breathless—just like it'll be when she has sex with you.

■ **Chocolate**
Why it works: It kickstarts the natural stimulant (phenylalanine) that tells her she's in love (on second thought, maybe you'd better hold off on this one).

■ **Dr. K's Dream Cream**
Why it works: Works like Viagra, but you smear it on her vulva to increase blood flow. But we figure if she's already letting you spread cream on her nether regions, you don't need any aphrodisiacs.

■ **The smell of licorice and cucumber**
Why it works: According to the brainy bloodhounds at the Smell and Taste Treatment and Research Foundation in Chicago, the fragrance of Good & Plenty candies and cucumber proved to be the most arousing to women. The least unarousing? Men's cologne.

■ **Ginseng**
Why it doesn't work: Known in Eastern cultures as "man root" for its resemblance to the, er, man's root, ginseng is, alas, only a mild stimulant, like a cup of black coffee. You'd have better luck showing her a picture of its phallus shape.

■ **Spanish fly**
Why it doesn't work: Maybe because it can kill you? This legendary concoction of ground-up beetle parts was used to irritate the urogenital area of frigid cows. Her ex might call her a heifer, but slipping livestock drugs to your girlfriend can cause an E.R. visit.

■ **Alcohol and illegal drugs**
Why they don't work: Sure, her guard's down, but drugs and alcohol can actually diminish desire and make it more difficult, if not impossible, for her to have an orgasm, which isn't exactly going to get her bragging to her friends about your masterful sexual techniques.

SCREW YOUR HEALTH: EIGHT MEDICALLY SOUND REASONS YOU MUST HAVE SEX EVERY DAY. LIKE YOU NEED 'EM.

Back in the 1940s, a renegade shrink named Wilhelm Reich recommended an orgasm every day to stay healthy. It was part of this thing he called the "sexual revolution." Unfortunately, folks were strung pretty tight back then, and they threw Reich's ass in prison, where orgasms aren't nearly as much fun. But thinking this guy was onto something, we called some of the planet's most renowned M.D.'s to find out if he was right. Guess what? He was. Unless you're moving from girl to girl like Camryn Manheim moves through a six-pack of cling peaches in heavy syrup, a daily love session is just what the doctor ordered, for you and your partner in crime. Here are eight reasons to never get out of bed.

1 THE BODY YOU WANT

When you cut your finger, does Ragú ooze out? Does the idea of exercising induce suicidal pork chop binges? We can think of one way to have a blast and get in shape simultaneously. "Sex is a vigorous form of exercise," says Dr. Michael Cirigliano, M.D., Medical Center of the University of Pennsylvania. "The physiological changes in your body are consistent with a normal workout. Your heart and respiratory rates rise, and you burn calories." How many? Screwing three times a week for 20 minutes a pop for a year will burn some 7,500 calories (that's the equivalent of a 4½ pound wheel of brie). If you do it every day, you can shave off a pound of lard in two weeks. Of course, the more athletic the sex, the better the workout. See you in the emergency room.

2 FORGET THE ZOLOFT

Ever lie back after a good screw and think, Damn, the world's a pit of misery. Why not end it all? Of course not! That's because sex is an antidepressant. During the act your body's producing pleasure-inducing fluids besides the ones that shoot out of your body. "You're releasing endogenous opioids. They're like drugs, but they're manufactured internally," says Alice Ladas, Ed.D., a psychologist and one of the authors of *The G Spot*. In fact, studies show that merely touching someone can raise the level of serotonin in your brain, which is similar to what Prozac and other antidepressants do. Just think what an orgy with a troop of swimsuit models would do for you.

3 HURTS SO GOOD

So she's got a headache, huh? Arthritis? A fresh chain-saw wound? No excuse: Thanks to the endorphins released during sex, a rowdy belly dance can actually ease her suffering. "Pain threshold in women is elevated 60 to 80 percent during pleasurable stimulation," explains Beverly Whipple, Ph.D., a professor of neuroscience and past president of the American Association of Sex Educators, Counselors and Therapists. In one recent study, Gina Ogden, author of *Women Who Love Sex*, experimented by attaching a clamp to a woman's finger and squeezing, first while she was at rest and later while she was getting some. As her subject climaxed, Ogden pinched past the point at which the woman routinely howled, with no response at all. "In the midst of orgasm," Ogden noted, "she apparently feels no pain."

4 DAILY INJECTIONS

Want to help ease those nasty PMS symptoms? Studies show that a woman's overall reproductive system benefits from frequent penile insertions. "Sexual activity helps strengthen the pubococcygeus muscles, which in turn help keep the pelvic organs in shape and where they belong," explains Ladas. Regular love sessions can also postpone the onset of menopause, stimulate fertility, and regulate the menstrual cycle.

5 OLD FAITHFUL

Frequent erections keep blood flowing through your capillaries, so the flesh in your bone stays nourished, which can help to ward off getting-it-up trouble later. And more important, an erection is an athletic reflex. "The more you train the coordination between nerve and muscle, the easier it is to perform," says Dr. Andre Guay, M.D., head of the sexual function center at the Lahey Clinic in Peabody, Massachusetts.

6 THE GLAND OF MILK AND HONEY

Yeah, the prostate's a funny little gland. It's key component in your pleasure machine (and a male G-spot, if you know how to find it), but it tends to swell as we get older, causing agony for lots of guys. To keep it from bugging you, take saw palmetto (an over-the-counter herb supplement that relieves symptoms of prostate enlargement), and keep ejaculating. "Most of the fluid you ejaculate comes from the prostate and the seminal vesicles," says Guay. "When someone stops having orgasms, the fluids back up and the glands can become swollen." When prostatic congestion occurs, the gland squeezes your urinary tract, pain shoots through your guts, and you have a hard time taking a leak. Talk about a spent fuel rod.

7 BONE UP

Bet you didn't know that testosterone is responsible for sex drive in women as well as men. Yup, a lady with no testosterone will be drier than an AA meeting. Plus, testosterone is a steroid that regulates the body's metabolism, enabling it to use energy more efficiently. And the more sex you have, the more testosterone you're producing. "A consequence is that your body is able to stimulate tissue replacement and bone growth,

which, among other things, helps prevent osteoporosis," says Susan Rako, M.D., author of *The Hormone of Desire*. "Higher levels of testosterone can also promote an overall feeling of well-being."

8 LONG TIME COMIN'
Want to live longer? Try adding a little sex to your diet. In 1997 an inquisitive British doctor published a study that followed 918 men between the ages of 45 and 59 for 10 long years to determine how sexual activity affected their life spans. Here's what he found: Men who had two or more orgasms every week were half as likely to croak as those who averaged fewer than one orgasm a month. And, hey, guys never lie about this kind of stuff, so we're sure the data's right on the money.

ASK DR. MAXIM

Quit worrying so much. Here's the scoop on everything from women swallowing to STDs in your mouth to sizing the old snake.

Is it possible to get a yeast infection by having sex with a woman who has a yeast infection?
While a yeast infection sounds like an STD you might get from the Pillsbury Doughboy, it's actually a common female ailment, though not as common as the number of Monistat commercials on Lifetime indicates. Put down the sandwich and get ready for an excursion to the vagina. Yeast infections are caused by a natural fungus getting out of control in the vagina when the environment becomes favorable, often because of persistent or excessive moisture. Symptoms include itching and burning in and around the vagina, a white discharge that looks like cottage cheese (don't test further), and pain during intercourse. Imagine jock itch, then imagine it inside your body. Like menstruation, this is not a subject to joke with her about.

Still with us? Here's how this affects you. While you lack what scientists call a "vagina," you can actually get a kind of yeast infection, called thrush, inside your mouth. (If you're uncircumcised, you can also get an infection under your foreskin). Additionally, 12 to 15 percent of men develop a penile rash following contact with a yeast infection, so you might want to hold off while she brings the fungi under control (usually three to seven days). Not that abstaining from cottage cheese sex should be a problem.

If a woman with a cold sore goes down on you, can you get herpes?
Believe it or not, the answer is yes. Here's why:

Herpes is a dark family secret: An estimated one of every five Americans over age 12 has it, and no one talks about it. Herpes simplex virus comes in two types, conveniently named HSV-1, the usual cause of oral herpes (cold sores), and HSV-2, which causes the majority of genital herpes. Both have similar symptoms—a periodic outbreak of blistery sores—and both are extremely contagious. If you get recurrent cold sores, there's a good chance you have oral herpes. But don't check into a leper colony yet: Seventy to 90 percent of Americans get HSV-1 at some point in their lives, and it's fine as long as it's dormant. But if your infected girlfriend goes down on you while she's active, she can give you genital herpes—about 30 percent of all new cases of genital herpes are caused this way. The same can be said if you've got a cold sore and decide to yodel down the valley—she could wind up with genital herpes.

A doctor can administer a test to find out whether the sores are caused by HSV-1 herpes or something else, like gingivitis. Unfortunately, there's no cure for herpes, so you've got it for life. But look on the bright side: If you're currently experiencing an outbreak, it's a convenient excuse to stay uptown until the symptoms fade.

What's the danger of having sex with a woman during her period?
The crimson wave's probably gonna stain the bed, but intercourse with a menstruating woman presents no additional risks then when she's not on the rag, according to Nardone. "You can get any STD whether she's bleeding or not," he stresses. "The chance of a guy getting an infection if she has her period is no less and no more than if she doesn't have her period." If you're the one carrying the dick disease, she's equally in danger of contracting something from you whether it's that time of the month or not. Since there's always the possibility that an infected partner will transmit the virus or bacteria to the other person, use a barrier contraceptive.

How does diet affect my semen and her discharge?
Contrary to what your buddies told you back in high school, no food or beverage product works as a contraceptive, says Belker, so don't believe that bullshit about Mountain Dew preventing pregnancy. However, what a person eats can affect how he tastes down below. Such alkaline-based dishes as meats and seafood can produce a fishy flavor (insert your own girlfriend-tuna joke here). If you're gonna have a nightcap, stick to brands of liquor that are distilled the old-fashioned way, as chemically processed booze can leave a tangy, acidic taste. You might wanna eighty-six the coffee and cigarettes before bedtime, too: Not only can caffeine and nicotine leave you jittery, the java-and-cancer-stick combo also makes for some nasty-tasting joy juice. Other foods that can foul up your flavor and essence include dairy products (high levels of bacteria cultures), asparagus (ironic, considering that its high vitamin E content spurs sex hormone production), and garlic and onions (do we need to explain this one?). On the other hand sweet, acidic foods (fruit, fruit juices) and naturally fermented beers tend to bring about a subtly sweet taste.

Doctors are less sure about how the smell and taste of her secretions change with certain foods, but maintaining a healthy, well-balanced diet helps keep her love tunnel in fine working order. Bingeing on sweets and excess alcohol can alter her vaginal pH, making her more susceptible to yeast infections. "She'll secrete more sugar in her discharge, and since yeasts love sugar, they may thrive a little more in that environment," explains Nardone.

Do women ejaculate?
Yep, but not all women can, and those who have that nookie-nectar-releasing gift don't spurt every time they have sex. Located around the urethra, the Skene's glands are the chick counterpart to your prostate gland, and they secrete female ejaculate through the urethra that's chemically similar to prostatic fluid. A female can release greater quantities if her G-spot, or even her clitoris, is stimulated during sex play, but she might hold back for fear she's shooting out pee instead. Ya see, her bladder sits above her vagina and can feel the aftershocks of stimulation down below, and G-spot swelling can put pressure on her urethra. Make sure she visits the john before you and she get busy.

"WOMEN HAVE SEX DREAMS THAT CAN LEAD TO VAGINAL LUBRICATION AND EVEN TO ORGASM."

Do women have wet dreams?
"Women have sex dreams that can lead to vaginal lubrication and even to orgasm, but I don't think women ejaculate during those dreams very often," says Kaminetsky.

What, if any, are the advantages of putting on two condoms for intercourse?
The CDC have no proof that double bagging makes sex any safer than slipping on only one jimmy, Michael

Stalker, at the American Social Health Association, adds that using male and female condoms at the same time may cause the female condom to dislodge during intercourse. Chances are pretty good, too, that the friction between two rubbers makes them likelier to break than a single condom used correctly.

When it comes to contracting HIV, are any sex acts safer than others?

Getting the AIDS virus depends on these three factors, says Stalker:

1. HIV can only be transmitted from an HIV-positive individual; two uninfected people aren't gonna pass it between themselves.

2. The virus has to exist in adequate amounts to cause infection, but the concentration of HIV varies from one bodily fluid to the next.

3. HIV must make its way into the bloodstream either directly (for example, shooting up with an infected person's dirty needle) or via the mucous membranes of the mouth, vagina, penis, or anus.

That said, here's what you need to know about the risk levels of different sex acts. (If both of you are HIV-positive, the Centers for Disease Control and Prevention [CDC] recommend using latex condoms during all kinds of sex acts to avoid reinfection from a drug-resistant strain of HIV and infection from other STDs.)

■ **Unprotected oral sex on the vagina, penis, or anus**
Low risk—it's less dangerous than unprotected vaginal or anal intercourse, but infection technically can occur if people get vaginal secretions, blood, or precome or semen in their mouths, since HIV can be absorbed through the mucous membrane. (The risk might increase a little with the presence of bleeding gums and other mouth traumas.) The lucky guy or gal receiving oral sex is at even lower risk. But no cases of HIV transmission from giving or getting head have ever been reported. Anus-licking carries a much greater chance of transmitting hepatitis A and intestinal parasites than HIV.

■ **Unprotected vaginal intercourse**
High risk—though some research suggests the male might be slightly less at risk. A woman can contract the virus from semen or preseminal fluids, especially if she has a vaginal infection; likewise, a man can get HIV from vaginal fluid or blood entering his bloodstream via the urethral membrane or through cuts, sores, or inflammations on the penis.

■ **Unprotected anal intercourse**
High risk. The guy seems to be at somewhat less risk for HIV infection, though blood or vaginal fluid can enter the urethra or be absorbed through cuts or sores on the penis. He can also develop urethritis as a result of dipping his unprotected dick into what is basically a sewer. HIV can enter a woman's bloodstream via blood, semen, or pre-cum directly absorbed in the mucous membranes of the anus or vagina. Her risk is highest if her partner ejaculates into her anal cavity, as well as if she has any infections in the anal neighborhood, and if she uses an enema or is fisted or fingered before or after unprotected anal sex.

What's the risk of birth defects if she conceives while she's on some kind of hormone-based birth control?

A woman who's pregnant and still taking the pill probably doesn't know she's knocked up, but birth defects are not necessarily inevitable, explains Nardone. "She'd still want to minimize the baby's exposure to these manufactured hormones." If something's weird about her period, she should get to a doc's office for a pregnancy test and to find out if her birth control hormones' dosage is affecting her cycle.

If my penis is really long or thick, could I damage her insides? Is it possible for her to become too loose?

Simmer down, Dirk Diggler. A woman's vagina is elastic enough for a baby to pass through, so she can definitely accommodate your one-eyed monster. However, "It's very important that she's adequately lubricated and stimulated," advises Nardone. "Even if you're huge, eventually a woman can be dilated to your size, but you both have to be patient." Deep, hard, fast penetration can lead to vaginal lacerations or even the rupture of an ovarian cyst; endometriosis—when the uterine lining somehow gets out into the abdomen—can also cause dyspareunia, or painful intercourse. This means you two have got to try something different, such as altering her position or changing your thrust speed and depth. "Pain tends to shut down the pleasure nerves, so if she's in pain she's not gonna climax," adds Nardone.

My penis rubbed up against my girlfriend's vaginal area very briefly. What are the chances she's pregnant?

Slim to none, says Nardone, assuming you did not shoot your load anywhere near her box and you did not penetrate her. You can, though, pass STDs between each other via this kind of unprotected skin-to-skin or mucous membrane contact.

I've recently started dating this girl who enjoys sex but can't seem to climax. What's wrong?

Unfamiliarity with or insecurity about her body, stress, guilty feelings about sex, memories of traumatic events such as rape or incest, substance abuse, or female reproductive trouble can all cause anorgasmia, the inability to orgasm. A sex therapist or gynecologist can help her get to the bottom of most of these problems. And if she's not masturbating already, she should learn how to pleasure herself (with or without mechanical assistance), then guide you as she learns how her little pink pearl works. When in doubt about how to rev her up, remember an old children's story: Slow and steady wins the race.

Will urinating inside a woman's vagina cause infection?

It's pretty much impossible for you to penetrate her and pee inside her at the same time. But anything—such as your urine—that can change her birth canal's chemical environment, even for a short while, can lead to an overgrowth of the normal, healthy bacteria living in her vagina, leaving her vulnerable to infections such as cytomegalovirus (CMV).

If she drinks like a fish or does drugs like Keith Richards, what happens to the effectiveness of her hormonal contraceptive?

According to Nardone, alcohol might interfere with the pill because both are metabolized in the liver, as well as disrupt her body's estrogen levels, and, as a result, alter her period schedule. Controlled substances can potentially affect her cycle, too: The hypothalamus, which is part of the central nervous system (CNS), controls her periods, and psychotropic drugs alter the CNS. Anything that can cause a CNS glitch might wreak menstrual havoc. "Around the Christmas holidays, I have female patients talking about having weird periods, which can be a result of keeping late hours and drinking," observes Nardone. Maybe you're looking for an easy lay—and party girls almost always fit the bill—but you also have to consider that you probably can't trust 'em any further than you can throw 'em. "How reliable is she about taking the pill at the same time every day if she's partying all the time?" points out Nardone. If the female in question is already involved in risk-taking behavior like drinking and drugs—and sleeping with you—who's to say she's not at risk for STDs, too?

The condom broke, so my girlfriend went on emergency contraception (EC). One day after finishing her dosage, we had sex, and the condom broke again. Can she still get pregnant?

Postcoital contraception, a two-dose regimen of certain kinds of birth control pills taken within 72 hours after one instance of unprotected intercourse,has been shown to be effective in preventing some pregnancies. But more than one prescription of EC pills in such a short amount of time can seriously screw up her menstrual cycle, making it tough to figure out when she'll ovulate next. Such a high dose can also make her so nauseated that she'll vomit and not absorb the hormone needed to keep from getting knocked up.

Is it unhealthy for her to swallow my cum?
To swallow or not to swallow is a matter of personal taste (get it?), but it's safe for her to down your Johnson juice so long as you're not infected with a sexually transmitted disease. (And just in case you didn't already know, she cannot get pregnant sipping from or sucking on your schlong.)

Whenever we're bumping uglies, why does she sometimes pass gas from her vagina?
Commonly called a "quiff," that squeaky *pwish* sound from between her legs occurs as a result of the vaginal walls filling with blood and expanding, then contracting, during arousal and intercourse and when air enters and exits her as you enter and exit her.

However, a total absence of love liquid upon orgasm may indicate retrograde (or backward) ejaculation, a harmless but embarrassing condition in which semen shoots back into the bladder and is then eliminated when you pee; its causes include diabetes and antihypertensive medications.

How damaging is a kick to the crotch?
Minimally so, declares Belker: "The usual kick to the groin results in swelling of soft tissue, but no significant testicle harm or injury to other organs. Actual damage that requires surgical repair can take place, but that's rare." You've still gotta check your potato sack to make sure all's well down below. Look at and feel around both testes to make sure they're still hanging low and that there's no external bleeding from a scrape or scratch. (Should you find that they're high up or bloody, get to the doctor's office, pronto.) Head off swelling and even more pain with an ice pack. Oh, and don't wear tight jeans for a few days, cowboy.

Why do I fall asleep after sex?
According to Masters and Johnson, sex occurs in four phases (and no, dinner isn't one of them): arousal, plateau, orgasm, and resolution. In men the last stage contains a refractory period in which the blood flows out of the penis and the body relaxes. In addition, when you ejaculate, your brain shoots out various substances (think of it as an exploding scoreboard) that can include melatonin, oxytocin, and endorphins (your body's natural painkillers). Combined, these factors may do for you what the movie *Waterworld* did for Kevin Costner's career: in other words, good night and thanks for coming.

Okay, so how come she's still awake and yappin'? In case you haven't noticed, women were designed to reproduce and continue the species. To do this they needed to scrounge the healthiest genes, and that meant staying awake in order to be inseminated by the greatest diversity of males possible. Back there on the savanna, nature decreed that the first guy in the tribe to get lucky with a particular female would need some downtime after making his deposit, allowing the other males to take their shots at playing the gene pool. In light of these rather nasty revelations, Dr. Maxim recommends that you not invite your girlfriend over for sex if your roommate is lurking in the next room.

"IS THERE SUCH A THING AS NOT ENOUGH SEMEN? HOW MUCH SEMEN IS TOO MUCH?"

Is there such a thing as not enough semen? How much semen is too much?
Stop comparing yourself to porn stars already—those rivers of jungle juice are actually cum shot scenes filmed from several different camera angles that are pieced together in the editing room. If spewing like a geyser (well, almost like a geyser) is really that important to you, keep your daily ejaculation to a minimum, like once a day.